PRAISE FOR *BED*___

M000282331

"It is said that each time a story is told, it breathes life into the culture. In *Bedside Witness,* Kay Adams brings out the dignity of her patients and families through their stories. She shows us that humanness transcends aging, dementia, and illness and that our culture is filled with the many colors of life behind the doors and walls of hospice and dementia care."

—Amelia Schafer, Senior Director, Alzheimer's Association

"Kay Adams shows us that illness, disease, and ultimately death offer us unlimited gifts if we are able to open our hearts along the way. Through Kay's eyes, we are able to see that rather than fear what lies ahead, we have the opportunity to embrace the journey."

—Karl J. Shackelford, MDiv, BCC, Founder, We Grieve

"*Bedside Witness* should be required reading for anyone in the fields of hospice, geriatrics, mental health, palliative care, and dementia. Through her stories, Kay Adams shows us that being a witness and companion goes far beyond checking off boxes. It requires sitting with, listening to, and understanding those we serve."

—Tracy Ellen Lippard, MD, FACP, Internal and Geriatric Medicine

"Kay Adams writes about caregiving, dementia, and the end of life with a deep compassion that shines off the page and warms your heart. *Bedside Witness* is for caregivers who are looking for a sign that they are not alone as they hold their loved one's hand through the most difficult journey imaginable, and for anyone—social worker, nurse, aide, therapist, doctor—who wants to understand the experience of patients in memory care or hospice and their caregivers."

—Amy Delpo, Librarian and Caregiver

"Kay Adams is the perfect voice to bring a powerful understanding to the impact dementia can have on people living with the illness, their families, and caregivers. Her compassionate look at navigating these life-changing moments is inspiring and educational."

—Cynthia James, Bestselling Author and International Speaker, President and CEO, Cynthia James Enterprises

"Kay's stories envelope you as you witness the extraordinary, honest, and difficult moments that others go through during one of life's most challenging times. Glimpses into Kay's gift with people bring you through a rainbow of emotions and leave you with a heartfelt desire to offer companionship and support to others when they need it most."

—Lindsy Moore, PharmD, Geriatric Pharmacy Specialist

"Having watched my mother slip away from the effects of dementia, *Bedside Witness* brought comfort, knowing that other families like mine have survived this loss with a sense of humility and heart. Through her stories, Kay illustrates the commonalities we share as human beings, families, and caregivers and draws on those connections with bright colors to inspire us all."

—Mary Gaul, Caregiver, Owner of Success Magnified Business Coaching

"Kay is a storytelling alchemist with an extraordinary gift that teaches and inspires. Her firsthand accounts of persons living with serious illnesses and their loved ones are transformed into powerful testaments of humility and compassion. Kay captures what matters most: an essential skill of a palliative care social worker."

—Melissa Coleman Palmer, LCSW, JD, Palliative Care Specialist—University of Colorado

"Adams is a master storyteller, taking us inside her world of compassionate caring for older people with dementia and other end-of-life issues. Her stories emphasize the importance of seeing beyond the person and understanding the impact—blessings and suffering—their illness has, not only on them but on their family and caregivers. By knowing our patients' stories, we come close to understanding their pain and their journey. Adams shows us the reward that all of us experience in working with patients like those in *Bedside Witness*. Adams has written a compelling book that will be a must-read for all of us who work or will work in this field."

—Michael Weitzner, MD, FRCPC,
Geriatric Psychiatrist, Kamloops, B.C.

"Kay Adams shares her journey as a social worker with care, sensitivity, dignity, and grace. Her beautifully written vignettes are so palpable you literally feel and experience her journey in a way that transports and places you in the room where it happened. They not only touch the heart but break it wide open and simultaneously transform it with wisdom, tenderness, and humor. *Bedside Witness* challenges each of us to determine what we *must* do and *can* do in order to honor humanity and transform into the highest version of self."

—Nadine Roberts Cornish, CSA,
Gerontologist and Chief Care Strategist

Bedside Witness

STORIES OF HOPE, HEALING, AND HUMANITY

KAY M. ADAMS

Foreword by Jane W. Barton, Author of *Caregiving for the GENIUS*

Bedside Witness: Stories of Hope, Healing, and Humanity
Published by Crown Hill Publishing
Denver, CO

Copyright © 2022 by Kay Adams. All rights reserved.

No part of this book may be reproduced in any form or by any mechanical means, including information storage and retrieval systems without permission in writing from the publisher/author, except by a reviewer who may quote passages in a review.

All images, logos, quotes, and trademarks included in this book are subject to use according to trademark and copyright laws of the United States of America.

ISBN: 978-0-578-37370-6
Diseases & Conditions / Alzheimer's & Dementia

Cover and interior design by Victoria Wolf, wolfdesignandmarketing.com. Copyright owned by Kay Adams.

The stories and conversations in *Bedside Witness* all come from the author's recollections; however, names have been changed and events have been compressed. The stories do not represent word-for-word transcripts. Rather, the author has retold the stories in a way that evokes the feeling and meaning of what was said, and in all instances, the essence of the dialogue is accurate.

All rights reserved by Kay Adams and Crown Hill Publishing.
Printed in the United States of America.

To all of the caregivers—past, present, and future—who are the unseen and unsung heroes of our time. Without fanfare, under the radar, and out of the limelight, you play an essential role in our families and in society as a whole. More often than not, you are doing this alone, under difficult circumstances, and hidden from view in a culture that is greatly indebted to the gifts *you bring* and for the great gift *you are*. Your magnificence is not lost on me and continues to be my motivation and inspiration every day in my work.

CONTENTS

SECTION 3: Breaking Open to Break Through

"We have been battered by modern times into obsessive problem solvers, but as life pares us down into only what is essential, it becomes clear that the deepest sufferings of heart and spirit cannot be solved, only witnessed and held."

—Mark Nepo, *The Book of Awakening*

FOREWORD

I love a good story. Always have. I'm not unique in that regard. Love of story is seemingly embedded in the DNA of human beings. Perhaps that's because stories help us make sense of life. Whether sharing or hearing a story, there are moments when something clicks and clarity is achieved. An aha moment! No doubt, you will have many ahas as you read *Bedside Witness*.

Storytelling is a process of weaving the disparate threads of our existence into a meaningful, rich tapestry—a tapestry that reveals who we are, how we are, and perhaps who we are becoming. Although we all have stories to tell, some are better at spinning yarns than others. As you will soon discover, Kay is a masterful weaver of tales. In the following pages, she recounts the poignant, powerful, and priceless experiences that taught her what it means to be fully human. The lessons learned transformed her understanding of life and thus how she chooses to live. Perhaps your view of life (and death) will be transformed as well upon reading this book.

Kay's stories will grab your heart and resonate in your bones. As you flip through the following pages, be prepared for an emotional roller coaster. One minute, you'll be laughing out loud; the next minute, you'll find yourself tearing up. The stories will transport you through the highs and lows, the twists and turns, and the ups and downs of life. Every emotional button on your body will be pushed. So, fasten your seat belt and get ready for the ride of your life!

I should also offer fair warning that the topics of discussion are not for the faint of heart: caregiving, dementia, dying, and death. These are serious issues that Kay addresses with incredible competence and compassion—along with a generous smattering of humor appropriately interspersed. As a result, you will learn that no matter how dire the circumstances, you can always find something for which to hope. You will recognize that healing can be achieved without necessarily curing a disease. And, you will realize what it means to be human—finite, vulnerable, and inextricably linked to other people.

It's obvious from page one that Kay doesn't shy away from the inherent messiness of life. Instead, she wades into the deep end of the pool to meet people where they are—to serve as a courageous companion and unwavering witness. Kay's stories are not mere observations of the trials and triumphs of those she has served; the stories are a testament to lives lived and lives lost. As a witness, Kay chooses to invest her entire being in those she serves. She has and continues to be a tremendous resource for individuals and families challenged by aging, illness, and the end of life.

As you read each story, allow the words to flow through your mind and heart. Pay attention to the emotions that bubble up. Reflect on your visceral response to the situations described in *Bedside Witness*. Are you inspired? Challenged? Humbled? Frightened? Amazed? Angered? Bereaved? Consoled? All of the above? Well, in all likelihood, you'll experience all of these reactions and then some! But ultimately, I imagine you will feel incredibly grateful. Grateful for your life, for this moment, and for this extraordinary book. It is a gift indeed.

Blessings,
Jane W. Barton, MTS, MASM, CSA
Speaker, Writer, Listener
Cardinal, LLC
Author of *Caregiving for the GENIUS*

PREFACE

Relish the Ride

I have told my friends, family members, and coworkers for as long as I can remember that "I know I have a book in me somewhere; I just don't know what I'm supposed to *write about!*" That was true until I was introduced in the fall of 2001 to the text *Final Gifts: Understanding the Special Awareness, Needs, and Communications of the Dying* by hospice nurses Maggie Callanan and Patricia Kelley. I devoured that book and all the great lessons it had to teach me during the beginning of my tenure as a new hospice employee. Afterward, I gained a visceral sense of *knowing* that I would someday write my book of vignettes about the patients and families I companioned who were facing life-threatening illnesses. I knew I would tell the tales from the perspective of a medical social worker and clinician. Over twenty years later, that day has *finally* arrived!

Bedside Witness is a collection of the most powerful, poignant, and personally compelling stories that have moved, saddened, inspired, and motivated me to think long and hard about the choices I make in my life, the people and relationships I need to attentively nurture and love, and the regrets I hope to avoid when *my time* on the planet draws to a close. My hope is that by sharing these vignettes, they will give voice to the army of extraordinary teachers whose stories have helped to shape and guide me on every level while also endowing me with invaluable lessons I couldn't have gleaned anywhere else other than from my unique vantage point as a "bedside witness." Fueled by their examples, I've come to understand what it means to have hope amidst the darkest of times, to heal even if you can't be cured, and to drink deeply from the well of humanity when we are most in need of quenching our thirst for connection.

The stories I've captured are for all the patients and families I've had the privilege to serve and learn from, the colleagues who have patiently mentored me along the way, and for *anyone* who needs to be reminded that the messy, complicated, and beautiful odyssey we're all on can be made ever sweeter when we focus on what *connects us* as human beings rather than on what *divides us*. In so doing, we can celebrate the common ground over which we all traverse during our earthly travels and commit to not taking another step of our precious journey together for granted.

May you relish the ride.

PROLOGUE

Kay and Einar's Great Adventure (Where It All Began)

"Whatever you do, Kay, do not stop!"

Sometimes life seems to randomly present us with unique challenges, and when we find ourselves in the midst of those trying situations, we have absolutely no concept of why they are happening or what we're supposed to be learning from them in real time. We just know that we are faced with obstacles in our path and somehow have to find our way through them. And then, as often happens, months, years, or even decades later, those lessons learned come back around to serve us in unanticipated and wonderful ways that we could have *never envisioned* at the time they occurred. Such is the case with the valuable lessons I learned from my Grandpa Einar over forty years ago during the infamous story of "Kay and Einar's Great Adventure." I guess you could say this is where it all began for me.

Grandpa Einar was the youngest of fourteen children—seven of whom died early in life. My grandpa and his family had emigrated from Denmark to the Nebraska plains when he was thirteen. Even at that young age, Einar had proved himself to be a highly gifted violinist who wanted to remain behind in Denmark so that his musical talents could be nurtured to their fullest potential. But his parents opted to bring him along to America, despite Einar's fervent protests to stay.

It took thirteen days for the ship to sail from Denmark to Ellis Island in New York, across the treacherous and stormy Atlantic Ocean. For the rest of his life, my grandpa was deeply suspicious of the number thirteen because of those harrowing experiences and the "bad luck" that came in their wake.

Grandpa Einar never fully embraced the solitude of the rural lifestyle that was thrust upon him after moving from his urban home in Denmark to the breadbasket of the United States, where there were far more cows than people. Einar wasn't cut out to be a farmer, either physically or mentally. He was of shorter stature and slight build and was not well-equipped for the backbreaking labor required of him on the farm as a child, nor did he ever plan to continue that occupation as an adult. But due to the far-reaching and devastating effects of the Great Depression, no other viable options for gainful employment ever came his way.

Despite being a farmer for decades, Grandpa found the isolation of that solitary lifestyle to be difficult. He came to life when he was surrounded by lively conversation, laughter, good food, and the chance to put aside his loneliness through much-needed social interaction with other people, whether for a few hours or a few days. When I was a kid, my grandpa's biggest joys were playing music on the piano, accordion, or violin for people who "came on The Place," indulging in my grandma's fabulous home cooking (especially the "forbidden sweets!"), and having family and friends come to visit. Nothing delighted Grandpa more!

My grandpa and grandma lived on a remote farm in Nebraska about thirty minutes from "the big city" of Sioux City, Iowa. I only got to see my grandparents about three or four times a year when my family and I would pack up the car and make the 150-mile trip to the farm. I can hardly recall a time when I ever saw Grandpa "looking like a farmer" on any of those memorable visits, aside from one occasion when he donned his overalls to drive his tractor into the fields while I rode shotgun by his side. He capitalized on the infrequent opportunity to have guests in his home by dressing to the nines for the occasion. Most of the memories I have of Grandpa are of him wearing a crisply ironed button-up shirt and tie, dress slacks, and a fedora hat—tilted stylishly to one side. He was a proud man who relished any excuse to look his "Sunday best" for company, even if it happened to be on a Tuesday.

Over the years, I became increasingly aware that Grandpa's typical jovial moods were more unpredictable, as were his personality and behavior. He started saying and doing things that were quite out of character for him, sometimes forgetting events that had happened not long before. But nobody in my family ever talked in front of me about those changes, so I didn't either. I knew that my grandpa's memory and behaviors were becoming harder for my grandma to deal with, but the only term I ever heard anyone in my family use to describe Grandpa's mental changes was "hardening of the arteries," and I truthfully had no idea what that phrase even meant. In those days, no one mentioned the word "dementia." All I knew for certain was that Grandpa was different, and I didn't know why.

As I grew older, it became more obvious that the sustained stress my grandmother had been living under for years was taking its toll on her. My grandma's health was in jeopardy due to working herself to the bone day in and day out with almost no assistance from her husband. Grandma had to take care of the majority of Grandpa's needs after he had to have his right leg amputated below the knee due to complications of his "non-compliant" diabetic diet (he couldn't resist my grandma's homemade sweets!) and resulting gangrene. In addition to that, Grandma had to manage the land and their old farmhouse without any modern-day conveniences like indoor plumbing or running water. She did all of her cooking on an ancient corncob stove and had just one potbelly stove on the main floor to heat their drafty old two-story home during those cold Nebraska winters.

Shortly after I turned sixteen, my mom was extremely worried and stressed about how to provide assistance to her folks on the farm when we lived two and a half hours away. Then one day, my dad said, "You know, I think we need to move your parents to Lincoln where we could be closer and more helpful to them." My mom jumped for joy at the idea and sprang into immediate action.

When my mom shared Dad's suggestion with Grandma, she was excited about the prospect of relocating, but Grandpa didn't receive the news nearly so well because he didn't understand *why* a move was necessary. Grandpa had no insight into his declining abilities or any real awareness of the incredible stress that his wife was under due to all of her unending responsibilities. As a result, Grandpa dug in his heels and informed us in no uncertain terms that he wasn't going *anywhere* that he didn't damn well want to go, and *nobody*— including his family—was going to make him!

Despite Grandpa's stubbornness, the search for a house in Lincoln began. When the perfect home was found only three blocks away from where my parents and I lived, Grandpa became even more resistant and angry, refusing to sign the contract on the new property. Luckily, my mom's perseverance and influence over her father prevailed in the end. Grandpa reluctantly signed the paperwork, and the planning began.

However, before Grandpa and Grandma could make the move to Lincoln, they had to sell their farm and liquidate all of the belongings they couldn't take with them, so an auctioneer was hired, and a farm sale ensued four weeks later.

I had only had my driver's license for a few months by the time of my grandparents' move. About a week before the farm sale and auction took place, my father elected me to drive my eighty-one-year-old grandfather alone from the farm to Lincoln, with the general hope that Grandpa would be less belligerent with his youngest grandchild than he would be with anyone else in the family—at least that was the working theory! The plan was for us to caravan back to Lincoln in our respective vehicles the minute the farm sale ended: me and Grandpa in my 1967 Ford Mustang, Mom in the family car with Grandma, and my dad in the big truck packed to the hilt with what was left of my grandparents' treasured belongings.

Before we all loaded into our cars for the commute, Dad pulled me aside and earnestly implored, "Whatever you do, Kay, do *not* stop the vehicle between the farm and home and let Grandpa out of the car for any reason, as you will *never* be able to get him back in again!"

Dad undoubtedly shared this sage wisdom with me because my grandfather was well-known for removing his prosthetic leg at the most inopportune times, and my father wanted to avoid that situation from happening, if at all possible. Grandpa had a reputation for yanking off his "fake leg" due to the phantom pain he felt in it following his amputation. There was no predicting when he might get the wild hair to do so, and there was not an extra inch of space in my Mustang for Grandpa's walker, should anything like that happen.

As we made our way down the winding country roads toward my grandparents' new home, Grandpa became increasingly agitated and confused. In his anxious state, he tried diligently to remove his "real" left leg instead of his prosthetic right leg. The harder he tried to take off the leg that was still attached to his body, the more frustrated he became. Grandpa started cussing like a sailor when nothing he tried seemed to work. Some of the colorful language he used during that car ride included words my young ears had never heard before, and I had never witnessed that intensity of rage in my grandpa (or anyone else, for that matter) prior to that day. His display of anger was terrifying—especially in the cramped quarters of my 1967 Mustang. I held my white-knuckled grip on the steering wheel, repeatedly assured my grandfather (and myself) that "we are almost there, and everything is all right" every few minutes, and silently implored God to get Grandpa and me to Lincoln without either of us dying in the process.

If all of that wasn't bad enough, Grandpa Einar kept repeating, "I have to pee like a racehorse. Stop this damned car and let me out!" My heart was beating wildly in my chest from the stress of the ride. I felt incredibly scared, helpless, and overwhelmed. There was no adult to turn to for help or guidance, and my teenage brain had *no clue* what the hell I was doing or how to handle the insanity of the situation. I tried my best to outwardly appear calm and under control, but inside, I was panicking and trying to remember to breathe. Despite the temptation to pull over to the side of the road and cry my eyes out, I dutifully did as my dad instructed and kept driving straight ahead—pedal to the metal on those country roads until we reached the capital city of Lincoln.

Looking back on that drive all these years later, I realize that I had absolutely *no plan* for what I would have done if Grandpa became even more upset and tried to jump out of the moving vehicle. Or what I would have said if he peed all over my bucket seats. And I certainly had no idea how I would have responded if Grandpa decided to clock me over the head with his fake leg—if he'd been able to get it off, that is! To say that I was grossly unprepared to handle that complex situation is a grand understatement, but it may have been where the seeds of my social work career were planted and where my strong interest in dementia took root.

The good news is that we made it from the farm to Lincoln in one piece and lived to tell the tale of "Kay and Einar's Great Adventure." I can look back now and laugh at that story because it's been over four decades since that fateful drive took place. But even through my laughter, I can still *feel* the fear in my gut and my wildly beating heart in my chest when I reflect on that day.

I wish so badly that my dad was still alive so I could ask him *why the hell he thought it was a good idea* to put his teenage daughter behind the wheel for that crazy journey, and how he would have felt if my efforts to drive Grandpa to Lincoln had not turned out so well in the end.

In hindsight, it's clear to me that my sixteen-year-old self (and maybe my whole family) was completely oblivious to the trauma my grandfather must have been going through as he was packed against his will into my crammed little car—leaving behind in the rearview mirror his sense of belonging, control, independence, and familiarity. I drove my grandfather down those dusty gravel roads that he knew like the back of his hand and delivered him into a strange new world two and a half hours away, where everything was foreign to him all over again.

I am acutely aware now that our "adventure" that day was actually *anything but great* for Grandpa and that his strong resistance and rage had more to do with feeling overwhelmed, powerless, and frightened than anything else. Looking back, I've come to believe that the whole experience of being uprooted from the familiar landscape of his life on the farm triggered unsettling memories and anxiety for Grandpa of the long-ago migration he had to make nearly seventy years earlier. The fear, sadness, and uncertainty that Einar undoubtedly experienced when, as a child, he was forced to leave his beloved homeland of Denmark and sail for thirteen grueling days across the unforgiving seas to a new country he never wanted to come to had left an indelible mark on his psyche that would last a lifetime.

I'll never know what my grandfather was thinking on our road trip back then, but I do know this: when we got out of my car in the driveway of Grandpa and Grandma's new home, my grandfather's mood improved almost immediately. My brother Joe had been waiting at the front door to welcome Grandpa to his new abode, and there was a visceral sense of relief written all over Einar's face when the rest of the family arrived safely in tow shortly thereafter. Grandpa even danced a little jig of joy around the kitchen floor on that prosthetic leg of his in celebration! We all laughed and breathed a silent collective prayer that we had actually *pulled off* moving Einar and Marvel to Lincoln after the challenging months of intense planning and requisite efforts leading up to that day. Now, our hope was to ensure that the remaining years of their lives could be spent in greater peace, harmony, and ease than all the previous decades they had spent toiling in hardship, isolation, and strife.

Because my grandparents only lived three blocks from us, we got to see them multiple times a week instead of only a few times a year, and that was a huge change and blessing for everybody involved. Living in such close proximity allowed me to witness in a much more personal way the progressing changes to Grandpa's memory, mood, personality, and day-to-day abilities as he continued to decline over time. And still, no one ever really discussed what was going on with Grandpa's "hardening of the arteries" because, in truth, no one in my family really knew or understood what was causing his brain changes. As a result, we all muddled through the best we knew how and just tried to provide as much support as we could to my grandmother, who was providing the lion's share of the care for her husband of sixty years without ever once complaining.

As time went on, Grandpa became more of a loose cannon when it came to speaking his mind. I vividly remember working hard for many months to lose a significant amount of weight when I was in college, and I was incredibly proud of my major accomplishment. When, on one occasion, Grandpa offered to make a game out of guessing my new weight at a family dinner, I eagerly agreed to the fun and was already anticipating his complimentary words, when he suddenly blurted out, "I bet you weigh at least a ton now, Kay!" I was shocked, crestfallen, and mortified, to say the least, as I tried to wipe away my tears before anyone else in the room noticed.

I had always seemed like a bit of an enigma to Grandpa because of my size, since the average woman that he grew up around in "the Old Country" was significantly shorter and more petite than I was at my Amazonian-like five foot nine inches. I grew taller than my grandpa by the time I was in my early teens and not only inherited my father's height but also his broad shoulders and love of sports. Because of these features and my tomboy nature, I never lived up to my grandfather's vision of what a true "lady" looked or behaved like.

Grandpa's hurtful comment to me at that family dinner was well over four decades ago, and yet I remember it as if it were yesterday because of how disappointed and ashamed it made me feel inside. I was furious with my grandfather for speaking such horrible words to me and then laughing about it as if it were a joke. I had *no idea* that his dementia had poked holes through the social filter in his brain or that he had lost the cognitive skill of understanding what was "appropriate" to say or do anymore. Nor did I comprehend that Grandpa was no longer able to read the wounded expression on my young face and apologize for his rudeness, let alone possess the insight, empathy, or ability to even care.

I recall another time that Grandpa's behavior caused significant angst for me. My grandparents' home was of modest size, and the living room was only large enough to fit a couch, an armchair, and their old piano and bench seat. In his confusion, Grandpa became utterly convinced that the couch did not belong to them and would therefore not allow anyone to sit on it despite the limited seating options available elsewhere. I remember arguing with my grandmother about the injustice of having to sit on the floor when there was a perfectly good sofa available, but she would only say, "Now, Kay. Daddy doesn't want anyone to sit on that couch, so we just have to find someplace else to be."

On another occasion, I remember dropping by my grandparents' home on a hot and humid summer day at the end of a long bike ride. I thought I would spend time conversing with Grandpa and Grandma while I recovered from my exertion, but when I entered their house, it felt like a stifling sauna inside. All the windows were tightly shut, and the air conditioner was not running as it should have been to combat the ninety-five-degree weather outside. When I implored my Grandma to turn on the AC and cool down the house, she simply said, "Daddy thinks the temperature is just fine in here." I had to cut short my visit for fear of passing out from heatstroke on their kitchen floor.

Despite our collective ignorance about dementia, my family did an impressive job of lavishing my grandparents with generous amounts of love, attention, and support during their final years of life. My grandma took amazing care of my grandpa, even though she had no real understanding of his disease or what it was doing to her husband's brain and functional abilities. Even when Grandpa was confined to a wheelchair after his second leg amputation and he became significantly testier, delusional, and difficult to handle, my grandma tirelessly catered to his every need without any formal support and with a seemingly endless supply of patience.

In the modern technological age in which we now live, we have instant access at our fingertips to incredible amounts of information and resources about dementia, yet I know from personal and professional experience that millions of people in the world are still armed with little more knowledge or skills to navigate the care for their family member living with this formidable illness than my family and I had when I was sixteen. *That* sad and tragic truth is what drives me every day to compassionately coach, companion, and educate care partners so they feel confident in their abilities to support their loved ones struggling with brain changes while also enhancing their own well-being in the process.

My ardent interest in dementia may have begun with Grandpa Einar on those country backroads of my past, but I am determined to ensure that his story and legacy don't end there. Instead, I intend for them to continue on through my work to empower other families faced with similar challenges today and into the future.

SECTION 1

Moving Into
the Unknown

A Long Journey with
No Straight Lines

One of my favorite quotes is by outdoor enthusiast Ron Lizzi, author of *Go Outside and Come Back Better: Benefits from Nature That Everyone Should Know*, who wrote, "Life rarely follows a straight line. Success is a process of trying, reacting, and changing." For me, those words sum up perfectly the processional journey I've been on since my early twenties. You see, I haven't always been a dementia coach and educator. In fact, the road I've traveled to become a "bedside witness" has been long and circuitous, spanning over four decades of my career.

It all started when I was enrolled at the University of Nebraska in Lincoln, struggling to figure out what to major in. For many of my friends, this decision seemed to come easily and intuitively, but not for me. I ultimately decided to major in psychology—partly because that was the subject in which I had accrued the most credits during my first two years of college, but also because I have always been wired for empathy and connection. I also possessed a keen interest in understanding what makes people tick. The only thing I knew for certain as a fledgling undergraduate student was that my deepest interests lay in discerning the motivations for human behavior and the underlying messiness of our emotions. I could think of no better subject to study that would prepare me for a career in working with people.

My dad spent over twenty-five years moving up through the ranks as a top-notch and well-respected police officer in Lincoln before being elected as sheriff of Lancaster County when I was a junior in high school. He served two four-year terms as sheriff and still held that prestigious position when I was in college. I had been working part time at Arby's during my first two years at the university, and when I finally declared my major in psychology, Dad thought it would be a great idea if I left the world of fast food and instead got a job as a correctional officer at the Lancaster County jail. By doing so, he thought I could learn firsthand how systems work and the complexity of human behavior, while doubling my income at the same time. So I traded in my brown polyester Arby's garb for a khaki green "jailers" uniform, with only a weekend in between to mark that enormous transition. It was the first of many massive job changes that I would make during the next forty years of my career, and it was probably the hardest one of all for my young, naïve mind to wrap my head around.

I went from making roast beef sandwiches and hanging out with my friends after our shift to working in a maximum-security adult jail surrounded by suspicious strangers who knew that I was "the sheriff's daughter" before I even started. They all figured I got the job handed to me on a silver platter and, as a result, decided to break me into the world of corrections in style. To say that I underwent a "baptism by fire" would be an enormous understatement. It was more like a hazing that went on continuously for the two and a half years I managed to survive in that hostile environment. As a white woman in my early twenties who had been raised in a protective, safe, and respectful household, the jail was like entering another solar system altogether. It was a world that, up until that point in my young life, I never even knew existed, let alone had ever witnessed.

To be sure, my dad was right about the plethora of opportunities such a job held for observing human behavior, along with studying the underbelly of society. The lessons I learned were plentiful and painful and wreaked havoc on my tender heart and spirit. I was an innocent, trusting, heart-on-your-sleeve type of person, so the experiences I was exposed to as a correctional officer were shocking and upsetting to me. I witnessed the disparities between the haves and have-nots and the oppressed and the oppressors. I saw the differences between integrity and debauchery, and I stood by helplessly as people of color and women were targeted with abuse in unfathomable ways that other inmates were never subjected to in that restricted setting. When I attempted to speak up and challenge the injustices happening all around me, I was met with threats to my safety and well-being, aimed at keeping me quiet, afraid, and disempowered.

Even though my mom was thrilled that I had landed a county job with great benefits, I intuitively knew within months of starting at the jail that I was not destined for a life of riding herd on incarcerated individuals. I found myself bringing in books from my college classes on topics like addiction and domestic violence to share with the female inmates I developed relationships with. I preferred helping inmates with kitchen duties instead of just ordering them to complete the tasks while I stood idly by and "supervised." I was frequently accused of "acting like a social worker instead of a guard" by the people I worked with; in actuality, I was developing the underpinnings of my social work roots within the walls of that institution.

I knew it was time to get the hell out of the jail when my direct supervisor started bragging about dressing his children in "kill a commie for Mommy" T-shirts and forcing his Vietnamese wife to walk two steps behind him in order to "show her who was boss." My budding sense of feminism was outraged by such disgusting actions, and I lost all respect for my fellow officers who were complicit in reinforcing such behavior with people like him who were in charge. I started passively bucking the system at work when I violated the strict dress code by wearing wildly colorful socks along with a clip-on button on my uniform that read, "I used to be apathetic, but now I don't care." It was my first foray into being insubordinate and losing my faith in the decency, trust, and humanity of others.

Although my mom was somewhat disappointed when I left behind my "golden handcuffs" job (i.e., well-paying with great benefits) in corrections, my dad totally understood the reasons why I had to get out of that environment before it was too late. As a seasoned cop himself, my papa had been dealing with the most unpleasant aspects of our society for decades, but he learned the hard way that he couldn't protect or shield his only daughter from being constantly harassed, objectified, and disrespected in ways he never thought humanly possible when he encouraged me to leave Arby's. As a gentle but strong, intimidating-looking man, my dad had never been subjected to the kind of treatment that I, as a young woman, had to endure at the hands of coworkers, supervisors, and inmates when I donned my green uniform and entered the locked doors of the county jail. I was usually outnumbered at least forty to one by the men in the building on every shift I worked, and being subjected to so much constant harassment made me angry, bitter, and hardened.

By the time I left the jail two and a half years later, I had turned into a completely different person than when I'd first started. I had become cynical instead of hopeful, guarded instead of open, angry instead of upbeat, and much more resentful than I was grateful. I had become distrustful of life on every level and developed a deep belief that people were more evil than good, more greedy than generous, and always out to get you in the end. I didn't like much of anything by the time I left that job—especially the woman I'd become.

My next job was with an agency in Lincoln that ran group homes for adults with intellectual and developmental disabilities (IDD), which I began three days after leaving the correctional facility. I was hired to be the manager and "house-parent" of one such home that housed five female residents who had a host of physical and mental disabilities to contend with. Even though I had never done anything remotely similar to that kind of work, it felt like a breath of fresh air to me after spending more than two years "behind bars" in my last position.

For the next two years, I spent four overnights a week with the women in that group home. I learned to communicate with them, despite their limited vocabularies and intellectual challenges, and to understand and manage their often unpredictable and odd behaviors that I had never before encountered. I began to love helping "my girls" eat, dress, bathe, and do all of their daily living activities to the best of their abilities. I built strong relationships with their families and with my staff and even brought some of my residents along to my parents' home for the holidays if they had nowhere else to go on those special occasions.

By working in the field of developmental disabilities, I began to see the good in people once again and to trust those around me in ways I hadn't done in years. I began to let down my hypervigilant guard that I'd had up for so long and to celebrate the humanity of the clients I worked with. In so doing and because of that paradigm shift, my perspective on life changed for the better. I enjoyed the work so much, in fact, that when I decided to uproot myself after twenty-five years in Lincoln and move to the Twin Cities of Minnesota in the fall of 1997, the first job I applied for and got was in a group home for residents with severe IDD in a northern suburb of Minneapolis—thirty miles away from my home in St. Paul.

I eventually grew restless for a new challenge and change of professional scenery. I made another huge career leap when I was hired as the intervention coordinator for a domestic violence program in a rural setting east of St. Paul. Once again, I found myself in a job unlike any I had experienced before. I went through another baptism by fire of sorts as I learned the political ropes of advocating for battered women in the courthouse by day, making home visits at night to women who had just been assaulted by their intimate partners, and managing the twenty-four-hour hotline as well.

Although I enjoyed the challenging nature of my work, I became aware that the interpersonal dynamics happening in our office were anything but normal. Within a few months of being hired, I discovered the hard way that the executive director of our program was not who she appeared to be on the surface. It became glaringly obvious to me that she employed the same tactics to control her staff as perpetrators of domestic violence did in their relationships: with coercion, intimidation, threats, and emotional abuse. I learned that my boss was every bit as manipulative and dangerous as the violent men in the community that our agency was tasked with protecting women against. I had been a target of this kind of subversive behavior before by the men I'd worked with in the jail, but I was completely caught off guard to find this same dynamic playing out within an all-female organization whose mission it was to keep women safe from abuse in the first place.

When it became apparent that my boss would not change her evil ways, I started cautiously searching for other employment. I tried to be as secretive as possible, fearing the wrath I would face if my attempts to leave were discovered. During this time, the *monster in charge* came into my office one day with a devious smile spread across her wicked face and informed me that "no employee ever leaves this place unless I say so. I will sabotage every attempt you make to get another job, and I have a long reach in this community, so don't think you'll ever get away from here unless I want you to!"

It was because of such threats that I found myself applying for a position in a court-ordered diversion program serving inner-city delinquent youth in downtown Minneapolis—forty miles away from the monster's sphere of influence. I ended up back in the *land of corrections* that I had promised myself I would never enter again, but at the time, it felt like the best escape plan I could hatch.

For the next four years, I worked as a counselor in a day treatment program with felony-level offenders between the ages of thirteen and seventeen. The kids who were court-ordered to our program were primarily African American boys who had gotten into serious trouble with the law by stealing cars, selling drugs, carrying guns, assaulting others, and engaging in highly dangerous gang activity in the community. My co-counselor, Derek, was a wonderful, six-foot-four black man with an infectious laugh that filled the room, and he generously welcomed me to my new job like we'd known each other forever. His acts of kindness toward me were incredibly healing after being treated like shit by the woman I was forced to flee in my last position.

My job consisted of doing individual, group, and family counseling; making home visits to the families of the kids on my caseload; and trying to get the teens I counseled to successfully complete our day program, obtain an education, and avoid violating the terms of their probation and thereby get "sent up" to out-of-home residential treatment facilities where they could spend up to two years sequestered away from their homes and communities. Unlike my work in the adult jail, I enjoyed that job a great deal because I wasn't trying to constantly assert my authority over the kids in our program. Instead, I was focused on working collaboratively with the teens, their families, and key individuals within the juvenile justice system to help our clients gain access to important knowledge, tools, and resources. They could then have a chance to carve out a better future for themselves rather than run the mean streets of Minneapolis for the rest of their lives.

My work with those teens changed me as a person. I witnessed devastating poverty, discrimination, child abuse, racism, police brutality, and many other forms of social injustice that opened my eyes to issues I had never had to face as a white woman in this country. I also saw incredible strength, fortitude, resiliency, and pride among the youth and families I worked with, and I was humbled by how carefree my life seemed in comparison to theirs, by virtue of the color of my skin. I learned what it felt like to constantly be the minority in the room. I came face to face with my own prejudices that

I wasn't even aware I had and discovered that every person's access to "The American Dream" in our country is far from equal.

It was intensely uncomfortable for me to go through the arduous process of being confronted daily with deep distrust and outright contempt because of what I looked like on the outside. My clients seemed to automatically judge me harshly because of it—a dynamic they had to navigate every day of their lives as people of color in this country.

I didn't think of myself as "the enemy" but was often treated as such. I didn't view myself as privileged but realized that indeed I was—in ways that hadn't been obvious to me before. The amount of introspection and personal transformation I had to go through in order to genuinely understand and be effective with the kids and families I worked with in that job was nothing short of agonizing for a sheltered white girl from Nebraska. However, the important lessons I learned from my clients and coworkers became an essential building block in my development as a helping professional, as well as a citizen of the world.

Our team was blessed when a highly skilled African American educator named Bill was hired as a consultant to help us create more success with the kids in our program. Bill was instrumental in teaching me about the true legacy of our country's racial inequality that I had never been exposed to in all my years of school. He compassionately taught me about the beauty, strength, wisdom, and values of African American culture and mentored me on the importance of racial humility and cultural competence in my work before those terms became part of our mainstream vernacular.

The kind of "on-the-job training" I received during those four years was invaluable. The hard-earned insights I gained changed me in dramatic ways and ignited a burning desire inside me to make the world a better place for us all to live in. So, with Bill's strong and loving encouragement and beautifully written letter of recommendation, I finally enrolled in graduate school to become a social worker at last.

I spent three years attending the weekend college program at Augsburg College (now University) in Minneapolis on a part-time basis while I continued to work full time. I eventually had to quit my job and live off student loans during the final year of my social work program because there literally weren't enough hours in the day for me to complete my internship, go to class, research and write a hundred-page thesis, and punch a full-time clock. Something had to give, and it ended up being my gainful employment.

While in school, I made another promise to myself: I vowed that after I graduated from Augsburg, I would never take another job in the field of corrections—youth or adult—because I was already burned out from the intensity of that difficult work. I longed to forge a new career path once I obtained my master's degree. Unfortunately, my plans didn't exactly turn out as I had hoped.

Due to complicating political factors in the new social work program's accreditation process, for an entire year after our first class of MSW students graduated, we were technically considered ineligible to qualify for a wide variety of open social work jobs in Minnesota. The educational institution was deemed "non-accredited," and therefore, our degrees were considered inferior. So, despite the promises I made to myself two years earlier, I ended up getting a job as a social worker in a residential treatment center for delinquent youth—the very same place where the kids I had previously worked with often went when they got "sent up" for violating the terms of their probation.

Those next three years were full of continued learning, growth, and expansion for me both personally and professionally. Although I was familiar with the kinds of youth we had at the "home school," it was an entirely different stressful dynamic to work in a treatment setting where the young men in our care were on-site twenty-four hours a day for months or years at a time. Although I tremendously honed my clinical social work skills while employed on that campus, I was growing weary of the trauma and intensity of that sequestered environment and the frigid Minnesota winters I had already lived through for ten years.

I had been saving up money for some time with the dream of moving out west. My "mountain moving fund" made it possible for me to leave behind yet another set of "golden handcuffs" and start anew. I moved to Colorado without a job, which seemed crazy to many people, especially to my parents who had raised me to never quit one position before I had secured another. But by that time, I had enough confidence in my skills and was certain I could land another job without difficulty.

I applied at different counseling agencies in the Denver area but soon discovered that I was already being pigeon-holed professionally because of my years of experience in the juvenile justice field. So, against my better judgment, I accepted a position as a mental health clinician for a boot camp program called Youthtrack that served incarcerated teens. It was housed on the campus of the maximum-security youth correctional facility known as Lookout Mountain in Golden.

I lasted all of a year in that position—which was the longest period any clinician had made it in that crazy environment. Each boy who was court-ordered to attend Youthtrack was sent there as a consequence of their criminal activity in the community. The boot camp model was loosely based on the concept of "scared straight," whereby the sentencing judges tried to "scare" the kids to straighten up their acts by removing them from their homes for three weeks and placing them in an altered reality system on the Lookout Mountain campus.

Upon arrival to the program, each boy got their head shaved, was forced to wear a neon-orange jumpsuit, and had to march around all day doing a bizarre combination of calisthenics run by a military-style staff member, and then was required to attend treatment groups for the remainder of the day.

I saw an endless parade of kids in my office who were anxious, depressed, suicidal, and completely overwhelmed at what they were being put through. Unfortunately, I could do little to help them because of the way the program was structured. That only added to my feelings of angst and was a contributing factor for me to accept a new job located a mere forty yards away on the same campus.

My mom seemed excited about the new position because it sounded prestigious on paper. I was recruited and hired as a faculty member of the University of Colorado Health Sciences Center in Denver and stationed in one of the many residential "cottages" on the Lookout campus. Each cottage housed around forty court-ordered young men ranging in age from thirteen to twenty. Unlike the kids I worked with for years in the Twin Cities, who were primarily African American and from two main gang-laden areas of North and South Minneapolis, the boys at Lookout were literally from every corner of the state. Some of the kids were from bigger cities like Denver or Boulder, but others were from small, distant towns I'd never heard of. There were far more white kids in the program than I was accustomed to, as well as a large population of Hispanic youth from the various agricultural communities throughout the state.

The one thing all of the kids at Lookout had in common was that they were considered the most serious juvenile offenders in Colorado. They were sentenced to out-of-home placement in that maximum-security facility for up to five years or until they turned twenty-one and "paroled out"—whichever came first.

The crimes these young men had been convicted of were divided into three distinct categories, including property offenders (car theft, shoplifting, burglary), violent offenders (assault, gang activity, weapons possession), and sexual offenders (indecent exposure, rape, child molestation). Regardless of the fact that their crimes were classified differently, all of the youth were housed together under the same roof, which was the complete opposite of how the cottages at the home school in Minnesota had been arranged. As a result, the "mental health kids" on my caseload were sent there because of the unlawful actions they had committed against property or people or both.

Thinking back on those days, I now realize that I was probably burned out before I even started that job. However, the university paycheck far exceeded what I had been making as a clinician in the boot camp program, so I didn't feel like I could turn down such a lucrative offer at that point in my career. Plus, my mom was elated about my faculty status and benefits, so that had to count for something!

I spent another two years of my life counseling kids and families within the dangerous confines of that institution and became increasingly miserable and depressed from the long-term effects of being immersed in such a toxic work environment. Things went from bad to worse on April 20, 1999.

I had just finished facilitating a ninety-minute "violent offender group," and as I walked from the therapy room into the central area of the cottage, I was met with an image I'll never forget. The kids and staff were all standing in stunned silence in front of large TV monitors. Every one of them was watching the horror of the Columbine High School shooting as it unfolded in real time on the television screen, while the actual events were taking place only twenty miles away in Littleton. It was the most shocking thing I had ever seen, as it was the first mass school shooting in our country's history, but unfortunately, it was far from our last.

For an entire year following that tragic event, a law enforcement "movement" began taking place around our shocked and grieving state. Countless teenage boys were rounded up, arrested, and charged with crimes related to planning their own school shootings or for posting content on the internet that was deemed criminally violent enough to pose a threat to public safety in Colorado. It felt like total mayhem everywhere I looked.

Most of those juvenile offenders eventually ended up at Lookout, and my job became even more unbearable as I had to don more layers of emotional armor just to make it through another exhausting day. I knew with every ounce of my being that I had to get out of that place before the last shreds of my sanity and humanity were gone. I just wasn't sure how.

Stepping into My
Hospice Skin

"Get out of that chair! My husband's sitting there!"

I t was my first week of employee orientation as a brand-new hospice social worker, and I was *way* beyond nervous! Six months earlier, I had abruptly quit my job working at Lookout Mountain. I used to tell people outside of that industry that in order to survive, you had to "don your emotional armor" before entering the secured gates of the institution every day and assume that everything the court-ordered kids told you was a lie until proven otherwise, because if you didn't, you'd get eaten alive. That relentless negativity took its toll on me over time—especially since my natural way in the world is to be open, vulnerable, and trusting.

I had never before vacated a job without having *some kind of plan* as to what I would do next to support myself. However, a graphic death threat from one of my clients served as the perfect motivating factor for an immediate career change. I turned in my notice and freed myself from that emotional bondage without a clue what I would do to keep a roof over my head. All I knew for certain was that I was *done for good* working with self-destructive young men in lockup! Other than that, I prayed that I would find a new job where I felt safe and valued, one that had the potential for me to receive more thank-yous than f-yous at the end of the day. Many months later, when I came across a job ad for a hospice social work position, for inexplicable reasons even I didn't understand, I decided to apply.

Most social workers *with any sense* at all would not make the leap from working with teenage offenders to caring for 75- to 103-year-old patients who were facing the end of their lives, but that's exactly what I did—which explains *why* I was feeling so panicked and overwhelmed during my first week of training. I had absolutely no background or education to prepare me for this next chapter in my professional life, and it was terrifying.

On day four, I left behind all the stacks of paperwork that every new hire had to complete and was sent out into the real world to shadow a well-seasoned social worker named Lynn. The goal of those eight hours was for me to prepare for my new role and responsibilities by observing her in action. I literally had no clue what to expect, as it was also my first time entering an assisted living community where many of the hospice patients resided.

Lynn stopped in the beautifully decorated hallway outside of Roxanne's apartment to prep me for the patient I was about to meet. Lynn explained that Roxanne had been slowly declining for over five months due to heart failure, but now she was significantly changing and starting to "transition." *Transition to what?* I remember thinking. I had no concept of what Lynn was referring to, but I was about to find out.

I trailed behind Lynn into the once-spacious abode that was now crowded with wheelchairs, oxygen concentrators, and a hospital bed in the center of the room. Roxanne was lying on her back in bed, her arms raised high above her head with her eyes tightly closed. Her lips were moving as if she were speaking to someone we couldn't see, but no sound emanated from her mouth.

Lynn announced our arrival in the room, but Roxanne did not acknowledge our presence in any way. She continued on with her silent conversation as if she hadn't heard a thing until Lynn softly inquired if she would like a drink of water. Roxanne surprised me by opening her eyes just enough to view the cup that Lynn was holding, while lowering her arms to reach for it. I watched as Lynn skillfully assisted Roxanne in taking a few tiny sips of fluid into her parched mouth and was amazed to see her clamp her eyes and lips shut once more as soon as her thirst was quenched. It seemed that Roxanne had rapidly retreated into a secret world of her own, and we were definitely *not* invited to join her.

I wanted to be unobtrusive and out of the way, so I sat down in the only empty chair, which was adjacent to the bed. My rear end had barely touched the seat when Roxanne suddenly opened her eyes, looked right at me, and emphatically stated, "Get *out* of that chair! My husband's sitting there!" With a rush of adrenaline born of pure fear, I leapt out of the chair as if I were spring-loaded.

It took every ounce of restraint I had to keep from bolting out of the room, away from the building, and into a different career as far from hospice as I could possibly find! Luckily for me, Lynn prevented my untimely and embarrassing exit by sauntering up beside me, calmly placing her hand on my shoulder, and offering a genuine apology to the patient on my behalf for the mistake I had made. The only thought in my mind in that instant was, *Oh my God! What the* hell *was I thinking when I took this job!? I must be* insane!

My memories of the rest of that visit are far less vivid, due to all the cascading stress hormones that had flooded my brain following that inter-action. For a while, my anxiety was so high that I had to literally will myself to remain close to the bed so that I could continue to observe Lynn working her social work magic. But once I became calmer and more able to fully pay attention to what was transpiring around me, I realized how masterful Lynn was in the way she provided care, support, and counsel to Roxanne in a manner that was solemn and yet also joy-filled and reverent. I watched in awe as Lynn compassionately ministered to the shell of a woman before her with tenderness, humanity, and dignity. I had never before witnessed anything like it in my career, and it shook me to the core.

We left Roxanne's room and found a private place in the building to debrief what had taken place during the visit. Lynn calmly told me how Roxanne's husband, Tom, had died the previous week in that same apartment. Since that time, Roxanne had unequivocally insisted that Tom was "sitting vigil" in that seemingly empty chair next to the bed, patiently waiting for her to join him. Others before me had also attempted to sit in that same vacant chair, with the same startling results.

Lynn spent a few minutes educating me about how people who are nearing death frequently have a "welcoming committee" hovering in the room that only they can see. Lynn explained that this committee is comprised of important people in the person's life who have already "passed over to the other side" and are waiting to chaperone the individual who is dying across that thin veil that separates the world of the living from the world of the dead.

The look on my face must have spoken volumes about my extraordinarily high level of ignorance and discomfort with the subject matter, as Lynn gently assured me, "Don't worry about all of this right now, dear. After you've been doing this job for a while, it'll all begin to make perfect sense. Just give it time."

Lynn gave me ample opportunities to ask her questions, which she answered in a deliberate, kind, and unrushed fashion so that a novice like me could understand. She also created space for me to process my feelings around the visit with Roxanne and to share my observations in an incredibly safe and nurturing manner. I had never before been mentored in such a loving way by anyone in my professional life, and it felt refreshing after spending so many previous years in the "sink or swim" world of corrections.

During the time I spent observing the interactions between Lynn and Roxanne in that small apartment, a huge and profound awareness was beginning to take root deep inside of me. It was like being transported to another dimension of time and space without my feet ever leaving the ground. I realized that I "wasn't in Kansas anymore," as the classic line goes, and that this new path I had stumbled upon couldn't have been further away from my previous road in the not-so-merry land of juvenile jail. Little did I know then how safe and respected I would eventually come to feel in my hospice skin or how gratifying and life-changing I would find the journey.

I can't honestly say that I never encountered occasional difficulties or conflicts with the people I served as a hospice social worker, but I *can say* that no one ever dropped the f-bomb on me during that time. Better still, I have a cherished collection of cards and letters that were given to me by grateful families, thanking me for the care, compassion, and support my team and I provided to them and their loved ones during a most difficult, vulnerable, and sacred time. That correspondence fills a special drawer in my home and a hallowed place in my heart.

During my last few months as a burned out and disillusioned social worker in youth corrections, I used to sarcastically joke with my colleagues about my fervent wish to "parole" from behind the barbed wire fences and madness of that job before I turned forty. For some reason, it never dawned on me that I could resign and walk out whenever I pleased. Because, much like the young men who were locked inside that institution, I, too, felt utterly trapped—imprisoned by my limited thinking and perceived helplessness. Were it not for the death threats I received that fateful day, which made "paroling" not only a viable option but an absolute necessity, I might never have had the courage to leave that position, despite how miserable and ineffective I had become. *Who knew* I'd owe a debt of gratitude to the rage-filled young man who threatened to take my life in such a violent manner? I now believe that young man showed up on my path as an unlikely savior whose abhorrent behavior woke me up, drove me to action, and probably *saved my life* in more ways than I can count.

Even with all of the unexpected twists and turns that took place over the six months leading up to my career change, I never imagined in my wildest dreams that my emancipation from that important but incredibly taxing work would lead me to a place where I would companion people who were dying. Or that I would discover so much about myself in that process by bearing witness to the miracles that can happen when you finally get the chance to combine your natural gifts and abilities with a warm and receptive audience that graciously welcomes all the love, trust, and kindness you have to give.

I realize now that my job in hospice offered me much more than just a way to earn a paycheck without threats of daily harm. It afforded me the chance to grow, to heal, to connect, and to get clear on what *really* matters, as well as what doesn't. Working with people who were dying or facing life-threatening illnesses gave me a much deeper appreciation for how beautiful life can be when we stop taking it for granted, start breaking free from our own mental servitude, and finally escape to where we were meant to be all along.

My Greatest Teacher

"I would have gladly read a thousand books on grief and loss than have my dad die within eight months of starting my hospice career, but that's not the cards that I was dealt."

started my job as a hospice social worker in October 2001 with absolutely *no* idea of what I was getting into. I vividly remember writing my cover letter numerous times in a desperate effort to make it *sound* like I was *actually qualified* for the position. There was a pile of crumpled-up papers on the floor from my failed attempts at making myself sound remotely capable of meeting the basic job qualifications. Then I got a great idea: Rather than try to sell myself as something I'm not, I should just be honest and transparent about my shortcomings in the letter. After all, up to that point in my career, I had never worked as a medical social worker, had no prior experience in palliative or end-of-life care, and had never seen anyone die except on television.

However, I did have years of counseling experience behind me and was well-versed in working with every imaginable kind of client and family system—the mainstay of a social worker's skill set and life. So, despite my low expectations, I rewrote the cover letter one last time and mailed it off with my resume—never expecting anyone to even bother to call me back.

To my great surprise, my phone rang, and the woman on the other end invited me to come in for an interview. The manager and other social workers I met in that setting exuded incredible kindness, compassion, intelligence, and a gentle, peaceful presence that instantly put me at ease. It couldn't have been more dramatically different from my last job interview years before, which took place behind barbed wire fences in juvenile jail.

When I got the job offer for the social work position the following week, I couldn't have been more shocked or elated. For reasons completely unknown to me at the time, I was magnetically drawn to hospice work despite feeling completely incompetent, ignorant, and ill-prepared for what I was stepping into. I *just knew* I had to take that job at the time, but I had no idea *why*.

The learning curve was overwhelming, but instead of the "baptism by fire" mentality of new-employee training that I had always encountered in previous jobs, my manager and peers in hospice patiently mentored me, tenderly counseled me, and graciously companioned me down this new and foreign path of end-of-life care. I felt utterly supported in a way I never knew was even possible in a place of work. Little did I know that I would need that kind of incredible benevolence a short time later. My world was about to turn upside down, and I never saw it coming.

On December 1, 2001, I was out of state attending the funeral of a cherished friend's mother. The day before the funeral, I got a phone call from my mom, who lived many states away in Nebraska. From the instant she said, "Hello Kay," I knew something was terribly wrong. I had never heard my mom's voice sound like it did that day. The tone was completely new and terribly grave. I could tell through the phone line that she was trying mightily to hold herself together and not break down. She called to tell me that my dad had been diagnosed with "treatable but not curable cancer" that day. Treatable. But. Not. Curable. Cancer. I was stunned.

I don't remember much else that she said after that—a common occurrence when your brain goes into shock to protect itself. I had only worked in hospice six weeks by that time, but six weeks was long enough for me to know that "treatable but not curable" meant *terminal*. My beloved father was going *to die*, and probably sooner than later. Life as I had always known it was about to change forever.

I remember hanging up the phone and sliding down the wall into a sobbing lump on the floor. My heart cracked wide open with a kind of pain I find difficult to describe in words. I cried and howled. I beat on the floor. I made guttural noises like a wounded animal left for dead and experienced pain that cut so deep, it seared through my soul like wildfire. I remember my friend coming out of the bathroom in her white bathrobe with an alarmed and questioning look on her face. I simply stated, "My dad has cancer," and broke into racking sobs.

My friend held my limp body against her own while my tears flowed down my face and onto her shoulder. She instinctively *knew* that I *needed to be held* and comforted. She understood that my heart had shattered into a million pieces in under five minutes during that phone call and that when there are *no words* of solace that one can reasonably offer in such a tender and vulnerable time, the gifts of silent presence and human touch are enough. I was to learn this lesson well during my years of hospice work to follow.

Those next six months leading up to my dad's death on June 25, 2002, were among the most challenging of my life on every level. Trying to learn a new job as difficult and inherently taxing as hospice when my personal world was imploding was unbelievably hard to navigate. Driving home five hundred miles every month to see my father growing weaker and weaker, while simultaneously trying to companion patients who were dying and their families, was an emotional tightrope walk of epic proportions. I constantly prayed that the proverbial net would catch me when I fell, which it did, over and over and over again.

The anticipatory grief process I went through was excruciating as I contemplated what my world would be like without my father in it. As I would later recount to new hospice staff and volunteers each year, "I would gladly have read a thousand books on grief and loss than have my dad die within eight months of starting my hospice career, but that's not the cards I was dealt."

What I came to understand and recognize was the hidden gift of my papa's untimely passing. I believe I would have eventually become a *really good* hospice social worker because of who I innately am and how I walk in the world, but I turned out to be a *really great* hospice social worker because of the upheaval I went through so early on in my job. My personal journey of grief leading up to my father's death prepared me to serve as no book or mentor ever could. He was, is, and continues to be my greatest teacher.

Going to the Well

"I learned a long time ago that there's no point in worrying about things you can't control. Life's a whole lot easier that way."

I remember the first time I laid eyes on Trudy. She was sitting in her wheelchair, a blanket draped across her lap, in the tiny, dilapidated nursing home room where she'd been sent for rehab therapy following her recent release from the hospital. The sun was brightly shining on Trudy's face when I knocked on the door to introduce myself. She looked up and greeted me with the warmest brown eyes and smile I'd ever seen, which instantly transformed the dour mood I'd been in prior to that moment. I had spent most of my day driving from one intense hospice visit to another in unrelenting Denver traffic before arriving at Trudy's room, and the stress of it had taken a toll on my frazzled nerves.

Trudy had just been admitted to our hospice program after being diagnosed with inoperable rectal cancer the week before at the age of seventy-eight. Much to the chagrin of her husband and daughters, Trudy had elected hospice care over pursuing any aggressive treatment measures, which her family had pushed for. After spending only a few minutes in Trudy's company, I could fully understand why her family had hoped that their beloved matriarch would choose radiation and chemotherapy over palliative care options so she could "fight to stay around longer."

Trudy explained: "Richard and my daughters tried their best to convince me to go the treatment route and get whatever radiation and chemo my doctor wanted to give me so that it could 'buy me some time.' But that just didn't make a lick of sense to me since there's no curing this cancer, even if I put myself through all of that. Why would I want to spend the last weeks or months of my life feeling sick and beaten down from all that medical mumbo jumbo in order to buy myself a few extra days on this earth? I'd just as soon enjoy every day I have left and skip all that needless sufferin' in between."

It dawned on me that Trudy was like some sort of an enlightened Buddha disguised as an ordinary-looking elderly woman in a wheelchair. I *just knew* that this unassuming and delightful being would teach me profound lessons in her simple, down-to-earth manner. We had barely met, but I already wanted to spend as much time in Trudy's company as I possibly could. After working as a hospice social worker for almost two years by then, I had learned the skill of intuitively knowing within the first thirty minutes of meeting them, which patients would steal my heart, and Trudy most definitely fell into that category in record time.

After we had conversed about all the transitions Trudy had been through the past few months, including her numerous hospitalizations, rehab admissions, and the discovery that she had terminal cancer, Trudy asked if I wanted to go somewhere else in the building where we could have a change of scenery for a little while. I immediately agreed to her suggestion and offered to take Trudy to the family lounge, which was located at the opposite end of the facility. I asked her if she would like me to give her a ride in her wheelchair or if she preferred to travel by propelling herself. She told me she would gladly take me up on my offer for a ride because it was challenging for her to wheel herself long distances.

"I only have one good arm these days, and it's my right. Since the stroke, I am partially paralyzed on the left side of my body, so my left arm is nearly worthless to me anymore. I'm just thankful that I don't go around in circles all day long since I only have one arm to steer with! Now wouldn't *that* be a sight!" We broke out laughing at her comment, and my bond with Trudy was cemented in that tender, funny moment.

A few weeks later, Trudy was transferred out of her rehab facility and permanently relocated to a nursing home in the foothills of the mountains outside of Denver, which was only a mile away from her home and husband of over fifty years. The hospice team continued to provide weekly care to Trudy in her new location, despite the fact that technically, the facility was located outside of our normal geographic service area. Everyone on the hospice team, including the nurse, chaplain, certified nursing assistant, and me, had gone to bat with our manager to make sure we could continue to care for Trudy after her move—if not for *her* sake, then for our own. Each of us on the team had fallen in love with Trudy for our own personal reasons. We would almost invent reasons to "go up the hill" to visit this adored patient, even if she wasn't having a pain crisis or any acute issues that needed to be urgently addressed.

I'll admit the obvious fact now: we often went to see Trudy not because of what she needed *from us* but because of what we all so freely received *from her* by just being in her presence. It was like "rare air" to be in Trudy's company. It was a distinct privilege to support her on her dying journey, a replenishing and nourishing experience for one's soul to just sit by her bedside. I referred to that phenomenon as "going to the well," and we all collectively understood what that phrase meant when it came to our beloved patient.

Trudy was a simple woman from Tennessee—unassuming in every way—but she had a folksy wisdom that was undeniable and a magnetic personality that drew you to her. She would say things that were so wise, yet she said them in this down-home, salt-of-the-earth sort of way that it almost sounded like poetry coming out of her mouth. I remember vividly talking with Trudy one day about how she had to give up driving years before when her stroke left her too impaired to operate a car any longer.

As part of that conversation, we discussed how close Trudy now lived in proximity to her home and husband, but how she would never be able to leave the confines of the long-term care facility to make it there again because of her physical limitations. I asked Trudy how she maintained such a positive outlook on life when she had so many losses to grieve, not the least of which was her incurable cancer. Trudy grinned at me with her infectious smile, her chocolate-brown eyes almost melting in kindness as she held my gaze and unpretentiously stated: "I learned a long time ago that there's no point in worrying about things you can't control. Life's a whole lot easier that way."

Oh, how I wanted to ask Trudy exactly *how* she navigated such difficult obstacles in her life with such apparent ease when most people would find themselves completely overwhelmed in her place. I longed to ask a million more questions about *how* she managed to avoid anger, resentment, self-pity, blame, and spiritual angst when so many hardships had come her way, and yet she was one of the calmest, most contented and grounded people I had ever met. I wanted to know *how* she was able to embrace her new calling as "the hall monitor" in the nursing home and shepherd her lost and confused comrades when their dementia prevented them from finding their rooms on their own. But I refrained from asking all those questions. Instead, I soaked in Trudy's words and memorized the look on her face and the lilt in her voice as she spoke in that soft Southern drawl that I found so endearing.

I wanted to remember *how it felt* to be in Trudy's presence for the rest of my days, especially the way she held my gaze with her smiling eyes and found remarkable joy in the simplest experiences. I wanted to embody the unconditional love and kindness that Trudy seemed to effortlessly bestow onto every person she met and to learn to follow my instincts when making difficult choices about what *I believe* is best for me, even when others who love me may not agree.

I selfishly longed to learn from Trudy's deep wisdom so that when life delivers loss and misfortune my way, as it does to us all, I can be ready. I longed to be able to call on my memories of Trudy in those challenging times; draw on the lessons of her strength, humor, and quiet courage in the face of my own adversity; and hopefully, muster even a fraction of the grace and acceptance I witnessed in her for my journey ahead. That, indeed, would be drinking from the well.

Thankfully, Trudy died as she had lived. Peacefully, without a fuss, and surrounded by family and caregivers who loved her so much. Despite the basket-ball-sized cancerous tumor that had grown in her abdomen, Trudy remarkably never had any pain. I'll never know if it was because of her incredibly optimistic and accepting attitude about her illness or just God's way of protecting one of his flock from such excruciating discomfort; either way, it was a blessing that she never had to endure any suffering as her time on earth drew to a close.

On what I had guessed would be my last visit to Trudy based on her declining condition, we discussed her impending death and thoughts about what happens next. Trudy had a deep faith and was excited at the idea of reacquainting with relatives long since passed. She was ready to explore what the next Great Mystery had in store for her. I couldn't resist the temptation at that moment to ask her if she would be nice enough to say hi to my dad when she got to Heaven and tell him how much we all missed him.

My dad had died almost a year before, and the hole in my heart was still gaping without him in it. Trudy looked at me with those beautiful brown eyes and said she would be honored to deliver that message to my dad for me and very much looked forward to meeting him "if he's anything like you, dear."

Some might call it coincidence, but I'm not so sure there wasn't a Divine Plan unfolding when Trudy died peacefully three days later—on the one-year anniversary of my father's death. So, when I remember and honor my papa every year on that sacred date, I also remember Trudy and feel confident that my message was delivered to Dad in style.

423-8150

"Send me a sign when you get to where you're going."

When I started out in hospice, I had no prior experience working with people who were terminally ill or with supporting families through the intensely difficult process of losing someone they love. In fact, during my undergraduate training in psychology or when I was getting my master's degree in social work, I never had a single class that specifically focused on death and dying, grief and loss, or remotely similar themes. As a result, when I started my new job in hospice, I did what I always do when I'm facing situations I've never experienced before—I read everything on the subject that I could get my hands on and asked everyone I knew to share their wisdom and tricks of the trade with me.

One of the first books I was introduced to during that time was called *Final Gifts: Understanding the Special Awareness, Needs and Communications of the Dying* by Maggie Callanan and Patricia Kelley—both well-seasoned hospice nurses. In vignette form, the book described the changes and challenges that people who are dying face in a way that made sense to my brain and in a manner that I found easy to assimilate. That book changed my life and enhanced my ability to competently companion patients and families who were grappling with terminal illnesses. It provided me with the knowledge and tools I needed to communicate with my patients who were dying in a way I could quickly integrate and apply to my life—both personally and professionally.

Final Gifts laid the groundwork for me to begin to comprehend the complexity of death and dying through reading the simple but informative heartfelt stories, and it was the primary resource I suggested to families. In truth, reading *Final Gifts* also inspired me to "someday" author my own book of vignettes written from the social work and family perspective.

One concept that book revealed was how those of us still living frequently look for signs that tell us our loved ones who have passed on have safely made it to the other side—or to whichever destination they may have hoped to go after they died, depending on their belief systems.

My father was a man of deep faith who believed there was a Heaven and that loved ones who died before him would be awaiting his arrival at the Pearly Gates. For the majority of my life up to that point, my parents had lived in the same house on Woods Boulevard in Lincoln, Nebraska. For decades, their phone number remained unchanged—like a North Star I could always count on. I used to joke that if I ever got dementia, one thing I would probably *never forget* when everything else was gone was my parents' phone number. That's how etched in stone it had become in my mind.

For days leading up to my dad's death, I sat with him at bedside and asked if he would send me a sign when he got to where he was going. Papa agreed to my requests with a soft-spoken "yes," a squeeze of the hand, or by a tear that silently slid down his cheek—depending on his energy level that day. So, for months after my dad died in June 2002, I constantly looked for signs informing me that the man I loved so deeply had made his celestial transition safe and sound.

One night many months after Dad left this world, my sign finally came. I was in a deep sleep, and Dad appeared to me in my dream *so vividly* that I could actually *see* and *feel him* with every ounce of my being. In the dream,

I told Dad how much I missed him and how desperately I longed to talk to him again. He answered in his typical calm and laidback fashion by saying: "Kaycee, if you want to talk to me, honey, all you have to do is dial 423-8150, and I'll be there."

I remember so many feelings rushing over me in my dream that night. Feelings of elation that I had seen my dad and knew he was all right. Feelings of frustration that I had missed so many months of talking to him when I could have simply picked up the phone and gotten him on the line, and feelings of exuberance that I had found a way to communicate with Papa Dale once again. That is, after all, what I had been praying for every day since he drew his last breath.

As I slowly awoke from my deep repose, I was at first overjoyed that I had reconnected with my father after such a long absence. I remember thinking that I needed to jump out of bed and call him before another wasted minute went by. But then, as wakefulness fully set in, I became conscious of the tear-soaked pillow beneath my head and painfully aware that I couldn't simply dial 423-8150 to talk to my dad any longer, as sad as that fact was.

However, the gift of his long-awaited "sign" that night allowed me to *know* beyond a shadow of a doubt that Papa was still out there, still watching over his "Little Bug" as he's always done, and that signs are all around us that our loved ones who have passed on are close by—even when our human eyes can't see them. When we take the time to *get still*, to tune into a *different frequency* of faith and knowing, and to *listen* with the part of our hearts and souls that neither time nor space can ever come between, they will always answer our call.

The Promise of
Something New

*"You know, there's just something about you that
I like, but I can't quite put my foot on it!"*

I pulled my old green Subaru into the nursing home parking lot near the storied Red Rocks Amphitheatre in Morrison, Colorado. It was a beautiful spring day with clear blue skies above and a distinct crispness in the mountain air. I was coming to meet a new patient named Doris, who had been admitted to our hospice service the previous day.

When I entered the front doors of the long-term care facility, I was struck, as always, by how depressing those settings can appear at first blush. Looking at all the elders slumped and dozing in their wheelchairs at ten o'clock in the morning was never an easy sight to see. When I first started in hospice, I used to cringe every time I had to go into one of those places, as it forced me to be subjected to all the uncomfortable sights, sounds, and smells that most of us like to avoid even thinking about, let alone experience.

In the early days of my job, it could take me at least fifteen minutes to get from the entryway of a building to my patient's room at the other end because I would stop every time a resident called out, "Help me, help me!"

or attempted to grab my hand as I was passing by just to have some human touch. It took me a long time to learn the fine art of navigating those crowded hallways in a respectful manner without overstepping my bounds by trying to meet the infinite needs of every lonely soul I encountered along the way.

I located Doris's small room just past the nurse's station on the north wing of the facility. When I knocked on the door to introduce myself, Doris looked up from her wheelchair, which was sitting near the window overlooking a bird feeder that was teeming with feathered friends of every kind. Doris had a colorful afghan draped over her knees, and when I inquired if it was okay for me to come in and chat for a minute, she quickly replied, "By all means, Dearie! All I've got is time!" I knew in that instant that Doris and I would be fast friends.

After introducing myself to Doris, I pulled the one tattered old chair from the far side of the room up closer to her so we could start our conversation. Reading the information I had received from the hospice nurse who admitted Doris to our program the previous day, I learned that Doris had been residing in that facility for the past two years. She had been placed there by Adult Protective Services after one of her close neighbors called to report concerns about the well-being of her friend across the street.

When APS investigated the matter, they discovered that Doris's fifty-seven-year-old son, Marvin, had been living in the basement of his mother's home for over a year under the pretense of being her primary caregiver. Prior to his arrival, Doris's Alzheimer's disease was already in the moderate stages. She was having difficulty accomplishing everyday tasks, like feeding and dressing herself, bathing, using the bathroom, and ambulating safely due to her impaired short-term memory.

Doris had also begun to experience significant problems performing her instrumental activities of daily living—those seemingly routine tasks that allow a person to live independently in a community setting in a self-reliant fashion. For instance, Doris had been getting lost driving to the grocery store and back, despite making that same trek for over two decades. She had become unable to sequence tasks to prepare meals or follow a recipe and frequently forgot to eat at all because of her memory changes.

When Doris could no longer manage her home, medications, finances, or her life because of her progressing dementia, Marvin moved in to "help his mom out" so she could remain living in her familiar environment as long as possible. The only problem was that Marvin did *anything* but actually "help."

Based on the findings of the APS investigation, it was determined that Doris's son was not at all the "caregiver" he had led people to believe he was. Marvin had a long history of reckless and irresponsible behavior and hadn't been able to hold down a steady job for over twenty years. Marvin had a gambling addiction and, without his mother's knowledge, had been using her considerable assets to put toward his mounting debts. Even though this wayward son had outwardly acted as if he were devoted to his mother's care, he could usually be found at the local bar or casino from early afternoon until closing time many nights of the week, leaving Doris alone at home—hungry, confused, scared, incontinent, and wondering what she was supposed to do next.

The APS investigation uncovered that among his countless egregious acts, Marvin had financially exploited his unassuming mother out of all of her hard-earned savings in order to bankroll his gambling habit and had borrowed so much money against her house that Doris owed more debt on it than it was worth. All of those atrocities took place outside of Doris's awareness due to her brain changes and dementia. When the APS investigation finally ended, Marvin went off to jail, and Doris was moved to a semi-private "Medicaid" room in a care facility because her only son had left her not only homeless but penniless.

There are few obvious "silver linings" when it comes to having a disease like dementia that can decimate someone's cherished memories, independence, and personhood, but in Doris's case, one of them may have been the inability to comprehend or remember what her offspring had done to her under the guise of "caring." In many respects, Doris was lucky that she couldn't recall the events leading up to her admission to that nursing home. She didn't remember being hungry and frightened night after night when Marvin was at the bar, or how he would yell at her to "Shut the hell up!" when she repeatedly asked him the same question. Doris didn't remember the way she sat for hours in her soiled clothing, waiting for Marvin to change her, or how confused she got when she didn't even recognize her own reflection in the mirror. And thankfully, Doris didn't have a single memory of the child she raised stealing everything she had worked her whole life for in order to feed his addictions and destructive lifestyle. Due to her nearly annihilated memory, Doris did not dwell on the misfortunes of the past but rather lived firmly in the present moment, where joy was accessible and where every moment held a promise of newness.

From our first encounter, Doris and I shared a bond that was quite magical. During her first six months in the facility, she had a stroke that left her semi-paralyzed and confined to a wheelchair. As part of my weekly visits, I took Doris outside so she could watch the squirrels frolic in the courtyard, listen to the birds singing in the trees, and feel the sunshine warm her withered body. Doris's childlike delight in watching the natural world bubbling all around her was obvious in the way her eyes lit up and in the look of pure joy that spread across her face as she intently observed all that was happening around her. Doris had a way of enjoying life's simplest pleasures that, up until meeting her, I had never taken the time to *truly notice* or appreciate.

Learning from the exquisite example that Doris set, my ability to become more mindful in the present moment irrevocably changed as well, and that is one of the greatest gifts Doris ever gave me.

Every time I arrived at the door to her room, Doris greeted me like a long-lost friend. Yet, because she could never recall who I was from one week to the next, I learned to introduce myself accordingly. I have no way of proving it, but

I always had an intuitive sense that deep down inside, Doris recognized me on some basic level, or at least had an emotional memory of how I made her *feel* when the two of us were together. Even when I briefly stepped outside into the hallway of the nursing home to get her some fresh water to drink, when I returned moments later, Doris would address me as if for the first time—like I was a fresh new source of delight for her to revel in. Instead of feeling annoyed by this behavior, it only endeared that precious woman to me even more.

One experience I looked forward to on my visits with Doris was the amount of laughter we shared. During one of my favorite visits, I had to leave her room numerous times to fetch some coffee, a box of Kleenex, and a nurse to administer pain medication. When I returned again after my third errand, I sat back down in the tattered chair next to my beloved hospice patient. Doris looked over at me, patted me lovingly on the leg, and said, "You know, there's just something about you that I like, but I can't quite put *my foot* on it!" That slight but hilarious word choice error sent me into a fit of uncontrollable laughter. As often happens, my laughter became contagious, and Doris started to chuckle right along with me, even though she probably didn't have a clue what I found funny in the first place. At one point, we were laughing so hard that tears were streaming down our faces. Just then, the nursing assistant entered the room to bring Doris her mail and looked at us incredulously, as if we had both completely lost our minds, then scurried out of the room as quickly as she had come. That only made us laugh harder.

A major stroke took Doris's life long ago, but her memory lives on in my heart and spirit. Every time I watch the squirrels frolic in my backyard, tune into the sweet song of the birds outside my window, or warm my aging body in the sun's glowing light, I think of Doris. And whenever I am able to quiet my busy mind long enough to be mindful of the present moment instead of dwelling on the past or worrying about the future, I remember Doris—a woman whose sense of joy was always readily accessible and who lived the last chapter of her life relishing the wonder and promise of something new.

The Cowboy

*"Why didn't Dad just sign that goddamned DNR form
like I asked him to? Now I am forced to make that decision
for him, and I have no idea in hell what to do!"*

veryone affectionately called him "The Cowboy," but his name was
Jack. After being introduced to Jack by the nursing home staff on my
first hospice visit, I could easily see where Jack earned his nickname.

Jack was eighty years old and dressed in faded Wrangler jeans that were
held up by a belt adorned with a huge silver buckle. He wore black weathered
cowboy boots and a Western-style button-down plaid shirt. His tattered
cowboy hat lay nearby on his bedside table next to the oxygen tank. Jack's
small, crowded room was stacked with old Western movies that he loved to
watch over and over again to break the monotony of the long, lonely days
in the nursing home. They also helped take his mind off his wife, who had
just been admitted to the emergency room of a nearby hospital for a brain
aneurysm two days before.

Jack talked slowly and deliberately, with a deep Southern drawl that
permeated his speech with every word he spoke. When he smiled, his weathered face cracked wide open like the parched Oklahoma soil he ranched on
for years when he was a younger man and still "riding the range." But smiles

were few and far between today because Jack was worried. Worried about his wife and if she was going to live or die. Worried about his own health since his chronic obstructive pulmonary disease (COPD) had grown progressively worse from years of smoking three packs of cigarettes a day to the point where he now found himself on hospice and facing the last six months of his life.

Jack's previous heart attacks only added insult to injury when it came to the condition of his fragile health. However, Jack wasn't focused so much on his own potential demise as he was on getting better so that he could leave the nursing home and go care for his precious wife, who Jack wanted to be with more than anything else in the world.

For nearly sixty years, Jack and Betty had been married. They raised their son, Tim, on the ranch in Oklahoma and lived a good and happy life there for decades before relocating to a small town on the eastern plains of Colorado to be closer to their Denver family. Only in recent years had they moved into the "big city" so they could see Tim and their grandkids on a regular basis and get the extra support they needed in their twilight years.

Jack's shortness of breath had become significantly worse since moving to the Mile High City, and he was now completely reliant on many liters of oxygen a day, which he detested, to keep him alive. Even the smallest of tasks, like walking ten feet to the bathroom, could exhaust him for hours, but that didn't mean that Jack was even close to giving up. To an old cowboy like Jack, you get back up on the horse after you fall and keep on riding. Giving up or giving in to his illness was simply not an option that Jack would ever consider. Not now. Not ever.

One of my tasks as a hospice social worker was to address whether my patients had completed their advance directives and, if not, to assist them with that process, if desired. Advance directives consisted of living wills, medical durable powers of attorney, and other documents that clearly spelled out a patient's wishes for future medical care if and when they reached a point where they were unable to speak or advocate for themselves due to a medical crisis or a significant change in their health status.

One medical document we always addressed was the DNR (do not resuscitate) form. Over 95 percent of the clients on our hospice service chose to sign a DNR form, stating that they did not want to be resuscitated should their heart and breathing stop. Given the terminal nature of the illnesses that all of our hospice folks were facing, it was typically a pretty straightforward choice for them to make. These patients and families were well-informed that the likelihood of going through such a medically intrusive endeavor would only serve to make their already compromised health even worse, should they survive the traumatic intervention at all. However, for The Cowboy, that argument was "total horseshit" and one that he refused to even entertain.

Before his admission to hospice, Jack had a well-documented history of opting out of signing a DNR form whenever the topic was brought to his attention during one of his countless hospitalizations and rehab stays. The Cowboy was fervently opposed to even discussing the issue since he wanted to be resuscitated at all costs. Jack's singular focus was to be there for Betty when she woke up from her coma in the hospital, and he couldn't very well do that if he were dead then, could he?! And Jack had good reason to believe that he was tough enough to live through being revived if necessary—he had already done so three times in the past and lived to tell about it! So, clearly, neither Jack's son nor the hospice team could convince him that he couldn't get the same results a fourth time.

I visited Jack on countless occasions over the coming weeks and talked to his son by phone to offer support after every visit. To say that Tim had a lot on his plate was a huge understatement. Tim was the appointed medical decision-maker for both of his parents, being the only child. His mom was in a coma on life support in a Denver hospital, while his dad was across town facing the final months of his life under hospice care and half out of his mind with worry about Betty. How much stress can one caregiver realistically expect to handle at any given time?

In every conversation I had with Tim, he pleaded with me to try to get his dad to sign a DNR form, given Jack's deteriorating health. Although it was a topic that Jack hated to discuss, I did my best to broach the subject for Tim's sake, but I never gained any ground despite my considerable efforts. Jack would just "not go there."

Then one day, the inevitable happened. Jack had another heart attack and was rushed to the emergency room at a nearby hospital. Because he was a "full code"—meaning that if his heart or breathing were to stop, Jack wanted to have all possible resuscitation procedures provided to keep him alive, the paramedics and medical team performed every heroic effort they could to save him. They administered CPR and had to crack his ribs in the process. They "gave him the paddles" and somehow managed to shock his heart back into rhythm with a defibrillator in the ambulance.

At the hospital, The Cowboy was placed on a ventilator because he was no longer able to breathe on his own. So, Jack got his wish of "being saved" at all costs once again, only this time, the price tag was extremely high. This was especially true for Tim—with two parents teetering on the edge of life in separate locations, in one unfolding nightmare of family drama.

For almost a week, Jack remained hooked up to tubes and numerous machines in the intensive care unit. In his confused and agitated state, he required four-point restraints in his hospital bed to prevent him from ripping out the tubing that was keeping him alive. Along with being available to make decisions regarding his mom, Tim now had the added burden of having to "play God" and make the excruciating decision of when to "pull the plug" and disconnect his dad from all life-sustaining treatment. I talked to Tim numerous times a day during this period, and all I could really do was listen and empathize when he said over and over, "Why didn't dad just sign that goddamned DNR form like I asked him to? Now I am forced to make that decision for him, and I have *no idea in hell* what to do!"

As it turned out, Tim was never forced to make that heart-wrenching decision because his dad pulled through one last time. Jack was weaned off all his life support and began breathing on his own—with only the aid of his oxygen concentrator. Jack now required the maximum amount of oxygen that his concentrator could produce due to the damaging effects of his latest heart attack.

Jack left the hospital and returned to his tiny room in the care facility, but he was not the same man as the one who had left for that last ambulance ride a week before. Jack had suffered an anoxic brain injury due to a lack of sufficient oxygen to his brain during the few minutes between when his heart stopped and when the paramedics arrived on the scene to perform CPR. Jack returned to the care facility a profoundly different man who barely resembled the gentle soul he had been all his life. He had become agitated, paranoid, and extremely confused. Jack was like a caged animal who trusted no one and who rejected all offers of help and comfort that the facility staff and hospice team tried in vain to provide.

Shortly after returning to the nursing home, Jack was found in his room, cutting up his oxygen tubing with a pocketknife. He became combative with the caregivers when they tried to assist him with the tasks of daily living. In his paranoia, Jack came to believe that the staff were his captors who were trying to hold him hostage in an attempt to keep him away from his wife's side, where he still desperately wanted to be.

When I visited Jack after his return to the care facility, he had no recollection of having ever met me before his hospitalization. Jack also had no interest in having visitors anymore and could no longer follow the plots of the Western movies he used to enjoy. The Cowboy had become extremely weak and confused, and the only thought that held his interest was trying to figure out how to escape from his perceived captivity so that he could rescue his bride and be free once again.

If there *is* a happy ending to this story, it is not because Jack got better and was able to recover enough to care for his wife, as he fought so long and hard to do. Instead, Jack died a few days after his return from the hospital, and his wife slipped deeper into a coma and right out of her body shortly thereafter—as if her spirit knew it was time to join her husband. I'd like to think The Cowboy and his lady are out riding the range somewhere now— galloping across the open plains, unencumbered by illness and separation, and disappearing into that Ultimate Sunset that we all hope to see one day.

The Hospice Daughter

"I'm not afraid of dying. I'm afraid of what
happens between now and then."

I was fairly new to my job as a home team social worker when I met Ruthie. So far, home visits had included a wide range of dwelling types, from multimillion-dollar mansions to one-bedroom senior housing apartments in low-income sections of the city. Ruthie's home was another type: she lived in a small trailer home with her husband, who was also in his eighties, along with their beloved cat, Theodore.

To say that Theodore was a large cat was *no exaggeration*, for he made Garfield—the obese cat of cartoon fame—look anorexic. Theodore was so fat, in fact, that he had to use a step stool to get onto the kitchen chair, and from there, he had to be lifted onto the kitchen table by Ruthie. He loved to sprawl on the table as Ruthie drank her morning coffee and read the newspaper. He was in that exact spot when I met Ruthie for the first time.

Ruthie was a simple woman who was the matriarch of her family and beloved by all her children and grandchildren. The week before I met her, Ruthie had been diagnosed with lung cancer despite never smoking a single cigarette in her life. She was round and soft with an infectious smile that I fell in love with instantly. In comparison, her husband was a wispy man, but his kindness and generosity mirrored that of Ruthie's in every way. He seemed to understand that Ruthie was quite sick, but he didn't grasp that she was dying. Maybe that is why Ruthie insisted that Mel wait in the living room while she met with me alone in the kitchen that first day. She was trying to protect Mel from knowing how ill she really was until it was absolutely necessary. As I was about to learn, Ruthie had a way of orchestrating her life to fit her beliefs, and only an issue as serious as cancer could throw her off her game.

In theory, one is not supposed to have "favorites" among their patients, but I could admit it then, as I can now, that Ruthie *was* my favorite patient at that time. I came to see her at least weekly, and she eventually allowed Mel to join us in some of our long conversations about living and what it meant to die a "good death."

I fell in love with Mel, too, and felt closer to both of them than I had ever felt emotionally to any of my grandparents long since deceased. I even got to meet many of their kids and grandkids along the way during my visits, and Ruthie always introduced me the same way to all of her family members. She would say, "I'd like you to meet Kay. She is my hospice daughter." No other patient had ever bestowed such a high compliment upon me, and no one since has ever referred to me by that term of endearment. I wanted to live up to what those words implied and tried to give Ruthie the best care I knew how to give at that early stage in my hospice career.

When I came to visit Ruthie, we always sat at her small kitchen table with the huge cat in the middle of it and discussed the unfairness of cancer. We talked about Ruthie's anger at developing this disease that "she didn't deserve," her fear of pain and suffering, and her worry about becoming a burden to her family. These obstacles were her biggest stumbling blocks on the road to dying, as was her worry that Theodore would not survive if Ruthie died before him. Their bond was that close. One day, Ruthie looked me straight in the eye and said, "I don't understand why we can choose the timing of when to put an animal to sleep and out of their misery, but we can't do the same for people. That just makes no sense to me!"

During this time in the early 2000s, Dr. Kevorkian was constantly in the news. He was the physician around whom the term "physician-assisted suicide" was coined. He believed the most compassionate care he could give his patients who were dying was to minimize their suffering and pain by providing medicines that would ultimately end their lives sooner than if their disease processes were allowed to take their natural course over time. Dr. Kevorkian was a highly controversial man who eventually ended up incarcerated for his actions that many found to be, at a minimum, against the laws of man and others found to be against the laws of God. In my line of work, Dr. Kevorkian's name came up daily, at least, and most of my patients wanted someone just like him in their corner when their time of death neared.

As the weeks passed, Ruthie became sicker and more afraid of dying. One day, she made the heart-wrenching decision to take her beloved Theodore to the vet and have him put down so that he wouldn't have to experience the pain and loss of living life without her. After his death, the empty baby bassinet where Theodore usually slept was a visual reminder of what lay ahead in Ruthie's path, and thinking about it made us all incredibly sad. Ruthie became increasingly anxious as the days passed, and her breathing became more labored from the cancer. She was petrified at the thought of suffering through her disease until death came to claim her. As Ruthie often said, "I'm not afraid of dying. I'm afraid of what happens between now and then."

Then one day, I received an urgent page to call Ruthie's husband. When I called him back, he informed me through choked tears that Ruthie had a gun and was talking about killing herself so that she could end her suffering on her own terms and in her own time. I made him put Ruthie on the phone, and we talked for a few minutes. She was in emotional anguish, as she was raised to think of suicide as a "sin," and yet, here she was, contemplating it at that very moment. She agreed to put the gun in a safe place and to let me come out to the house immediately, which I did. I called the hospice chaplain, and he joined me for the emergent visit because it was not one I felt prepared or trained to do alone. I also called Ruthie's son for backup. I needed all the help I could get.

The chaplain and I met for hours with Ruthie, Mel, and Ruthie's son Chuck. Chuck removed the gun from the premises, so we all breathed a collective sigh of relief. We talked in depth about Ruthie's fear of suffering in pain or gasping for breath as she was dying. We discussed the medications that the hospice nurse could give to Ruthie to control her pain and help her breathe more peacefully, as well as the emotional and spiritual support we could provide on an ongoing basis to her family. When Ruthie shared her deepest fear—dying all alone in some unfamiliar nursing home or hospital—we explained how we would do everything in our power to facilitate her wish of being able to die at home surrounded by her loved ones so that she felt a sense of control over her remaining days on this earth. Once Ruthie *truly understood* how much support and assistance the hospice team could provide for her and her family, her fears began to slowly dissipate, as did her thoughts of ending her life prematurely.

Ruthie's wish was granted a few short weeks later. I spent half of my day with her in that cramped little trailer house on the day of her death. Her husband was right by her side the whole time. Her children and grandchildren came in shifts to kiss and hug Ruthie, to tell her how much they loved her, how much they would miss her, and that it was okay for her to go.

The hospice nurse and chaplain were there, too, as was the hospice nursing assistant who was doing everything in her power to keep Ruthie clean and comfortable until the end. Long after the nurse could no longer feel a pulse in Ruthie's wrist, Ruthie was still hanging on by a thread, and we all knew why. As so often happens with people who are approaching the final stages of the dying process, they continue to exude whatever vestiges of power they have left to influence how the closing moments of their lives will play out. For some, they want to be alone when their last breath is taken and they are released from this earthly realm. For others, like Ruthie, they want to hang on as long as possible until everyone has had a chance to gather at bedside and say their goodbyes. In this case, her youngest son, Jim, had not yet arrived from Florida, and despite being in a deep coma, Ruthie knew it.

Once Jim arrived, he quietly entered the bedroom of his mother's home and gently took Ruthie's hand in his. He leaned down to kiss her cheek, and as soon as that tender moment happened, Ruthie took her last and final breath and slipped peacefully and beautifully out of this world. If a death could be considered "good," Ruthie's was exceptional. She ended her days exactly in the way she wanted and on her own terms. When *my time* comes, I can only hope to do the same.

The Eleventh-Hour Visitor

"I can't believe I get paid for this!"

I will admit it's a bit odd—this habit I have of cataloging former patients in my mind based on where they lived. First, I picture the facility—was it an old, rundown nursing home or a high-end assisted living? Did it have a beautiful open floor plan, or was it a cramped and closed-off unit that felt depressing just to enter? My patient Wanda lived on the garden level of a nice assisted living facility in an area that was devoted to serving residents with dementia. Wanda's "neighborhood" was known as "Reminiscence," or "Rem" for short. (I have always found these names somehow lacking and insufficient. Why do we call it "memory care" or "reminiscence" when people are there because they can't remember?)

As far as "secured dementia neighborhoods" go, this place was a nice one where I would have put my own family member should they have required that level of care. Wanda was there because her husband had died and her memory had begun to fail her over time due to her progressive Alzheimer's disease. Wanda was one of those people we all affectionately referred to as being "pleasantly confused," so it was always fun for me to spend time with her because she was almost always upbeat and jolly during my visits, which was frequently *not* the case with other patients on our hospice service.

It was a goal for all of us on the team to be just like Wanda should any of us develop Alzheimer's ourselves, because she seemed joyful every time we came and never developed any of the problematic dementia-related behaviors as do so many people living with that neurological disease. Wanda was always smiling, quick to laugh, and could be in the moment like nobody's business! Her favorite stuffed animal—a well-worn cat—was her constant companion, and as far as Wanda was aware, the cat was alive and well and not just some soft and tattered fabric in the shape of a feline. It was her prized possession, and she cared for it as such.

I remember spending hours outside on the patio with Wanda when the weather was nice. She loved gazing at the flowers, taking in the smells of earth and air, and she especially delighted in watching the many squirrels dart around the trees in search of food and fun. Wanda would throw her head back in laughter as she observed the animals chase each other from tree to tree, and we would hold hands and watch the sights together on sunny days. In times like those, I used to say to myself, "I can't believe I get *paid* for this!" It wasn't the image that most people had of hospice work, but in truth, those sacred moments happened a lot, and I relished them.

Wanda was on my caseload for close to a year as her dementia slowly progressed before she died. It was common for our hospice team to care for multiple residents of Rem simultaneously, so I spent hours in that "neighborhood" every week as part of my job. The unit was quite large and spread out over the entire lower level of the facility so residents could wander freely from room to room and always be found again. Wanda was one of the inhabitants who covered a lot of ground as she slowly shuffled from one end of Rem to the other in her daily wanderings.

But then an extraordinary phenomenon began to happen that none of us could explain. Over time, Wanda's travels became less aimless. Instead, she seemed to develop a kind of sixth sense for when her fellow residents were sick and close to dying. Wanda then began to consistently find her way into the rooms of patients who were transitioning from their earthly lives to whatever comes next when we die.

We would find her sitting vigil next to the bedside of dying patients, holding and stroking their hands, whispering softly to them in words that were often unintelligible but yet always reassuring. Agitated patients would breathe more easily and struggle less in her presence, even without an additional dose of morphine. Wanda brought a peaceful energy into the room that was felt by all who entered. And even though she no longer had the language skills or ability to tell us what she was doing or why, Wanda undisputedly had a deep-seated knowingness about how to care for her dying neighbors in a simple yet elegant way that those of us with years of training were humbled to observe.

The family members of those who were nearing death were at first alarmed and annoyed at this stranger who entered the room uninvited in the middle of a sad and vulnerable time. However, those families came to eventually realize that they, too, were witnessing a miracle of sorts by this eleventh-hour visitor, and instead of being angry and disturbed by Wanda's vigils, they became open and grateful for the sacred service she provided their loved ones when they needed it most.

In all my years in hospice, I never before or after saw another resident do what Wanda did for her fellow dementia companions during their final days. And even though I know that it might be a pipe dream, I secretly hope that someone like Wanda shuffles into my life when I am most alone, afraid, and in need of a comforting hand and reassuring words. Someone whose very presence transcends language and cognition and simply connects heart to heart.

Time Travelers

"Wait up for me, my love. I'm coming soon."

My face was well-known throughout the hallways of Summer Ridge—an assisted living facility I frequented at least three times a week for almost eight years. Our hospice team received many new patient referrals from the director of nursing in that building.

One of the most memorable experiences I ever had with any patient or family member of Summer Ridge involved a wonderful couple. Janet and Harry had been married for nearly fifty years. They were passionate about many areas of life—their faith, their children and grandchildren, and each other. But the experience they most relished throughout their marriage was traveling the world together, which they had been fortunate enough to do extensively for decades. Their apartment was a living testament to their adventures—it was filled with colorful and interesting souvenirs from all over the globe. Each one had a story they loved to recall in mixed company.

I first met Janet when she was admitted to our hospice service with a primary diagnosis of heart failure and a secondary diagnosis of Alzheimer's disease. Janet was confused but always full of joyful enthusiasm, and I looked forward to my weekly visits with her. Janet could be found seated in her wheelchair, carrying a purse or small satchel on her lap wherever she went. From one visit to the next, I was witness to the many interesting items crammed into and falling out of her bags, including bras, socks, currency from different places in the world, and other miscellaneous items suitable for travel.

Often, I would find Janet sitting in her living room with her sunglasses on, a bag on her lap, and a huge smile on her face. I got in the habit of inquiring where she and Harry had been since the last time I saw her, as she was always convinced they had just returned from one exciting trip or another or were about to embark on one momentarily, and I had arrived just in the nick of time to wish them farewell. In truth, Janet and Harry rarely, if ever, left the facility. I never argued this point or tried to orient Janet to that reality, however, for it was far less interesting than the one they inhabited together in Janet's mind. Although Harry didn't have dementia, he played along with "Janet's games" and was a good sport about it in the way only a spouse of five decades could be.

Janet would recount amazing tales of their trips to Southern Italy or the Greek Isles. Like Harry, I played along and joined her in the moment—reveling in her passion for life and adventure and for going places that were foreign and out of her comfort zone. That was part of the thrill, she always told me. On most of my visits, I would find Harry sleeping soundly on the sofa until it was mealtime, then he would get up and slowly push Janet in her wheelchair to the dining room. Without him, she would lose her way down those familiar hallways that seemed brand new for Janet every time she traversed them. Harry was her seasoned guide through the assisted living complex, and Janet was his eager companion along for the ride.

About nine months after I met Janet, Harry's health suddenly began to fail, and he was admitted to our hospice service as well. Harry was diagnosed with metastatic lung cancer, and his energy and life force began to dissipate rapidly before our eyes. Harry started sleeping for eighteen to twenty hours a day, and because he became too weak to push Janet down the hall to the dining room, the assisted living staff took over that responsibility. Janet would dote on Harry—covering him up with well-worn blankets, kissing his cheek, saying he was tired from their last big trip across the ocean, but informing us that he would be ready to go again soon.

Eventually, Harry was moved into a hospital bed in the middle of the living room. Janet would sit next to the bed, holding Harry's hand and stroking his arm softly, and sometimes she would talk or sing to him. Other times, she would simply sit in silence. One day, I arrived to find Janet looking distracted and worried. She said to me in a quiet, almost quizzical fashion, "Harry bought a ticket for the train, but he didn't buy one for me." I took my time to think of an appropriate reply and finally said: "Janet, Harry bought a one-way ticket because this is a journey that he has to go on alone. Soon enough, it will be your turn to buy a ticket, and then you can join him."

Janet didn't say a word, but she held my gaze for a long while as if she were contemplating my message. When she finally looked away from me and back at her lifelong traveling companion lying peacefully in front of her, she softly whispered, "Wait up for me, my love. I'm coming soon."

Harry died a few days later. Their family wondered what was the right thing to do—to tell Janet about Harry's death? To take her to the funeral? To ignore that it ever happened? To give her an excuse about why Harry had stepped out and tell her that he would be back later? In the end, they elected to take Janet to her husband's funeral to give her a chance to say bon voyage and to mourn. And mourn she did. Janet stood over Harry's open casket, and she wept inconsolably. She stroked Harry's face and asked, "Why did you go without me?" We all cried in Harry's honor and for Janet's broken heart.

A few days later, it was like Janet had entirely forgotten the fifty years of marriage to Harry. However, intermittently, she would suddenly say, "Harry died. He's left me. He's gone," and the tears would flow as the raw grief swept over her anew with each reminder that Harry's train had departed the station without her. Then, as quickly as that moment of clarity arrived, it would vanish into the fog of dementia until the next time something jogged Janet's memory, and the waves of grief would begin all over again.

Ten weeks later, Janet died, and the whole hospice team mourned for them both. We held a collective vision of Harry and Janet to remember them by. Two travelers sitting hand in hand on the celestial night train—expectant looks of anticipation glowing on their faces as they traversed through the dimensions of time and space to places known only to those who have gone before us. True travelers in time—linked by incredible love and by the joy that journeying to unknown destinations can bring when we travel lightly, carrying only our faith, sense of wonder, and never-ending thirst for adventure.

When You're Dead,
You're Dead

"I've never hoped to be more wrong about anything in my life!"

It would have been intimidating meeting Bill in any other setting or circumstance than this one. Bill was over eighty, but his six-foot-three-inch frame was still large and imposing, as were his quick temper and strong opinions that he enjoyed sharing liberally. To say that he was unhappy to meet me was a grand understatement, as I represented everything he hated and feared most—not being in control and the idea that he was going to die. I was the hospice social worker assigned to this newly admitted patient who had recently learned that he had incurable metastatic lung cancer, and he was mad as hell about it.

Bill had made the difficult decision to sell his beautiful home in the quiet outskirts of Denver and move into a large and bustling assisted living community near his only daughter, Becky. She had pleaded with her father to move closer to her and into an environment where he could get more care as his cancer progressed.

Bill was a scrapper from way back who would sooner knock your teeth out in a fistfight than ever appear vulnerable, weak, or in need of *anyone's* help. Defeat was a notion that Bill forcefully rejected with every fiber of his being, so it came as no surprise when he informed those of us on his hospice team that his "goals of care" at that stage of his illness included "fighting this goddamned cancer and kicking its ass!" We acknowledged and supported Bill's goals while simultaneously being aware that the likelihood of him beating this formidable opponent was slim to none. Such is the everyday heart of hospice work that we all reveled in doing but which others outside of our profession widely misunderstood and steadfastly avoided.

Bill had been widowed for many years by the time I met him, but when he talked about his deceased wife, Alice, his normally gruff tone always softened with a surprising tenderness. Alice was one of Bill's favorite subjects to discuss on my weekly visits to him, which, in the beginning, usually consisted of us taking robust walks together from one end of the long building to the other in order to observe the massive construction project that was taking place right outside of the grounds. It was from this vantage point of the third-floor windows that Bill told me about his career as a commercial electrician and the complex and tumultuous inner workings of the construction industry in which he had been a legendary force for decades. Bill learned to stand up to the labor unions, to drive a hard bargain, and to never let his competitors see him as anything other than competent, tough, and resolutely unafraid. He had a reputation to uphold, after all!

At first, Bill acted as if he were merely tolerating visits from the hospice team. For many months, he consistently rejected the chaplain's offer to visit—citing his atheist views as a rationale for not needing that service. It was Bill's staunch belief that "when you're dead, you're dead," so he never worried about an afterlife or about the need for any spiritual support or guidance. He felt certain that his final destination would end alone in a cemetery plot six feet under—he just didn't know when or want to be reminded about that eventuality. So instead, we all focused our energies on building relationships with

Bill, honoring his thoughts and wishes as best we could, and companioning him down the twists and turns of hospice care.

It was a gradual process for Bill to get to know and trust me, but over time, he decidedly warmed up to my weekly sojourns to see him and found joy in the deep conversations and belly laughs we would share. He also came to look forward to his biweekly visits from the nurse who monitored and managed his cancer pain while providing a safe and nurturing place for this once-fearless man to begin dealing with his anxiety about death and the biggest fight of his life that he so desperately wanted to win.

Slowly but surely, Bill's appetite began to diminish, as typically happens with cancer, and he began losing weight and became more unsteady on his feet. After numerous falls and injuries, Bill finally agreed to get a nice walker with a built-in seat that he could rest on when he became too fatigued to continue down those long hallways alone and needed a breather. Bill didn't relish the need for the walker, but he made the best of it in his own way.

During one of our now-slower strolls down the hallway with his walker, I recall Bill locking eyes with me and saying, "It's hard to act like a tough guy with this contraption!" I just smiled and joked, "Looks can be deceiving. I'm still scared of you," and he roared with laughter.

That was the yin/yang of the deepening relationship between Bill and me that so often happens in this sacred circle we call hospice care. We are *not* angels concealing our wings under our jackets, as the stereotype goes, but rather people who are privileged to walk with the dying, to learn from their collective wisdom, and to support them and their families in the most vulnerable of times. And our reward for doing this consecrated work is not money, fame, or even wings, but the opportunity to irreversibly change ourselves for the better because of it.

Unfortunately, the fancy walker was not of much use for long, as Bill continued to decline. He upgraded to a top-of-the-line motorized scooter that Becky again convinced him to purchase. It appealed to Bill's need for some control over his life because at least the scooter allowed him to be in the "driver's seat" once again. But a few short weeks later, Bill was forced to relinquish his new wheels after accidentally bumping into a couple of other assisted living residents due to the inability of his fine motor skills to effectively regulate the joystick any longer. I came to see Bill later that same day, and his usual macho demeanor had been replaced by a look of utter failure, embarrassment, and defeat. It was the lowest point he'd ever been at emotionally since coming on hospice, and the team rallied to support him through this dark and difficult time. The next day, the hospice nurse quietly had a wheelchair delivered to Bill's room, and any vestiges of normal independence in his life ceased to exist. The fighter had lost that round definitively.

The hospice nurse and I came to know Bill well and also formed a deep bond with his daughter, Becky. She would often call to request that one of us be present when she came to visit her dad, as she was terrified at how ravaged his body had become from the cancer and didn't know what to say or do when left alone with this man she hardly recognized as her father.

I remember a particularly poignant visit with Bill and Becky on a dark gray afternoon. Bill was lying in the hospital bed that his hospice nurse had ordered for him after he became too weak to get out of his own bed. He began discussing his many regrets, as well as how much he missed his wife of over fifty years. For the first time, I witnessed Bill crying uncontrollably. I could tell from the shocked expression on Becky's face that she wanted to bolt from the room and disappear, as she had never before seen that level of unveiled emotion in her tough-as-nails dad, and it made her incredibly uncomfortable.

I asked Bill where Alice was buried, and he informed me that because he was a World War II vet, Alice was buried in a nearby national cemetery in Denver—the same place Bill's body would go after he died. As we continued to talk, I asked Bill, the steadfast atheist, if he thought he would ever be reunited with Alice after he passed away, and he instantly replied, "No, Kay. When you're dead, you're dead! I'll never see my wife again!" At that, Becky ran sobbing from the room, and I was left alone to sit with Bill in his grief and despair and to hold space for the possibility that he just might be wrong.

As Bill's condition continued to worsen, he eventually acquiesced to letting the hospice chaplain visit, "If she can just talk football and not religion when she comes." Hospice chaplains are adept at following a patient's lead and at not forcing their belief systems on those they serve, so this situation was no exception. When she wasn't talking about the Denver Broncos with Bill, the chaplain was busy providing emotional and spiritual support to Becky, who was more fragile by the day, as her once-strong and scrappy father slipped further and further away before her eyes.

I recall the day when Bill finally agreed to allow the hospice CNA to start coming two to three times a week to provide personal care to him, as he was unable to do his activities of daily living by himself anymore. It was another in a long line of losses that Bill was accumulating on his journey to death's door, and he was gradually learning to surrender his need for control as his cancer progressed over time. Bill was now starting to admit that he probably wasn't going to win this fight after all, but instead of being so angry about that, he had become more loving and accepting, openly vulnerable, and outwardly grateful for every minute he still had left. The hospice team circled our wagons even closer to support Bill and Becky during this critical time, and they both acknowledged and thanked us genuinely for our efforts.

About a week before Bill took his final breath, I was sitting bedside with him in his cluttered apartment, holding his hand and listening intently as he whispered in a slow but deliberate tone about what was on his mind that day. His thoughts had again turned to Alice, and *this time* Bill said to me, "Kay, do you think I'm ever going to get to see my wife again?" I let that question hang suspended in the air for a few moments before softly replying, "I don't know, Bill. I thought when you're dead, you're dead." Tears began to roll down his sunken cheeks, and he replied, "I've always been a hard-headed son of a bitch who thought he knew everything. But, I'll tell you, Kay, I've never hoped to be more wrong about anything in my life than that!"

A few days later, Bill gently slipped into a coma and then out of his cancer-ridden body at last. I was summoned to attend his death one early morning, along with my nurse and chaplain colleagues. Becky was waiting in the assisted living lobby for us to arrive, as she was too shaken and over-whelmed in her grief to enter her dad's apartment alone. As the sun streamed in through the open windows, we shared tears over Bill's final battle coming to an end, but we also shared stories, hugs, and heartfelt laughter about this incredible man we had all come to love and respect. As the mortuary attendants arrived to wrap Bill's body and take him away, we shared one last collective hope and prayer between us—that this would not be the end for Bill and Alice but perhaps, a new beginning.

God's Retribution?

"Please stay."

I t was one of those first meetings you never forget—mainly because it was just so tragically sad. Rita was an obese woman in her early eighties with brightly colored red hair. She had just been admitted to our hospice service twenty-four hours earlier.

When I entered her tiny, cramped Medicaid nursing home room that day, I found Rita curled up in a semi-fetal position in her single bed, sobbing her eyes out. I had to rely heavily on my intuition in that moment regarding how to introduce myself to this grieving woman who was in obvious distress, as I possessed no handbook to guide me through what the right thing to do was in such an awkward situation.

Because Rita and I were total strangers to one another, I did the only thing I could think of. I sat down on the singular seat available in the room, which happened to be a bedside commode, introduced myself as the hospice social worker, and asked if she would like me to stay or come back at another time when she felt better. There was a long pause as Rita tried to catch her breath between racking sobs. At last, her tears subsided enough for me to hear her whisper, "Please stay." And so, I did.

What I learned during our first conversation was how horrendously upside down Rita's life had been turned in just a matter of days. She went from "knowing something was wrong with me but just not knowing what" for the past year to suddenly being diagnosed with stage 4 liver cancer. Her doctor had informed Rita that her cancer was incurable because it had already metastasized, spreading to multiple places in her body. She said he referred her to hospice because "there was nothing else he could do for me." Rita went from having her own apartment, her own car, her own routine, and her own life and independence only a week before to being placed in a long-term care facility in a foreign part of town where she felt as scared, overwhelmed, and lonely as anyone could possibly feel. She was living in a semi-private dingy room with a curtain separating her from her screaming roommate, as well as from any chance of seeing daylight through the window on the far side of the dividing wall. Who wouldn't be crying if they were in her shoes?

When I inquired about her family, Rita told me that she had been divorced for decades and that she had five children who all lived in the Denver metro area. I let her know that it was my practice to call families after every patient visit to offer support, resources, and updates on how their loved ones were doing and to answer any questions they might have. I asked Rita if she wanted me to reach out to all of her kids on a regular basis, or if there was one of her children in particular who would be a reasonable point person to disseminate the information I provided to the rest of their siblings.

I could immediately tell by the look in Rita's eyes that my question struck a sensitive nerve. She gave me the names and phone numbers of three of her children, without a word of explanation as to why she didn't offer to do the same for the two remaining kids, and I knew better than to ask.

Over time, Rita was moved into a private room in the facility where there was a little more light and much more privacy to talk during my weekly visits. Rita developed a massive amount of fluid in her belly from the cancer, and it had to be drained frequently by the hospice nurse. Rita struggled to find a way to rest comfortably and was always short of breath despite being on many liters of continuous oxygen. She also struggled to make sense of how she, of all people, could be dying from liver cancer when she had never had a single drink of alcohol in her life.

Rita's three adult children visited regularly and were quite involved in Rita's care. I got to know each of them well and eventually learned from Rita's son that his mother and two other sisters had been estranged from each other for many decades, even though they only lived a few miles apart at that time. When I tried to probe for more insight into the underlying cause of the estrangement, Rita's son only offered that his dad was an alcoholic and that it "was a long story" that wasn't his to tell. But then one day, many months after meeting Rita, she disclosed the painful truth behind the fallout she had had with her daughters, and it was a tragic story I'll never forget.

We had been discussing Rita's liver cancer, pain, and the remaining goals she hoped to accomplish before she died when suddenly, the admission came flying out of her like a fast-moving comet. Rita told me about her miserable marriage to her husband, whom she described as a "mean and abusive alcoholic." Rita married her husband right out of high school, and she began having her five children one right after another shortly thereafter. It didn't take long for Rita to become stuck in that marriage since she had little education, no job or money of her own, a domineering husband, and five children to raise while trying to protect them from their drunken, violent father.

Through tear-filled eyes, Rita went on to tell me that her two oldest daughters came to her when they were teenagers and informed Rita that they were being sexually abused by their father and had been for years. Rita began crying in earnest as she described how she responded to her daughters' allegations that day: with denial, blame, and projected anger onto them. Rita said she could not allow herself to believe their accusations at the time because she thought she had no way out of that abusive marriage herself. She felt trapped, beaten down, and utterly powerless to change her fate, let alone the fate of her children. So, the choice she made in that excruciating moment was to shut her daughters down, disregard what they said, and fail to protect them from the monster who was their father. Rita had been living with the festering guilt of that decision ever since, and she wondered aloud if getting liver cancer was "God's retribution" for not sheltering her daughters from "that sick son of a bitch" all those years ago.

I sat in stunned silence as Rita pondered those heart-wrenching questions aloud to herself—as if I served as some sort of bedside confessional where she finally decided to purge her burdened soul. I listened intensely to Rita with as little judgment as I could muster as she berated herself for the decisions of her past and mourned the terrible legacy those long-ago choices had indelibly left on her daughters' lives and futures. It was hard for me to be completely unaffected by Rita's admissions since I had worked directly with countless people throughout my career who had been raised in households full of addiction, secrets, and abuse and had witnessed firsthand the long-term consequences of that kind of childhood trauma on the survivors.

Rita's main wish before she died was to reconnect with her daughters, apologize for her transgressions, and ask for their forgiveness before she left this earth. Rita asked me if I thought that was possible. I told her that she would never know unless she tried and that I was willing to help her in any way I could with that process.

With Rita's permission, I outreached her two estranged daughters the following day. I told them that their mother was dying, that she had deep regrets she wanted to discuss with them, and that she was requesting to see them both before she passed. I also let them know that there wasn't much time left, as Rita's cancer was progressing by the day, and it wouldn't be long before the illness consumed her completely.

I wish I could say that I was able to help tidy up all the loose ends of Rita's life before it ended, that I was able to facilitate healing between Rita and her daughters, and that there was a "Hallmark ending" of sorts to this very sad tale, complete with a big bow on top. But that's not what happened. The best I could do at that juncture was to convince one of Rita's daughters to visit her mom in the nursing home before she died and the other to attend Rita's memorial service after her death. It wasn't at all the way Rita hoped her life would conclude, nor was it anywhere close to being a storybook ending for Rita's daughters, either. But often, it's as close as we ever come to making peace with the mistakes and regrets of our past. Sometimes we die the way we lived, and happy endings can be as elusive as comets and forgiveness.

The Unlikeliest
of Friends

"I'll give you a quarter if you would just shut your trap!"
"I'll shut my trap when I'm good and ready, and it'll cost
you a lot more than a quarter, you cheapskate!"

My hospice colleagues and I used to jokingly refer to certain memory care units as "the pink sweater clubs." Those were the places that seemed to cater to residents who were relatively low-maintenance, who didn't have a lot of dementia-related behaviors that the staff had to manage, and who had the financial resources at their disposal to privately pay for specialized assisted living when their memory and functional abilities began to change and fail. It was in one such building in a suburb of Denver where I had the pleasure of meeting Evie and Jane when they were both admitted into our hospice program during the same week.

When I was initially introduced to Evie, she was fashionably dressed in an elegant blouse and pants with perfectly coordinated accessories and patent leather shoes. I could immediately tell from her unmistakable accent that she originated from New York City—a fact that I would soon learn she took great pride in. Evie spoke with a rapid cadence of speech, and she was extremely entertaining to listen to. It was not apparent from the first few minutes of chatting with Evie that she had Alzheimer's disease. However, that all changed as soon as the telltale sign of conversational "looping" began, and I started to hear the same stories over and over again in a short period. One of those stories involved her love of authentic New York bagels and how her son had a dozen of them shipped to her each week straight from her favorite Jewish bakery back home. For Evie, there was no finer treat on earth than those bagels!

Evie was admitted into our hospice service under the primary diagnosis of congestive heart failure. It is a chronic and progressive disease that affects the pumping power of the heart muscles and eventually leads to a buildup of fluid around the heart and causes it to pump inefficiently. Evie's Alzheimer's disease was a secondary diagnosis on her hospice chart, as her doctor believed it would be the CHF that would take Evie's life within the next six months. Evie's dementia just made her end-of-life care more complicated since she was completely oblivious that *anything* was wrong with her physically or cognitively, and she told everyone who visited that her stay "in this resort" was short-term only. In her mind, Evie was merely waiting there until her family could arrange to take her back home to The Big Apple, where she belonged. Her Alzheimer's disease prevented Evie from comprehending that her son and his family arranged to have her moved closer to them in Colorado after Evie's beloved husband, Norman, died. It is a difficult choice that countless families have to make every day when their loved one is impacted by dementia and is no longer safe to remain in their home alone.

Directly across the hall from Evie lived a woman named Jane. Jane was raised in "the hollers" of West Virginia, where she grew up in the shadow of the Appalachian Mountains "in a town so small that you could spit from one end of it to the other." I quickly discovered after meeting Jane that she was chock-full of such colloquialisms that were deeply embedded in her Southern roots and speech. Jane dressed in jeans, checkered button-up shirts, and sensible shoes. She was the antithesis of flashy in every sense of the word in her no-nonsense kind of way, but what *wasn't* plain about Jane was her exceptionally warm personality, wicked sense of humor, and generous heart.

Five years before I met Jane, she had been diagnosed with vascular dementia resulting from a combination of multiple small strokes that she had had over a three-year period. Those events left Jane's memory spotty and her ability to remain safely independent in her own abode impossible. It also put her at an elevated risk of having another major cardiac event in the future, but Jane "paid no mind" to worrying about the past or what might come in the future. She simply took each day as it came and lived firmly and happily in the moment.

I visited Jane weekly on my hospice rounds. She would often talk to me about her relationship with her ex-husband, Carl. "He was lower than a snake's belly in a wagon rut and as worthless as gum on a boot heel!" Jane had a seemingly endless supply of these folksy expressions that I had never heard before in my Midwestern upbringing, and they cracked me up every time! The way Jane told it, there was no love lost in the marriage between Carl and her, and she never looked back on the day she finally decided to leave him. "That man was about as useful as a steering wheel on a mule! When the Lord was handin' out brains, that fool thought God said *trains*, and he passed 'cause he don't like to travel!"

Jane never felt bad about divorcing Carl, but she did have one major regret about her past that she often spoke of during our visits. She regretted ever letting her kids talk her out of leaving her beloved home in the foothills west of Denver after her strokes. Jane had lived there alone for twenty years following her divorce, and she went "kickin' and screamin'" from those beautiful rolling hills she so loved and into the sequestered memory care community where she had resided ever since.

With the brain changes resulting from her strokes, Jane couldn't fully comprehend the fact that she was living in a "neighborhood" designed specifically for people living with dementia, but she *was* savvy enough to know that something was different about her fellow residents. Jane would often confide to me in hushed tones that "the people who live in this place are older than the hills and a few bricks short of a load," but she didn't seem to mind their company, despite that fact. It was in that setting that Jane and Evie first laid eyes on each other, and where their unlikely friendship began.

Most "typical" friendships I've witnessed throughout my life usually start with two people being drawn together because of what they have in common—like a love of music, travel, cooking, politics, parenting, or spirituality. But the only obvious commonality that Evie and Jane shared was that of living across the hallway from each other in a dementia care facility. Aside from being "neighbors," they were opposites in every possible way, yet that never impeded their unique friendship in the slightest.

Hearing Jane talk reminded me of Vicki Lawrence's character "Eunice" on *The Carol Burnett Show* I watched as a kid. She spoke slowly and deliberately with a thick Southern drawl and a quick wit, and she delivered her punchlines in classic "straight-man" fashion. On the other hand, Evie was like watching the comedienne Lily Tomlin doing a standup act. She was extremely animated and expressive and quite a character in her own right. When Jane and Evie entered a room together, you could always count on the fact that a belly laugh was never far behind.

I often visited Evie and Jane over the lunch hour and sat with them at their table in the memory care dining room. On one such occasion, Evie was in rare form. She was talking incessantly to no one in particular, and she literally seemed unable to stop herself. Jane looked over at Evie across the table and snapped, "Hey, Lady! I'll give you a quarter if you would just shut your trap!" Evie immediately quipped back, "I'll shut my trap when I'm good and ready, and it'll cost you a lot more than a quarter, you cheapskate!" Jane looked at me, nodded her head toward Evie, and replied, "That lady is stuck up higher than a light pole! I don't know *who* she thinks she is!"

At that point, I totally lost it! I was reduced to tears from laughing so hard I couldn't see, and even though the Dynamic Duo had no real clue *why* I found their conversation so entertaining, they couldn't help but join me in the contagious and riotous laughter, just the same. It was times like that when I used to think to myself, *Everyone believes that hospice work is always so sad and depressing. If they only knew!*

Evie and Jane always hung out together in side-by-side chairs immediately outside of the dining room doors that were kept locked between meals. They would typically show up there at least an hour before the appointed mealtimes, as they no longer had an accurate concept of time. I would often pass them in the hallway and overhear snippets of their conversations. One day, I heard Evie say, "Who's in charge of this place anyway? I think they need some new management around here! The meals are always late, and there are not nearly enough men. I think we should file a complaint!" Jane retorted, "You're right! We just have to figure out who to complain to! Do *you* know who's in charge of this place?" And round the conversation would go. It was like listening to a new version of the old "Who's On First?" skit by Abbott and Costello, and every bit as funny.

On another occasion, I walked by Evie and Jane shooting the breeze outside of the dining room when loud sirens could be heard approaching the building from the outside. Moments later, two extremely handsome young paramedics arrived on the scene with their gurney on wheels. They had been summoned after another resident had a cardiac event, and staff called 911. Ever curious, the Dynamic Duo followed the strapping young men down the hallway and into the room, where an older woman was carefully being placed on the gurney for transport to the emergency room. Oblivious to the distress of their comrade, Evie and Jane were instead focused on the muscular lads in uniform.

I overheard Jane say, "Well, butter my butt and call me a biscuit! Those boys sure ain't hard on the eyes!" Evie nodded in agreement and then sidled up next to the stretcher, turned on her dazzling smile, and began flirting with the young men as if there weren't sixty years of age between them! Both of the paramedics turned bright red from Evie's unedited and colorful comments, including offering to remove the other resident off the gurney so she could ride in the ambulance with the two of them instead. I could tell that those medical professionals were hurrying even faster than usual just to escape the good-natured but embarrassing ribbing from Evie. As they were leaving the memory care unit, I heard Jane exclaim, "Those boys are faster than a one-legged man in a butt-kicking competition! Just *look* at them go!" It was the most exciting event that had happened in as long as Evie and Jane could recall, and they were enjoying every second of the ride.

Having witnessed firsthand the incredible and unlikely friendship between Evie and Jane, I often look back and wonder what it would take in this highly contentious world we're living in for us to foster such alliances with the people in our lives who we seemingly have nothing in common with, and to forge relationships with those we have come to inherently distrust and hate based on what *we think* they represent or believe that does not align with our own points of view. What seeds of friendship might be sown if we were able to build community with our neighbors—no matter how different they might appear from us? If we were literally able *to forget* about the issues that divide us and focus on our shared humanity and an abundance of belly laughs instead? Maybe *that's* the silver lining of the memory loss that comes with dementia, because that's *exactly* what Evie and Jane so beautifully demonstrated. It was not just a pipe dream; it had become an absolute *reality*.

Twinkle, Twinkle

"On the forty-five-minute drive to the patient's home at
3:00 a.m., I had a lot of time to think and to pray."

I t was one of those crazy nights in hospice when my pager never stopped. I
had already worked a full eight-hour day in the field, visiting my patients
and families in various care facilities around town and tending to the tasks
that needed to be done on behalf of my caseload. But at least once a month,
I was required as a social worker to be on call from five in the evening until
eight o'clock the following morning, on top of my already busy day.

For my first five years in hospice, most of my on-call shifts had been
relatively quiet nights consisting mainly of a few grief calls or an occasional
visit made to a patient's home or facility where someone was "impending"
and close to death or had just passed away, but the last three years had gotten
much busier and demanding. The social worker and chaplain were often
called upon to provide comfort and emotional support to family members
gathered at bedside who were in the throes of anticipatory grief as their
loved ones were minutes to days away from dying, or to provide bereavement
support to families whose loved ones had already taken their last breaths.

On this particular cold spring night, I was unusually busy and had fielded
numerous crisis calls to families, had made a post-death visit thirty miles

away to a nursing home, and had returned home to my warm bed in the early morning hours. With my pager perched close by on my bedside table, I hoped for a few hours of sleep before my full workday started again in a few hours.

I had just drifted off to slumber when the familiar "beep, beep, beep" of the pager abruptly awoke me. I slipped out of my room and called the night-shift coordinator to get the report on what I was being paged to do—all the while wishing I could still be dreaming in bed. When I talked to the nursing supervisor, she informed me that she needed me to attend a death in the southern part of the city to support the nurse who was on-site but having a difficult time managing all the dynamics in the home.

When I asked for more detail, she told me that the patient's name was Katrina and that she had just died an hour before from the complications of a terrible neurodegenerative disease. Katrina was a mother in her early forties who had two young children present in the home, as well as a grieving husband and extended family members on the way. The nursing supervisor also added that the family dog would not let the hospice nurse anywhere near the body and would growl and bark at her if she tried to enter the living room where the patient's body was lying. Needless to say, I selfishly wished this whole nightmare wasn't really happening, but my blinking pager reminded me that indeed it was and that I had to get dressed and go. Duty called.

On the forty-five-minute drive to the patient's home at 3:00 a.m., I had a lot of time to think and to pray. Pray that I would be a calming presence for this family when I felt so overwhelmingly sad and chaotic inside after just hearing but a few details of their tragic story. Pray that I wouldn't say or do the "wrong thing." And pray that I could deal with seeing those grieving children and their father without breaking down myself under the weight of their undiluted, raw grief.

When I arrived at the appointed street, I had no problem identifying which house on the block I was destined to go to, for it was the only one with all the lights on at that wee hour of the morning. I centered myself as well as I could in my car. I took long, deep breaths and asked The Universe to divinely guide me to be a compassionate presence for this grieving family on what must be the darkest night of their lives. I got out of my car and walked the short distance from my Subaru wagon to their front door and hoped for the best. The family dog actually greeted me at the door without a growl or a bark, so I took that as a good sign, given the nurse's experience earlier in the night. I came in and introduced myself to the patient's husband and the young, pajama-clad children who were gathered around their father's leg in the entryway. I petted the dog and went to talk to the nurse who had sequestered herself in the family's office, so I could get a report and update.

Monique, the night-shift nurse, was tucked safely away in the corner of the den with a stack of hospice paperwork and a pager spread out on the desk before her. She looked both relieved to see me and utterly exhausted at the same time. I walked across the room to introduce myself, and Monique told me that this was the third death she had attended since her shift began. She felt frustrated that she couldn't get near the patient's body or comfort the family without the dog going berserk.

Monique thanked me profusely for coming to help, pointed me in the direction of the living room, and wished me luck to be able to get close enough to the family and provide the grief support they desperately needed. She added that her plan was to stay in the den to complete all of her paperwork and the required phone calls to the coroner and mortuary until she was otherwise needed. Monique felt that the dog's protective reaction to her presence in the home only exacerbated the emotional intensity that already permeated every corner of this home, and she wanted to minimize that stressful dynamic as much as humanly possible.

After that came the hardest part.

I walked into the living room, where Katrina's body was lying silently on the couch. She was dressed in a flowing nightgown and loosely draped with a cozy blanket around her torso. My first thought upon seeing her was how strikingly beautiful she was, even in death. Huge framed family photographs that lined the warmly painted walls and sweeping stairway caught my gaze. The whole family looked perfect and so very happy in those photographs, a vision that was in stark contrast to the shocked, sad, and strained faces I saw all around me in that room when I entered.

I've never found an etiquette book that tells a person the socially appropriate things to do or say in such a situation. One just has to follow their heart and instinct and hope for the best. Mine led me to sit on the floor next to Katrina's body on the couch and to say how incredibly sorry I was for their loss. I quietly invited the family to tell me about their mother and wife, and then I just listened and let the rest unfold.

I heard stories about Katrina that were touching, painful, funny, and inspiring. While we were talking, the family dog decided to take up refuge across my legs—like he knew we both needed each other for comfort to get through this long, dark night. Katrina's parents arrived at the home during this time and kneeled over their precious daughter's body—wailing out the pain of their loss, which I didn't even attempt to soothe. Holding space for their grief was the best care I could provide in that moment.

Just when I thought things couldn't get any more heart-wrenching in that room, one of the young children disappeared for a minute and came back holding a violin case. Her sister admonished her not to play the instrument as it would "wake up Mommy," but the young girl continued, despite her protests, to unlatch the case and place the instrument in her hands. The precious child held that small violin and bow in her awkward grasp and played a slow and off-pitch version of "Twinkle, Twinkle, Little Star" as a gift to her mother, whose body was lying five feet away on the couch. It took absolutely every shred of emotional restraint within me not to start weeping in that tender, private, and sacred moment that I was witness to only by virtue of my job.

At the conclusion of her musical serenade, the little girl put the violin back in its case and burrowed into her grandmother's lap in the recliner. Everyone in the room was crying, and I was no exception, though I tried to hide my tears as much as I could so as not to distract from the family's mourning process. Moments later, the doorbell rang, and two mortuary attendants dressed in dark suits and ties arrived with a gurney to take Katrina's body away. Monique came out of the den to greet the new arrivals, and amazingly, the dog didn't even glance in Monique's direction this time, let alone bother to growl or bark at her.

The family vacated the living room while the mortuary personnel gently placed Katrina's body onto the gurney and draped it with a luxurious blanket in an age-old respectful ritual—except for her beautiful face, which they left uncovered. When the mortuary attendants re-emerged from the living room and moved Katrina to the entryway of the house, everyone gathered around to say their final goodbyes to their wife, daughter, and mother. Monique and I stood by in the background to offer our silent support and a shoulder to cry on, as needed.

After Katrina's body was driven away by the funeral home employees, Monique and I took our cues from the exhausted family members, said our condolences and goodbyes, and left the house shortly thereafter. All of the overwhelming feelings I had been trying to hold in for hours came cascading out of me like a tidal wave when I reached my car. I sobbed in solitude for the beautiful woman who died in her prime. I cried for her husband and parents, and for the huge hole in their broken hearts that only time could begin to heal. And I especially grieved for those young, motherless children who were too little to understand the permanency of death but could easily comprehend that somehow life was never ever going to be the same.

Today, no matter where I am or what I am doing, whenever I hear "Twinkle, Twinkle, Little Star," it always sounds much different to my ears than it ever did before entering Katrina's living room that night. The tempo was a little slower, and I must admit, somewhat off-key. But between every note played, I invariably hear the deafening sound of the never-ending love of a child for her mother.

Up, Up

"Do you mean to Heaven?"

One of the surprising facts I learned throughout my eight years of employment as a hospice social worker was that you don't have to reside in a memory care community in order to have dementia. In fact, I regularly encountered people living with dementia in their private homes, in independent living settings, in assisted living apartments, and in nursing homes during my daily visits to those diverse living environments. Only a relatively small number of patients with a dementia diagnosis assigned to our team actually lived in memory care settings, which was not at all what I imagined would be the case when I started out in end-of-life care. I realize now that I was ignorant about dementia in the beginning, that I based most of my conjectures about people with that disease on the stereotypes I'd made up in my head rather than on any facts I had ever been presented with.

It took me years of targeted education and exposure to people with neurological diseases to comprehend how dementia can be as devastating as it is misunderstood. As I came to discern, dementia is a general term for loss of memory, language, problem-solving skills, and other thinking abilities that are severe enough to interfere with daily functioning. Of the more than 120 known forms of dementia that currently exist, Alzheimer's disease is the most prevalent cause of *any* dementia, as well as the sixth-leading cause of death among people aged sixty-five or older in the United States, according to the Alzheimer's Association.

I'd become knowledgeable enough to understand that dementia is not a *specific disease* but rather a group of disorders caused by abnormal brain changes. These changes trigger a decline in thinking skills, also known as cognitive abilities, severe enough to impair daily life and independent functioning. Because the brain controls *everything*, dementia can *change everything* for the people living with it—including their behaviors, moods, and relationships.

A large percentage of the patients whom my hospice team cared for had an Alzheimer's diagnosis, as it accounts for 60 to 80 percent of all dementia cases. However, Alzheimer's can only be diagnosed with *absolute certainty* at the time of autopsy, when small sections of the brain are examined under a microscope. That is the reason medical professionals often inform their patients that they have "a probable diagnosis of Alzheimer's disease" based on the clinical assessment of their patient's cognitive and functional changes while they are still alive. It's a rigorous process of ruling out other possible causes behind the brain changes and then making the best educated guess and diagnosis they can with the information available to them at the time of the evaluation process.

Another confusing yet prevalent pattern of behavior that I became aware of while working in hospice was how we as individuals use language to describe people who are suffering from significant memory loss and cognitive decline. I regularly came across both professionals and laypeople who generally referred to a person as "having dementia" without ever specifying the *exact kind* of dementia they may have been dealing with, such as vascular dementia, Lewy body dementia, frontotemporal dementia, or Alzheimer's disease. People tend to do this in much the same way that we refer to someone as "having cancer" without ever acknowledging the *exact type* of cancer that the person may be battling, such as breast cancer, prostate cancer, liver cancer, or pancreatic cancer.

During the sixth year of my hospice tenure, I visited a particular senior living community about three times a week. One woman on my caseload for that facility was named Edna. She had a diagnosis of vascular dementia as a result of a major stroke that left her confined to a wheelchair and almost completely unable to communicate without great effort on her part and a lot of patience and guesswork on the part of the person on the receiving end of the conversation. Sometimes, Edna would get frustrated when I couldn't understand what she was trying to tell me, but more commonly, it was *me* who felt bad when I couldn't comprehend what that dear soul was trying to tell me, despite my best efforts to listen. Regardless of the outcome of our conversations, Edna was nearly always in a jovial mood during our visits and consistently greeted me with a warm and welcoming smile that was worth a thousand words.

Edna's assisted living apartment was located on the second floor of the facility, and the dining room was on the main floor—a quick elevator ride below. I was often in the building around noon when Edna was eating lunch. I often escorted Edna to the dining room in her wheelchair, sometimes shared a meal with her, and always checked in with her after she was done eating to see what she was in the mood to do next. Some days, she chose to attend a musical activity with other residents, watch TV, or sit outside when the weather was nice. Sometimes, Edna was tired and just wanted to go back to her room for an afternoon siesta. I could never predict which option she might choose, and trying to figure out what Edna specifically wanted was no fast or easy task because of her severe aphasia.

Aphasia is a disorder that affects a person's ability to speak, read, write, and listen. It is caused when a stroke occurs in an area of the brain that controls speech and language. Different aspects of our language centers are located in the left temporal lobes of our brains, and the type of aphasia that someone develops depends entirely on what parts of the brain, if any, were impacted by the stroke. For some stroke survivors, the aphasia is more "receptive" in nature and may cause difficulty in terms of their ability to *make sense* of the words they hear spoken or read in print. For others, the aphasia can be more "expressive" and create frustration when the person *knows* what they want to say but has trouble getting the words out correctly or struggles with writing down what they are trying to communicate in a way that others can understand.

People who have expressive aphasia may also use words that are somewhat close to what they intended to say but just a little bit off. For instance, a person might say they would like to "eat" when they *actually mean* "drink." In Edna's case, her stroke left her with expressive aphasia, so she could only communicate in short one- to three-word sentences, and it was challenging to ascertain what point she was trying to convey because even when Edna used the identical words or phrases during a single conversation, one couldn't assume that they carried the exact same meaning from one time to the next.

In an ongoing effort to improve the odds of us mutually understanding one another, I discovered little tricks along the way that helped me communicate more effectively with Edna and other patients on my caseload who had experienced stroke-related language changes. I asked yes-or-no questions; employed simple, short sentences; used hand gestures and visual cues when talking; and tried to make sure that Edna and I were in a quiet and unstimulating environment when we attempted to have a true interaction. I also knew to watch Edna's face for clues as to what she was trying to say and learned to tune in to any nonverbal communication that was available to me so that Edna and I could connect on a meaningful level.

On the days when Edna was fatigued after lunch and in need of a nap, she frequently smiled and told me that she wanted to go "up, up." Some days, she would say that phrase, and other days, she would merely point in an upward direction toward the second floor to indicate her desire, and I would wheel her back to her apartment so she could lie down for a while. This was a common pattern of communication between Edna and me for many months until her health began to fail and she became noticeably weaker and more withdrawn. Edna had only eaten a few meager bites of her lunch during one of my last visits and had recently lost a great deal of weight due to her progressively diminished appetite. When it was clear that Edna had lost all interest in her meal, I began to wheel her out of the dining room and back toward her room so she could rest her tiny, frail body.

Before we reached the elevator, Edna began pointing in the direction of a small conference room that was unoccupied at the time. I asked her if she wanted to go into that room, and she nodded "yes." Once inside the quiet room, I parked Edna's wheelchair in front of a bank of floor-to-ceiling windows and pulled my chair up next to her. I softly asked Edna how she was feeling, and she gave me a rather sad and pleading look and said, "Up, up." I inquired if she wanted me to take her right back to her room to lie down, but the expression on Edna's face told me that was not what she was asking. Edna again said "Up, up" a couple more times, but as she did so, she pointed out of the big windows toward the sky above. I asked, "You want to go up, up? Do you mean to Heaven?" A knowing smile spread across Edna's thin face. She reached out to grab my hand and said, "Go now. Up, up. Home. To Heaven."

I informed Edna that I would miss her very much when she was gone, but that I understood she was ready to die and that the hospice team was there to make sure she had the best days possible until it was time for her to go "home." She gently squeezed my hand in gratitude and reached over to wipe the tears away that were streaming down my cheeks. That was one of the hardest parts of hospice work for me—being able to "let go" of the patients I'd grown to love so that they could move on from this world unencumbered by my selfish wish for them to stay.

I took some deep breaths in an effort to get my emotions under control and sat by Edna's side for a few more pensive minutes—we gazed out the window at the clear mountain sky in silent unison. Then I softly told Edna how much she meant to me and that I hoped she could go "up, up" as comfortably as possible when it was her time to pass. Edna held my gaze for a long while with a knowing smile before pointing upward in the direction of her room, and I slowly wheeled her back to her apartment, savoring every step as I went, blissfully unaware that it would be the last time I ever got to do that.

Five days later, Edna was resting easily in her sun-filled, second-floor apartment when her spirit took flight. Edna was surrounded by her daughter, four grandchildren, the hospice chaplain, and me when she peacefully slipped out of her withered body and went "up, up" to the Pearly Gates. Obviously, God didn't have any trouble deciphering Edna's jumbled language or effortlessly granting her final request. I guess it's just the rest of us mortals down here on earth who struggle with such things.

Finding Purpose in My Passion

The Next Curve
in the Road

enjoyed my social work role in hospice so much that I was almost certain I would be employed in end-of-life care for the rest of my career. But as I had frequently experienced throughout the years leading up to that time, The Universe often had other plans for me beyond what I had ever envisioned for myself. Consequently, I learned to listen to that still little voice inside myself and to trust the process when new opportunities presented themselves out of the clear blue sky.

Our only son, Eli, was born on December 19, 2009. I had saved up every hour of vacation and sick time I possibly could in order to take three months of paid maternity leave to stay home with him. I know that everyone tells about-to-be-first-time parents that "a baby changes everything," and a truer statement has never been spoken! I was so fatigued and overwhelmed during those first twelve weeks as a new mom that I remember wondering how a person could possibly feel that exhausted and still be expected to adequately care for the nonstop needs of an infant. It was downright terrifying at times.

The week before my leave ended, I decided to schedule an appointment with a nurse practitioner to make sure all of my parts still worked before going back to my job. The hospice where I worked had switched over to a new insurance provider while I'd been home changing diapers and adjusting to motherhood. Since I had never had any previous interactions with the new HMO that was now in charge of my medical care, I was a little nervous about my appointment and meeting the nurse practitioner, Valerie, for the first time.

It must have been a slow day in the clinic for Valerie because when she found out that I was the mother of a three-month-old baby boy, she excitedly talked my ear off about how I should get a social work position within their organization. She highlighted the amazing pay and benefits I'd receive so that I could better support my growing family. She even went so far as to write down the name and address of the specific medical clinic where she thought I should apply, which was only seven miles from my home. I felt like I had somehow landed in the middle of some cosmic infomercial while sitting there in the sterile OB-GYN exam room. Afterward, I did the only reasonable thing I could think to do when I got home: I called up an old social work friend of mine whom I hadn't seen in over five years to find out if he was still working at the same clinic the nurse practitioner had recommended.

It was like the celestial wheels had already been greased for me because my transition from over eight years in hospice to my new job as a behavioral health therapist for the HMO happened quickly and with relative ease, given the enormity of that healthcare institution. Even though I certainly hadn't been looking to make a career change with an infant at home, I knew enough to follow my intuition right through the doors and into that medical clinic near my home, despite the fact that I had no idea why I was energetically being drawn there in the first place.

I spent three years as a therapist doing individual, group, and family therapy, and I learned a great deal about countless aspects of human behavior and mental health that I had never previously encountered in my career. However, I also felt like a fish out of water in many respects. My coworkers seemed to thrive on the independent nature of the work, providing services to an extremely wide range of clients ranging in age from seven to ninety. I, on the other hand, sorely missed my work with seniors and being an integral part of a high-functioning team. The isolation of my job was slowly killing me, but with an active toddler at home to support, the "golden handcuffs" I was wearing made it much harder to think about taking them off.

For that reason, when one of my coworkers informed me about a time-sensitive job opening within the company that involved working in the memory clinic with patients who were sixty-five and older, I jumped at the opportunity to apply.

It didn't take me long to fall in love with my job as a clinician on the team in the memory clinic. I was no longer isolated. Instead, I worked as part of a talented interdisciplinary team made up of geriatric psychiatrists, a nurse practitioner, a geriatrician, a clinical pharmacist, two social workers, and a medical assistant. All of my coworkers were off-the-charts smart, kind, helpful, knowledgeable, and extremely dedicated to their diagnostic work in dementia. In many ways, the memory clinic team reminded me of what I loved and missed most about my hospice career and the colleagues I'd left behind three years earlier. I hoped with all my heart that my new role would hold as many unexpected gifts as I had received when I made the major career change from youth corrections to hospice in the fall of 2000.

When I vacated my position at Lookout Mountain in the spring of 2000, I had a lot of time on my hands for soul searching while I diligently looked for a position that had absolutely nothing to do with teenagers or corrections. One day, I came across a job posting in the paper for a hospice social worker, and I thought I was hallucinating when the words on the page literally glowed and pulsated in bright neon colors within the black-and-white lines of the newspaper on my kitchen table. I had only known one person who had worked in hospice back in graduate school, and I didn't understand why anyone would choose such a "depressing" line of work at the time. Yet, as I stared at the brightly colored words practically jumping off the page in front of me, I knew with inner certainty that I had to apply.

Getting a job in hospice was truly a godsend in my life. Being surrounded by thoughtful and compassionate doctors, nurses, social workers, chaplains, nursing assistants, and volunteers was amazingly restorative for me after being in the trenches of juvenile jail for so long. And when my dad was diagnosed with terminal cancer only six weeks after I was hired, I couldn't have found a better work environment in which to learn, love, grieve, and grow. I came to truly understand the value of hospice early on when my dad spent his final days on earth receiving hospice care at home in Lincoln. Because of the heroic efforts of Dad's hospice team, he was granted his final wish of dying comfortably in his own bed surrounded by family, just six months after his cancer was discovered.

Although it was immensely difficult to be in a new job that was so emotionally intense and foreign to me and simultaneously working with people who were in the midst of facing their mortality while my own father was sick and dying, it turned out to be a great gift as well. I was literally surrounded by compassion, love, and understanding while I went through my own grief process. If a coworker stopped me in the hallway at work and asked, "How are you doing today, Kay?" I would often break down into tears born of raw grief that lived just below the surface. Unlike my work environment in corrections, where such open displays of emotion would have been viewed as weak, shameful, or downright dangerous, my hospice colleagues welcomed my tears and vulnerability with open arms and with ears ready to deeply listen to my pain. Without reservation or judgment, they unconditionally supported me through every stage of my long and extensive grieving process both before and after my dad's death. I remain extremely thankful for those glowing neon words that pulsated right off the page of the want ads section all those years ago, for they led me to the remarkable world of hospice—exactly when I needed it most.

Spending eight years at bedside with patients who lived in nursing homes, assisted living, and memory care facilities was like nectar for my withered soul. It opened up my heart once again and helped to deepen my faith in Spirit and in the human race. The job allowed me to shed my emotional armor and wear my heart proudly on my sleeve without apology. It helped me use my God-given gifts with people without having to pretend to be someone else in the process or to hide behind walls of emotional armor just to get through the day. My "sacred circle work" in hospice seemed to magically align with who I innately was, with the kind of work that I found exceptionally rewarding and the kinds of people who were appreciative of what I had to offer. That was made abundantly clear in the way I received heartfelt feedback and gratitude from the patients and families I worked with. That job also fanned the flames of my growing interest and passion for supporting people living with dementia, as well as their families and care partners.

As I would grow to understand, working in the memory clinic felt like a microcosm of hospice. My job revolved around educating and supporting patients and families who were frightened and facing life-threatening illnesses. It required a high level of clinical skill, knowledge, expertise, compassion, and the ability to hold sacred space for people who had just been told devastating news about their health, family, and futures. These were "gifts" I naturally possessed and had experience with. For the first time in years, I felt like I had found my professional home again, and my mental health improved immensely as a result.

The team of top-notch professionals in the memory clinic taught me more about understanding dementia from a variety of medical and psych-social perspectives, as well as how to be highly effective in my work. But one element to my job always seemed to be missing: the ability to develop relationships with the patients and families who came through our clinic. Those families hung on to our phone numbers forever because there was no other place within our medical system for them to call for specific dementia-related assistance. Those concerned caregivers continued to call us back for months and years after their loved one received a dementia diagnosis in our clinic—desperately looking for any help and guidance they could find as the disease continued to worsen and morph over time.

It became clear to me that the two appointments our clinic was staffed and designed to provide to each patient and family would never be enough to adequately meet their ongoing needs or my desire to help them more. Due to the relatively small size of our memory clinic team compared to the staffing patterns found throughout other departments of our healthcare organization, that dynamic was highly unlikely to improve any time soon, if ever, and that reality was even more difficult for me to bear.

The next four years flew by quickly before I decided to leave the memory clinic and accept a new position as a home-based dementia specialist within the palliative care department of our HMO. In that newly developed role, I had the opportunity to do home visits all around the Denver metro area with patients who were living with dementia, as well as with the people who were intimately involved in their care. I provided disease-specific education and emotional support, taught classes on dementia for caregivers, and assisted with completing their written advance directives, outlining their wishes for the kind of medical care they would or would not want to receive in the future. It was like a dream job for me in many ways, and I felt extremely blessed to be part of a large team of palliative care professionals who were all rock stars in their own right and whom I was fortunate enough to learn from and be mentored by.

After a time, my work worlds began to collide when I started to frequently run into patients and families who I had previously worked with in the memory clinic months or years before. It was wonderful to see them again in their living rooms and kitchens and outside of the sterile confines of a medical complex. However, it was also hard for me to witness the obvious progression of their dementias, as well as the weathered looks of overwhelm, sadness, and worry that had taken up residence on the caregivers' faces since I had seen them last. Getting reintroduced to Gertie and her family was a perfect example of time taking its toll.

Gertie's Wishes

"Now you're talking about that dementia thing, aren't you?"

At our staff meeting, each of us was asked to share any significant updates regarding the patients who had come through the memory clinic that week. When it was my turn, I said: "A woman by the name of Gertie stole my heart," and everyone laughed. I had a well-known reputation among my peers for falling in love with the seniors I was fortunate enough to meet in my job.

Gertie had been referred to our clinic by her primary care physician, who had concerns about her declining health and the ripple effect it was causing in the family. Gertie experienced a small stroke two years before and had been getting along relatively well until the past few months when her short-term memory deficits began to impact her day-to-day functioning more noticeably, prompting the referral for cognitive testing to evaluate the source of Gertie's memory changes.

Gertie appeared quite anxious when she arrived for her appointment but tried to hide the discomfort behind her nervous laughter by sitting close to her daughter, Ingrid. As she gradually relaxed, Gertie's radiant personality began to shine. I quickly found her to be an absolute delight to converse with, and I could tell that Gertie was enjoying talking with me as well. While

I gathered initial background information from her, one question I posed was whether Gertie had chosen anyone to be her medical durable power of attorney, as I did not find any evidence of that in her medical chart.

When Gertie asked me to explain what I meant by that term, I told her it involved choosing someone she trusted to make future medical decisions on her behalf if she ever became incapable of making those decisions herself due to illness or injury. I clarified that if Gertie were to get into a serious car accident, have another stroke, or have any kind of unforeseen medical complications that left her unable to communicate, it was crucial that she designate someone to make those important decisions for her. I also told her it was important to document her wishes in the form of a living will or advance directive. For good measure, I threw in the fact that our organization provided a free program called Advance Care Planning to assist with that process and that I was one of the facilitators trained to deliver that specialized service.

Gertie winked at me and said, "Well, if it gives me an excuse to come back and chat some more with you, my dear, then by all means, sign me up!" Ingrid and I chuckled at Gertie's playful humor, and I quickly set up an appointment for the two of them to return the following month.

When Gertie and her daughter arrived for the advance care planning appointment, the first topic we discussed was the results of Gertie's memory testing that had been completed since I'd last seen her. Ingrid explained that she and her mom had been informed by the physician in the memory clinic that Gertie had a "mixed dementia" diagnosis—likely the result of Gertie's stroke, combined with her history of a traumatic brain injury that Gertie had sustained after slipping on a puddle of water in the grocery store aisle five years before.

Gertie's random fall in the aisle of Safeway was more than just bad luck for her that day. It led to a week-long hospitalization, a month spent recovering in a rehab center, and ongoing headaches, dizziness, and intermittent short-term memory problems for at least six months after the incident. The long-term ramifications of that perilous accident had caught up with Gertie's brain and illuminated all the memory and functional changes she'd been experiencing for the past couple of years. Although these two lovely ladies were admittedly still in shock after receiving the unexpected news of Gertie's dementia diagnosis, they also had a close-knit family and a deep sense of faith, which fueled their confidence that, together, they would be able to face whatever challenges awaited them.

I spent the remainder of the visit facilitating a conversation between Ingrid and her mother to address Gertie's broad goals for her future medical care in the context of her new dementia diagnosis, and I assisted her with completing a basic advance directive. She readily chose Ingrid to be her primary medical decision-maker and two of her other children to be backups if anything ever happened to Ingrid.

We discussed Gertie's spiritual belief system and what she most valued at that point in her life. Gertie was clear that she wanted to remain independent for as long as she could and dreaded the thought of becoming a burden to her family—financially or otherwise. We talked about the active lifestyle Gertie was still fortunate enough to enjoy and the kinds of things that brought great meaning to her life, like gardening, reading, attending church, and spending time with her family and friends. When it came to discussing different medical case scenarios that could possibly happen to her in the years to come, Gertie consistently responded that she would always choose to live fewer years with a high quality of life and ability to be independent over living for a much longer period of time if her health and independence were severely compromised.

When our appointment was almost finished, Gertie and Ingrid both told me how helpful and enlightening it had been for them to talk about Gertie's wishes, as it was a topic they realized was important but had steadfastly avoided for years, even though she was eighty-two years old. In my line of work, that was, unfortunately, a common trend among the patients and families I encountered. Most tended to procrastinate to complete such documents in order to dodge the uncomfortable discussions about illness and death that came with them, instead of taking a more proactive approach to future planning. Gertie and Ingrid gave me hugs as they were leaving my office, and Gertie paused to thank me for putting her at ease during that emotionally taxing process. She promised that she *would never forget* the professionalism and kindness I bestowed upon them that day.

Two years later, while I was working as a social worker in palliative care, Gertie and I crossed paths again after her primary care doctor referred her to our department. Gertie's PCP requested that I make a home visit to his patient to access Gertie's worsening dementia and to update her advance directives that I had initially helped her create back in the memory clinic. According to the information in the PCP's referral note, Gertie had recently moved in with her daughter's family when it became unsafe for her to live alone as a result of her impaired memory and reasoning abilities. I was excited at the prospect of seeing Gertie and Ingrid again, as I vividly recalled how delightful my previous interactions had been with them.

When I called Ingrid to set up the appointment, she immediately remembered who I was and seemed genuinely eager for me to come to their house to meet with them. However, Ingrid also alerted me that her mother had little insight into the extent of her memory or functional changes and believed there was not a *damned thing wrong with her* most days. Ingrid went on to explain that her mother's lack of awareness regarding her own memory changes was a frustrating bone of contention for her and her husband because *they both knew* with absolute clarity that Gertie's perception of herself was *anything* but accurate.

This worried daughter sounded increasingly distressed as she told me how much her mom's personality had become markedly different over the past year and how "mean" her once-patient and loving parent could now be. Ingrid tearfully informed me that if I were going to make a home visit, I could do so only if I promised *not* to use the word "dementia" in front of Gertie because if I did, she would probably "throw me out the front door on my ass and never look back!"

I agreed to Ingrid's request and admitted it was sad for me to hear that the personable and funny woman I became enamored with during our past meetings had changed so much as a result of her progressing illness. I set up the appointment with Ingrid and quietly pondered what an absurd challenge would be awaiting me when I got to her house the following week. This was because a significant portion of my visit would be centered on updating Gertie's advance directives and asking her straightforward questions, like what she knew and understood about the mixed dementia diagnosis she had received two years before. I would also need to inquire about what information Gertie's doctor had provided to her regarding her incurable neurological disease and how she would apply that information to determine the kind of medical care she would or wouldn't want to receive down the road.

I thought to myself, *This is a frickin' joke! How am I ever supposed to complete those aspects of my job without uttering the "D-word" in the process?!* I had no clue how I would ever pull that off short of a miracle—I knew I would need all the help I could get to make that happen!

When I arrived at the house at the appointed time, Ingrid greeted me at the door with a huge smile and a hug and warmly welcomed me into her comfortable abode. Gertie was seated at the kitchen table when I entered the room, and I could tell from one glance that she'd aged a lot since I'd seen her last. Ingrid reintroduced me to Gertie, saying, "Mom, you remember Kay Adams? She is the social worker I've been telling you about for the past few days who was going to be coming out to meet with us. Kay was very helpful when we worked with her in the memory clinic a couple of years back, and then she was so kind to arrange another meeting with us after that to help complete all of that important medical paperwork for you. This time, Kay was willing to come right to our home so that we wouldn't have to drive anywhere in this cold weather."

Gertie cautiously shook my outstretched hand while saying to Ingrid, "Well, this gal looks friendly enough, but I've never laid eyes on her before today or I certainly would have remembered! How many times do I have to *tell you* to warn me in advance when we are expecting company because I'm really in no mood to be bothered by nosy strangers today!" I took a deep breath and said to myself, *I'm off to an amazing start! I'm sure the rest of the visit will be a cakewalk from here!*

I employed every skill in my arsenal to quickly build rapport and trust with Gertie once again so she would be comfortable enough to address some difficult topics with Ingrid and me, but that was no easy feat! It took at least twenty minutes of social banter before I sensed that it was safe enough for me to pull out the paperwork from my bag and attempt to have another advance directive discussion without Gertie flying off the handle. I still had *no idea* how I would accomplish that task while simultaneously honoring my vow of silence to keep from uttering the "D-word" in the process.

At first, I asked Gertie general and benign questions about how she had been feeling. How were her appetite and sleep? Was she having any pain or discomfort? Ingrid gently prompted Gertie's memory on some of the questions when she saw a look of confusion cross her mother's face. I slowly started to circle in closer to more pertinent questions that related to Gertie's advance directive. I asked if she was having any health problems that were of concern to her, and as commonly happens when I ask such questions to eighty-something-year-olds, I heard all about her bowels, glaucoma, ingrown toenails, hearing loss, and how "growing old isn't for sissies!"

I was silently praying for Divine Intervention of some kind so I could get to the *real issues* I was there to address, when Gertie suddenly blurted out, "Well, my family thinks my memory isn't what it used to be." I nearly leapt out of my seat in giddy exaltation. Now *that* was something tangible I could work with at last!

So, for the rest of our meeting, I used Gertie's language and followed her lead. I inquired about what she thought would happen if her memory kept getting worse. What were her worries? I asked Ingrid similar questions, and we talked about probable outcomes. Gertie occasionally got off track and went "down the rabbit hole," so I had to patiently wait and redirect her back to the topic at hand before I could proceed to the next question on my list.

I eventually was able to ask Gertie if she thought she would want a feeding tube if she ever got to the point in her disease where she lost the ability to swallow on her own. Then, as if the heavens parted and a rare moment of synaptic insight returned to Gertie's damaged brain, she looked me right in the eye and said, "Now, you're talking about that dementia thing, aren't you?" Thoughts began racing through my mind about how I had promised Ingrid I wouldn't use the word "dementia" with her mom, but since *Gertie* brought it up first, my gut told me I couldn't let that golden opportunity pass me by.

I decided that honesty was the best policy, so I said, "Yes. I was referring to dementia." Gertie replied, "Do you mean to tell me if my brain keeps getting worse that I won't even remember how to swallow on my own anymore?" I said, "Yes, that could certainly happen." Gertie then turned to her daughter and emphatically stated, "If I ever get like that, don't *you dare* do that thing to me!"

And so, the game of charades began as I strived to uncover what Gertie meant by that statement. We were slowly and painstakingly able to discern that what Gertie was referring to by "that thing" was life support. She did not want anything to prolong her life, including a feeding tube, if and when her dementia got to the point where, *by her own definition*, she had little to no quality of life left.

It took me over two hours to update Gertie's advance directives that day. It was definitely one of my most challenging palliative care visits but also one of the most gratifying. When Ingrid walked me back to her front door, she thanked me profusely for giving them so much of my time and attention and told me how much better she felt.

"This disease has been so hard on us all! In the beginning, I thought it was just going to affect Mom's memory. I was completely unaware that it could impact every part of her being and turn her into someone I barely recognize at times. When we met you two years ago, I *could never have imagined* that our family would be in the place we are in now, and I've felt at a loss as to how to deal with everything on my plate. Having this talk today and *hearing directly from Mom* what her medical wishes are have been an enormous relief for me as her daughter and medical proxy. Although it'll be hard if I'm ever actually faced with making those tough medical decisions for Mom someday, it will be much easier now that I actually *know* what her priorities and values are. I won't have to 'play God' and guess what she would have wanted me to do because she has already told me. That, alone, is one of the greatest gifts my mother has ever given me, and I have you to thank."

As I drove back to the office that day, I realized that even if a lot of people *thought* that what I did for a living must be deeply depressing, weird, or simply a job to avoid at all costs, I believed differently. What those other people didn't grasp about my vocation were the beautiful and intangible rewards I received from the fruits of my labor.

Knowing I had played an instrumental role in Ingrid receiving vital information and guidance about her mother's final wishes was tremendously satisfying. Understanding that the dialogue I was able to facilitate between Gertie and her daughter would one day enable Ingrid to avoid a great deal of emotional pain and provide some peace of mind was priceless. And knowing in my heart that I was able to create a safe space for Gertie to discuss and document what was most important for her in the final chapter of her life, in spite of her dementia, was like hitting the ball out of the park for me. It just doesn't get any better than that!

Bob and Ellie

"I wouldn't want your job for anything."

t was another tense day in the memory clinic. Ellie returned for her follow-up appointment accompanied by her husband, Bob, and their forty-five-year-old daughter, Jean. When they took their seats around the conference room table, Jean placed herself to the left of her mother. Based on the way that Jean kept shielding her face behind her hand and avoiding eye contact with everyone in the room, I had the sense that she was trying to hide the look of pained concern on her face so that none of us would see. Jean's sister Betsy had been able to attend the initial intake appointment in person with the family, but on that particular day, she was only able to participate in the meeting over speakerphone from her home in New England—over two thousand miles away.

Our job that morning was to review the results of Ellie's cognitive testing and the other assessments that our team had completed on her behalf during the previous two weeks. That initial ninety-minute intake appointment was one of the toughest I had ever experienced because of the collective anxiety, anger, and tension that was glaringly obvious between Ellie's husband and their two daughters during my extensive interview with the family.

As a social worker on the team, one of my roles was to gather pertinent information from family members about the changes they have observed in their loved one in terms of memory, mood, cognition, and functional ability. Those interviews were often highly charged with emotion and required all my years of counseling experience, clinical expertise, and family systems knowledge to facilitate. The data I was compiling on Ellie would be combined with the results of her cognitive testing and medical chart review—all essential elements of the overall memory evaluation process.

Despite being in his early seventies, Bob was still a force of nature to be reckoned with. It was clear from the start of the intake meeting that Bob was a man accustomed to being in charge and getting his way. He had run his highly successful company for decades and per his daughters, had also tried to micromanage their formative years with the same kind of scrupulous expectations that he demanded of his employees. According to Jean and Betsy, Bob's brash style of parenting was in total opposition to Ellie's patient and nurturing approach to childrearing. I learned a great deal about this family dynamic during my intake appointment interview with Betsy when she explained the reason she and her sister enjoyed such a close bond with their mom, whom they revered, and why their relationship with their dad was so incredibly tenuous and strained.

When Bob wasn't busy working, he was off traveling the globe with his wife, and he informed me that he had no intention of allowing Ellie's cognitive changes to keep them from continuing to enjoy doing what they most loved to do together. I inquired about changes in Ellie's memory, mood, and functional abilities that the family had noticed over time and addressed any questions that arose, such as what the difference was between normal aging and the memory loss Ellie had been experiencing.

Bob was edgy and angry throughout the intake appointment, and his mood only grew worse by the end when he learned that they would have to wait two weeks for a follow-up appointment in our clinic before they could find out the results of Ellie's cognitive testing, as was standard protocol.

After engaging in a few minutes of polite social banter at the beginning of the follow-up appointment two weeks later, Sandra, the nurse practitioner, skillfully reviewed the results of Ellie's memory testing with consummate professionalism—including delivering the difficult news that Ellie had a probable diagnosis of Alzheimer's disease. The family sat in stunned silence for a minute or two before Jean tearfully asked what she could do to help her mom so that her memory wouldn't get any worse.

Sandra carefully outlined the benefits of keeping Ellie socially stimulated, physically active, and mentally challenged as a way to maximize Ellie's current brain health and to try to slow the disease process from advancing any faster. She also talked about the importance of structuring Ellie's day so she had a consistent and predictable routine to follow in order to avoid the need for her to constantly adapt to new changes and stressors in the environment. Sandra gently asked Ellie if the world was becoming more of a confusing place to her. Ellie quickly nodded her head in silent agreement and averted her gaze to the floor and away from her family's watchful eyes.

Sandra had barely finished her last sentence when Bob sprang into action and began to vehemently refute every word she said. Bob was so upset that his hands were shaking as he talked, and his face was beaded with sweat. Bob was used to being in complete control of his universe, so hearing from a group of medical professionals that the love of his life had a disease no one was able to stop or fix was definitely *not* part of his agenda that day. Bob demanded answers. He demanded action steps and a treatment plan. He demanded facts and predictions. He demanded resources and a way for us to prevent this horrible illness from taking his beautiful wife further and further away from him. Bob demanded things that were impossible for our team, or any team, to deliver, and *that* made him even angrier.

The pressure in the conference room was so thick I could barely breathe. The emotional upheaval resulting from Ellie being informed that she had an

Alzheimer's type of dementia had reduced her to tears, and the deep grief emanating from Bob and Jean was almost palpable. I tried to offer hope and assurances, but there is little real comfort to give at such times when the shock of a life-threatening diagnosis shakes a patient and family to their core. Sometimes silence and holding sacred space for people's intense grief and hard emotions are the best medicines we can hope to provide.

After asking pointed questions about how we reached our diagnosis, Bob again expressed how important it was for him and Ellie to be able to continue their international travels together, as they already had three big trips booked for the coming year. Bob asked for our advice regarding how Ellie's new dementia diagnosis might impact their vacation plans. Sandra and I patiently explained how difficult traveling can be for someone who is living with a progressive brain disease like Alzheimer's.

Travel, by its very nature, is about going somewhere new and different. It's about having novel experiences you've never had before and getting out of your day-to-day routines. It's about being exposed to different sights, sounds, smells, languages, and cultures and doing activities you've never experienced before. Even for someone like Ellie, who had previously enjoyed traveling all over the world, leaving the comfort of her home and familiar schedule at this advanced stage of her disease could become frightening and discombobulating instead of stimulating and enjoyable. What a brain impacted by dementia needs more than anything else is structure, routine, and predictability to keep the person from becoming stressed and overwhelmed. As a result, extensive travel was not the antidote Sandra and I were recommending for Ellie, and Bob clearly resented our counsel.

The level of Bob's disdain for our suggestion to thoughtfully limit future travel plans went over like a lead balloon, despite the fact that he and his daughters had privately informed us that Ellie had become disoriented many times in the past during their trips to foreign countries and had been extremely fortunate that nothing more serious than increased confusion and embarrassment had ever resulted from her getting lost in those faraway lands. The look of distress on Bob's face continued to intensify as the meeting wore on. More than once, Ellie reached her small, thin hand over to Bob's arm, patted him gently, and urged him to "calm down, dear ... it will be all right."

But everyone in the room knew it wouldn't be all right. At least, it wouldn't ever be the same. And no matter how rich, powerful, and resourceful Bob may have been, he could not buy his way out of this situation. His projected anger and blame at those of us on the team were an emotional shield to protect himself from the harsh reality of his wife's incurable illness and the heartbreak that was sure to follow.

We spent the remainder of that hour-long appointment answering the family's questions about Alzheimer's disease, the pros and cons of having Ellie try a memory medication when none of the current ones on the market had robust success rates, and what to expect in the future.

Somewhere in the midst of our final minutes together, the energy in the room noticeably softened and transformed. It was as if the pent-up anxiety and intense emotions the family had been discharging throughout our meeting somehow magically dissolved the wall of tension that had encompassed the room only a short time before. Every one of us seemed to experience a collective out-breath of relief after such an exhausting hour. It was then I witnessed a shift in the overall demeanor of the family—from angry, sad, and guarded to a visceral level of acceptance that a *disease* was responsible for Ellie's cognitive and functional changes and that we as the memory clinic team were not the enemy after all—only the unfortunate bearers of bad news that *no family* ever wanted to hear.

As I looked around the room when the follow-up appointment drew to a close, Bob did not appear as defensive or angry as he had been in the beginning, Jean looked less pained and worried, and Ellie's tears had been replaced by a sad smile as she sincerely thanked us for our time and patience with her family. To my great surprise, rather than shaking our hands when he was leaving the consultation room, Bob extended his arms in a hug instead, and Jean and Ellie quickly followed suit. Sandra and I embraced each family member as they exited the room in single file. Ellie was the last one to hug me as she was leaving, and as we parted, she looked me straight in the eye and said, "I wouldn't want your job for anything."

Although I thoroughly understood her sentiment, I couldn't have disagreed more. Because for me, what had transpired between our team and those four people in only sixty minutes was profound. From delivering heartbreaking news to helping Ellie and her family process the medical information, along with their initial shock, anger, and raw grief regarding the new life-threatening diagnosis, we covered a lot of emotionally challenging ground in such a short amount of time. And to be rewarded for our efforts with words of gratitude and heartfelt hugs for the expertise and compassion we offered was genuine icing on the cake.

It was also what truly fed my spirit in that difficult job and what made it possible for me to be authentically present to the next five patients and families waiting in anxious anticipation to meet with us later that same day. And it was what enabled me to go home to my family that night and still have energy left in my emotional gas tank to give to those I cherish most and then to return to work day after day and do it all over again.

A Great Misnomer

"I'm not ready yet."

once read a note in a patient's medical chart years ago in which Sandra, our nurse practitioner, had documented a diagnosis of "alcohol-induced dementia, late-onset, uncomplicated" for a seventy-five-year-old man named Rex. I had been involved in both the intake and follow-up appointments with that patient and his wife and vividly recall thinking to myself what a great misnomer that diagnosis was.

Rex had come in for an intake appointment in the memory clinic, accompanied by Carolyn, who was four years his junior. I could instantly sense the thick tension between them from the moment we met in the lobby, but it wasn't until I interviewed Carolyn alone that I began to understand the reason behind it.

Rex and Carolyn had been married for forty years. Carolyn told me about Rex's prolonged history of alcoholism, dating back decades to when they owned a pub-style restaurant together. Carolyn disclosed to me that Rex would drink from early morning until late at night for years on end and that she had pleaded with him to quit drinking for most of their years together, but Rex's empty promises to get sober never materialized, which Carolyn admittedly resented.

Carolyn went on to tell me how Rex had squandered away their money throughout their marriage on bad business decisions made under a cloud of addiction. She explained that because of Rex's poor financial choices in the past, they were barely squeaking by on Social Security, so she literally *couldn't afford* to leave her "toxic marriage" because of that financial reality. Through her tears, Carolyn told me how she and Rex fought constantly and could barely stand to be in each other's company. She described "feeling trapped and alone" in the world, despite having grown children who lived nearby, because Carolyn strove to avoid burdening them with her marital woes—especially in light of the fact that her kids "detested" their father due to his extensive history of abusing substances, as well as them.

I listened intently as the woman before me described the never-ending turmoil of her marriage. Carolyn admitted that she was guilty of constantly screaming at Rex when he couldn't remember anything she said for more than five minutes because of his "nonexistent" short-term memory. She also stated that when they got into big arguments, Rex would pick up any object within reach and hurl it at her as hard as he could. This is what their marriage had devolved to after four decades: a living hell.

As our conversation wore on, Carolyn told me that her blood pressure was dangerously high and out of control. She said she wanted to try counseling or some other intervention that might help lower her blood pressure, but the unrelenting stress of caregiving, combined with Rex's increased dependency on her, made practicing self-care *of any kind* completely out of the question.

Carolyn inquired whether I thought Rex could be *faking it* on the frequent occasions when he claimed he couldn't recall things she'd just told him or asked how to complete simple tasks he'd done his entire life. She revealed that she found it nearly impossible to distinguish between her husband's historic pattern of "laziness and manipulation" with any "real" cognitive or functional changes that might be happening as a result of Rex "pickling his brain" with alcohol for decades.

In great frustration, Carolyn described to me how Rex was in total denial about his memory loss, which only served to heighten the conflict in their already volatile relationship. According to Carolyn, Rex had a well-documented history of verbal and physical abuse toward both her and their children long before the dementia hit, and those behaviors only intensified over time. Carolyn admitted to having lifelong struggles with anxiety and depression related to her noxious marriage, and they were only becoming worse due to the sustained level of stress she'd been living under for so long. In fact, Carolyn was worried enough about her own mental status and fear of developing dementia herself that she had undergone a memory evaluation in our clinic the year before. Fortunately for Carolyn, the findings showed no evidence of any dementia developing in her brain but *did reveal* that she had extremely elevated levels of anxiety and depression that were interfering with her daily functioning and making her feel like she was losing her mind in the process.

As my interview with Carolyn was drawing to a close, I felt certain of a high likelihood that the results of Rex's cognitive testing would align with Carolyn's description of someone who was experiencing advanced dementia, and the diagnosis and prognosis that would be delivered during our next visit would be anything but good.

When Rex and Carolyn returned to the clinic a few weeks later for the follow-up appointment, Sandra went over the results of Rex's memory testing, including his diagnosis of "alcohol-induced dementia." Carolyn instantly reacted to this news by screaming at her husband, "I don't *want* to take care of you! You did this *to yourself!* I hate you for this!"

Rex just stared at Carolyn with a blank look of apathy on his face, as if nothing his wife had just said in that moment of rage even began to register or compute in his broken brain. I sat silently pondering if I should step out of the room and call in security before the situation escalated any further but then decided against it when Carolyn's anger quickly dissolved into racking sobs across the table.

A little while later in the conversation, Sandra strongly urged Rex to consider giving up driving due to the severity of his memory problems, and Rex somehow miraculously followed the thread of her words just enough to scoff at them. Rex stated (and *erroneously believed)* that he was still an excellent driver and he wasn't about to give up his keys no matter what some doctor or anyone else said. Due to the advanced nature of his "uncompli-cated" dementia, Rex was incapable of recognizing the mental and functional losses he had undergone, let alone the mood and personality changes that were glaringly obvious to everyon*e except* him. Rex's common sense was nearly gone, as was most of his social filter. He tended to say and do things that were socially inappropriate and sometimes downright outrageous. The subtle nuances of expected human behavior no longer registered in Rex's diseased brain—just one of the hundreds of cognitive casualties that Rex would fall victim to because of his disease.

Sandra informed Rex and Carolyn that she would be sending a letter to the Department of Motor Vehicles to request that Rex be mandated to take an over-the-road driving test to ensure he was competent behind the wheel. Sandra periodically had to perform that unpopular duty with other intractable patients who were hell-bent in their belief that operating a motor vehicle was their God-given *right* and oblivious to the consequences that could happen when their dying brains could no longer be counted on to safely drive a car from point A to point B and back again.

I wondered to myself if Rex would pass that test, as Sandra had referred numerous patients to the DMV who had been diagnosed with advanced dementia, only to find out later that they had been allowed multiple attempts to take their road tests after they initially failed. Those same individuals were often granted the privilege of keeping their driver's license even when it seemed incredibly clear to us in the memory clinic that they were *long past the point* of responsibly operating a motor vehicle. Granting such driving privileges to people with severe cognitive impairment or dementia not only put *them* at great risk but also endangered the community in which they lived. As Sandra often stated, "In this job, it is far less difficult to give someone a terminal diagnosis of dementia than it is to tell them they need to stop driving. Those are fighting words that most people don't want to accept or hear."

I placed my usual memory clinic follow-up call to Carolyn two weeks after that appointment to see how things were going. Carolyn acknowledged that she should probably be researching facilities to move Rex to but added, "I'm not ready yet." In truth, Carolyn and Rex did not begin to have the kind of money it took to pay the $6,000 to $12,000 monthly out-of-pocket costs of memory care or assisted living in Denver and possibly wouldn't even qualify for Medicaid benefits to cover the bill if their meager Social Security income happened to be even a dollar over the strict financial cutoff line required to receive federal Medicaid funding.

Whoever first came up with the term "uncomplicated" to describe the innumerable changes and challenges that happen on every level for someone living with dementia and the people who are responsible for them must have *never* been a care partner themselves. Or perhaps they were just ignorant, or maybe both. Because from my vantage point, this heartbreaking illness, and the collateral damage it can leave in its wake, is *one of the most complicated* journeys any human being may ever have to take. I only wish that the diagnostic terms we've invented to describe it better reflected this grave but accurate truth.

Olga's Wheels

"You can't take my car away from me! It's not even paid for yet!"

It was the beginning of a three-month internship for our new social work intern, Hillary. She was both excited and nervous to shadow me for the day to observe and learn about the work that our team did in the memory clinic. The first call of duty was to meet with a patient named Olga, who was coming in for her initial appointment and battery of cognitive testing.

Olga was a seventy-three-year-old woman with a strong Swedish accent and a delightful countenance. She had a head full of thick white hair, twinkly blue eyes (a combination I am admittedly a sucker for!), and more personality in that little body of hers than ten people combined. Olga came to the intake appointment accompanied by her daughter Joan, with whom she resided and was the best of friends. Hillary and I had barely greeted Olga and Joan when they both double-teamed us with a barrage of questions about Olga's fitness to drive a car.

Apparently, Olga's primary care doctor had concerns about her driving after recently administering the SLUMS (St. Louis University Mental Status) test to Olga, on which she scored rather poorly. Her physician then ordered Olga to take another more comprehensive driving-related assessment to ensure that she and others who were sharing the road with her were safe. The results of that test had not yet been shared with Olga and Joan, so they were anxious with anticipation and singularly focused on advocating for Olga's ability to continue operating a motor vehicle.

It's hard to say which one of them spoke the most during our family interview, but suffice it to say that Olga's daughter didn't fall far from the family tree when it came to the talkative gene. The session ran twenty minutes over, despite my constant attempts to keep the discussion focused and on task. Both of those women were a force of nature unto themselves and would not be silenced until their points were firmly made. Those points primarily had to do with convincing Hillary and me that Olga was not demented in any way and that her beloved Honda Accord was in the safest of hands with Olga behind the wheel.

Olga eventually left the room with Sandra to do her testing across the hall. Meanwhile, Hillary and I interviewed Joan in more depth about any memory or functional changes that she had observed in Olga over the past six to twelve months. Joan consistently stated that her mother only had slight memory changes but nothing to be concerned about. She even told us, "If I thought my mom was unsafe in any way to drive a car, I would be the first person to take her keys away from her!"

Joan was well aware that her mom depended on that car to get to the fitness center every day and to frequently go to the grocery store, visit friends, and run short errands around the neighborhood. That car represented Olga's gateway to her continued independence, and she was not about to give up her driving privileges without a fight. That much was crystal clear.

Joan's forceful reassurances to us regarding her mother's flawless driving capabilities represented an argument I was quite familiar with after countless interactions with other families over the years. I discovered long ago that such fervent advocacy attempts by people like Joan were frequently motivated more out of selfish intentions than out of actual concern for their loved one's wings being clipped. In Olga's case, if she were no longer able to safely motor around town by herself, then that task would fall to *someone else*, and Joan's name was at the top of the shortlist of people who would likely have to take on that added responsibility—and burden—on top of everything else she was already doing for her mother.

It was not part of Sandra's standard practice to come back into the consult room while I was still meeting with a family, but that day was an exception. Sandra returned to the room to voice her acute concerns to Joan about the extent of her mother's memory problems. Sandra cited multiple examples to highlight her concerns. For instance, when Sandra asked Olga what year it was during the memory evaluation, Olga stated it was 1982 instead of 2015. When Sandra asked her what day of the week it was, Olga said it was Thursday, when it was actually Friday. There were other examples that Sandra gave to demonstrate her alarm, but Joan was visibly shocked at what the nurse practitioner was telling her and almost speechless for the first time that morning.

An hour after Olga and Joan left our office that day, Olga returned alone and unannounced. The front desk clerk brought her health insurance card back down the hallway to me and stated that someone was in the lobby who wanted to see me about changing the answers on her memory test. Hillary gave me a quizzical look, and I showed her the card with Olga's name emblazoned across the front of it. I told Hillary that nothing like this had ever happened to me before, so Hillary quickly inquired if she could tag along with me to the lobby to observe my conversation with Olga, and I agreed.

We found Olga sitting nervously in the lobby, gripping her purse tightly in her lap and looking completely distraught and overwhelmed. I quietly knelt down on the floor in front of her and asked Olga what she was doing there. She told me that Joan had become angry with her when they got to their car following the appointment. Joan had reproached her mother about her answers on the mental status test and asked her why she would ever say the year was 1982 when she clearly knew it was 2015, and she challenged her as to why she said today was Thursday when it was obviously Friday.

Unlike other situations I had encountered when my internal "radar" went off, warning me of trouble or violence within a family, I'd had no such concerns that day. Based on watching the loving interactions between Olga and Joan just a short time before, it seemed far more likely to both Hillary and me that Olga appeared incredibly distressed because she had disappointed her daughter, whom she adored, and she was scared that her future freedom was hanging precariously in the balance of her cognitive testing results.

Olga was clearly shaken as she pulled her checkbook out of her purse and, with trembling hands, proceeded to show me her checkbook register that had the date of 2015 recorded inside. "See," she told me. "I know the year is 2015! I have no idea why I said 1982. I was just so nervous about coming here today that I couldn't think! I want to change the answers on my test. Please! I can't lose my license. You can't take my car away from me! It's not even paid for yet!"

Hillary and I were both fighting tears of our own as we sat with Olga in the lobby that day. Her grief, fear, and anxiety were so *raw* that we couldn't help but feel deeply touched by her unfolding struggle. There was not a dry eye among the clerks who sat behind the front desk as they watched the interaction from across the room and silently prayed that this wouldn't be their fate one day.

A week later, Olga showed up at our clinic without warning, without an appointment, and without checking in at the front desk. Instead, she strolled straight back into the no-patients-allowed shared office space of the geriatric psych team and plopped herself down on a chair as if she owned the place. She was back to her amazingly cheerful self and started conversing with Sandra, Hillary, and me like we were longtime friends. She told us how sweet, smart, and wonderful we all were and how she was getting along so well and just wanted to stop in and tell us so.

The three of us looked at each other in amusement, as this, too, was a first for our clinic. No one had ever *just stopped by* like this before, and although the visit was delightful in a way, there was also a manipulative aspect to it. Olga was still trying to convince us that there was not a darned thing wrong with her noggin, and if there was, we would be hard-pressed to tell her so when she returned for her follow-up appointment in two weeks. Olga was determined to win our approval in every way she knew how and hoping with all her might that her award-winning personality would make up for whatever neurodegenerative disease might be lurking beneath the surface of her skull.

On the day of the follow-up appointment, Sandra and I were full of dread because of the bad news we were tasked with delivering to Olga and her daughter. At a minimum, we expected a lot of pushback, denial, and resistance when the disclosure of Olga's dementia diagnosis was made, and we were deeply concerned that Olga's bright spirit would somehow break when she learned she had a life-threatening illness that would, over time, radically impact her ability to remain independent and self-sufficient, let alone have free rein on the open road. Breaking news of this kind was the hardest and most emotionally taxing part of our job in the memory clinic, but unfortunately, it was a core aspect of our work as well.

Sandra and I entered the consult room to find Olga and Joan laughing and joking at the table as they were awaiting our arrival. Both of them were surprisingly jovial and appeared relaxed and eager to hear what the memory testing results revealed. After a few minutes of lighthearted banter, Sandra quickly got down to the business of reviewing Olga's testing results in great detail, including the words that *neither of them* wanted to hear: Olga was in the early stages of an Alzheimer's disease for which there was no cure. Sandra took her time in explaining what Alzheimer's disease is, what it does, and what to expect in the future as it slowly progresses.

Sandra gently explained why driving becomes a safety concern for those living with this brain disease that impacts a person's vision, wayfinding system, problem-solving abilities, response time, and safety awareness. Sandra went on to discuss how Alzheimer's disease also negatively affects a person's executive functioning skills, including the ability to control one's emotions or impulses, to plan and process information, to rapidly shift their attention, to remember things that happened a short time before, and to sequence tasks—all of which are vitally important skills in driving. Sandra also added that we were acutely aware of how difficult it is for most patients we meet to fathom the idea of giving up driving, but that as we all continue to live longer and longer as a society, most of us will eventually reach the point where driving ourselves around will no longer be a viable, realistic, or safe option.

Olga and Joan listened intently to the information Sandra and I presented and only interrupted a couple of times to ask pertinent questions. They seemed remarkably calm and accepting of what we had to say under those stressful circumstances, which was not at all what we had anticipated would happen. Much to our surprise and enormous relief, Olga and her daughter took the news with grace, humor, and gratitude. Olga even had a mischievous glint in her eyes as she hugged Sandra and me goodbye, and that's when we discovered the reason for her impish demeanor.

As she was walking away, Olga paused and cheerfully informed us that she had already made plans to take a driving test at the Department of Motor Vehicles the following week to prove her *exceptional driving skills* once and for all. Sandra and I broke out laughing and shook our heads in amazement at Olga's fortitude and unmitigated resolve to keep her four-wheeled freedom for as long as humanly possible, despite the countless barriers that awaited her. Sandra and I also silently prayed that our local DMV would *not* do what they had a well-known reputation for doing—granting people with cognitive impairment and dementia up to seven attempts to pass their driving tests, instead of erring on the side of public safety and taking away their driver's licenses for good.

I walked back to my desk and silently asked myself what areas of my life were so important that I would be willing to fight as hard as Olga was fighting to maintain them. How will I handle the prospect of my own mother's wings getting clipped by some disease or disability that takes away the last vestiges of her independence? What lengths will I be inclined to go to in order to prove myself to a world that doubts my abilities so that I can maintain my autonomy for yet another day? I don't know the answers to any of those questions yet, but I do know this: Olga certainly taught me the value of incorporating dogged determination and unfettered persistence into one's plan when facing adversity. And an extra dose of blind optimism and charismatic charm thrown in never hurts your chances of success!

If I Had to Live
Without You

"It's going to be fine, my sweetheart.
Everything's going to be just fine."

A gentleman named Sven came into our clinic for memory testing, along with his wife, Ruba. I sat down with them in the family consult room to gather some historical information about Sven.

Sven and Ruba had been married for nearly sixty years and had immigrated to the United States from Sweden in their early twenties. They had a son who was still residing in Sweden and a daughter in Colorado. Before his retirement, Sven worked as a mechanical engineer but now spent most of his free time involved in numerous "Swedish clubs" that he attended throughout the Denver area. Ruba was not the socialite that her husband was, and she preferred spending quiet nights at home, cooking Sven's favorite meals from the "Old Country," and making quilts for her family and friends.

I talked with this lively duo for fifteen minutes to collect demographic data from them before Sven was escorted across the hall to complete his cognitive testing. I spent the next forty-five minutes alone in the room with

Ruba to gather additional collateral information from her perspective as to what she thought might be going on with her husband.

I had come to learn over the years that the patients who came in for testing were frequently unreliable historians about their lives because of increased memory loss and confusion, so collecting background information from family members was an essential part of the memory evaluation for that reason. Besides, families usually felt far more at ease reporting any concerns or changes they had seen in their loved one when that person wasn't present in the room. Otherwise, they often felt like they were embarrassing their family member or somehow "talking out of school" about matters that should be kept private. Being able to quickly create a safe space for family members to feel comfortable enough to share their concerns with a total stranger in a medical clinic was an inherently difficult part of my job, yet a challenge I relished.

Ruba was more formidable than most spouses I had interviewed because of how closely she held her cards when it came to Sven. I asked her a series of questions about potential differences she may have noticed in her husband over the past couple of years. Were there noticeable changes in Sven's memory, in his mood and ability to do his day-to-day activities, in his functional abilities and reasoning skills, or in his level of interest and involvement with family and community events?

Ruba answered my questions in a terse manner. I could tell by her responses that she was trying hard to make Sven *look good* for my sake—even if that meant not being completely honest with me. However, I was acutely aware of the sheltering instinct that Ruba and other family members I had interviewed frequently displayed at such times. I was cognizant of the fact that we as human beings are deeply wired within our genetic code to try to protect those we love and how we sometimes have to fight against our internal programming to do what is "right" on their behalf. I could almost *see* the invisible tug of war that was happening inside Ruba's head as she silently weighed the options before her: to remain evasive with her answers in order to be loyal to her husband's public image or to be straightforward with me so she could access the help from our team that she and Sven were desperately seeking in the first place.

I waited in respectful silence for Ruba to make the difficult decision that my gut told me she was deliberating over in her mind. I was secretly hoping she would elect to be open with me so that Sven's cognitive assessment would be balanced and thorough by adding her valuable firsthand knowledge to the evaluation process, but I couldn't read the expression on her "poker face" enough to guess which option she would ultimately choose.

Finally, during the last ten minutes of my interview, Ruba decided to come clean about a few changes she had observed in her spouse. With a heavy sigh, she told me that Sven had recently stepped down from some of his leadership roles in many of his beloved Swedish clubs due to increased short-term memory loss and confusion. He was struggling to remember important dates and appointments and was beginning to make a lot of mistakes when managing their finances—something he had never done in the course of their long marriage. With tears threatening to escape her eyes, Ruba ended the appointment by sharing that Sven frequently couldn't remember the names of their four grandchildren, and sometimes even forgot that he had spent his whole career working as an engineer, which was one of his greatest accomplishments he had always taken deep pride in.

Two weeks later, Sven and Ruba returned to the memory clinic for the results of his cognitive testing. Ruba's stoic appearance began to crumble once our doctor gently conveyed the sad news that, in his best estimation, Sven had Alzheimer's disease, which was already in the moderate stages. Both Ruba and Sven looked shell-shocked after hearing the diagnosis that Dr. Kelly so empathetically delivered. From my vantage point in the room, I noticed that neither Sven nor Ruba looked at each other once the word "Alzheimer's" was spoken aloud. They both appeared to be trying diligently to control their outward emotions—probably in an effort to protect one another from the pain emanating from their broken hearts.

Later in the meeting, Dr. Kelly skillfully switched gears to a critical topic. He emphasized the importance of Sven and Ruba getting their advance directives in place, since neither of them had ever officially appointed anyone to be their medical proxy or discussed what they would want or wouldn't want in terms of their medical care in the future, despite being in their eighties. Dr. Kelly highlighted the timeliness of completing these exigent documents, as Sven was quickly approaching the point in which he would no longer have the decisional capacity to make some of those vitally important choices. I immediately offered to assist this wonderful couple with completing their advance care planning, as it was an additional part of my job that I truly loved. They readily agreed to my offer, and we set up a meeting for the following week.

Sven and Ruba returned for that appointment, along with their daughter, Genette. I sat down with them to facilitate a conversation about their choices for end-of-life care and to complete their advance directives—including a detailed living will and how to choose a medical durable power of attorney (MDPOA) or decision-maker whom they would trust to make medical decisions on their behalf if and when they became unable to make those choices themselves due to illness or injury. Sven quickly and easily chose Ruba to be his primary MDPOA and Genette to be the secondary or backup decision-maker, but the choices were not nearly so simple or straightforward for Ruba.

Up until two weeks before, when she was informed that Sven had Alzheimer's disease, Ruba would have automatically chosen her beloved husband to be her medical proxy without question or a second thought. However, when we discussed the potential problems that choice could create now that the love of her life had a progressive brain disease, Ruba understood the merits of giving medical decision-making authority to Genette instead, but it was absolutely excruciating for her to do so.

Tears streamed down Ruba's face as she wrote Genette's name on the line that asked her to declare who she would choose to be her primary medical proxy. I swear I could almost *hear* Ruba's heart being ripped out of her chest as she put her daughter's name on the form instead of her partner of nearly six decades. Watching Ruba's grief, but not understanding the reason behind it, Sven gently put his arm around his beloved's shoulder and simply said, "It's going to be fine, my sweetheart. Everything's going to be just fine."

Not being able to pick up on the nuances of our conversation and the deep mourning that Ruba was experiencing due to his brain changes was a silver lining of sorts. In that moment, Sven's dementia protected him from comprehending the level of emotional anguish his wife was going through when she had to pick someone other than the man she had always relied on *for everything* in her life to be her MDPOA and the implications of what that meant for both of their futures. It also shielded Sven from his own pain of not being able to serve in that incredibly important decision-making role for the woman he loved more than anything else in the world.

The last document I assisted Sven and Ruba with completing that day was a living will. I had a series of open-ended questions and statements that I posed to each of them. One of those statements was: "Life would no longer be worth living if I had to …" I had gone through this process at least fifty times before in similar advance care planning conversations with other families, and most of them replied with statements like, "Life would not be worth living if I had to be in a nursing home, if I didn't know or recognize anyone around me or myself, or if I had to be hooked up to machines to keep me alive." But on that day, I heard an answer I had never heard before.

When I posed that question to Sven, he instantly replied: "Life wouldn't be worth living if I had to live without my dear Ruba." Moments later, when it was Ruba's chance to answer, she said: "My life would not be worth living another minute if I had to spend it alone without my precious husband." And then, as if realizing for the first time that Alzheimer's disease would likely take Sven away from her much sooner than she ever expected, she dissolved into tears of grief once again. I hesitantly looked across the table and met Genette's gaze, and not surprisingly, neither of our eyes were dry.

I felt a distinct heaviness in my body for the remainder of that day and into the next. I wondered to myself what it would be like to love someone so passionately and for so long that you literally couldn't imagine living a single day without them on the planet. What would it be like to face losing your partner little by little to a disease as cruel as Alzheimer's can be and to still find the will to go on living yourself? I wondered how many people *ever* *really* get to experience the kind of incredible amore that Sven and Ruba had shared for almost sixty beautiful years. But mostly, I wondered if any of us spend enough time *truly being grateful and present* to the love that does come our way instead of taking it for granted and deluding ourselves into thinking that it is ours to hold forever.

Resigning Yourself
to Change

*"I have an obligation to my family to keep fighting and to not give
up. I love them, and they love me, and that's where I am trying
to keep my focus now. Not on everything that I have lost."*

I made a social work visit to a seventy-two-year-old gentleman in a long-term care facility by the name of Ted, at the request of the geriatric psychiatrist with whom I worked in the memory clinic. Ted and his wife had been married just shy of fifty years. They had two grown children, multiple grandchildren whom Ted adored, and many dear friends in their tight-knit community. Ted had always been a superior athlete with a long and lanky build. His six-foot-four-inch frame looked out of place in the wheelchair he now relied on since his life-changing fall eight weeks earlier. Prior to that accident, Ted had enjoyed an extremely high quality of life. He still worked part time in the successful family business that he ran with his children, golfed twice a week, and only gave up downhill skiing a few years back because he thought it was foolhardy of him to continue, given his age. But then the fall happened, and as is so often the case, everything changed on a dime.

Ted had experienced three falls on the same day, but the last one in the bathroom at home had been the worst. That fall resulted in Ted sustaining major fractures to his C-4 and C-5 vertebrae in his neck, which required over ten hours of surgery to repair. When he was finally released from the hospital following his operation, Ted spent numerous weeks in a rehab center before being transferred to a high-end nursing home nine days prior to meeting me.

Despite how hard Ted had willed himself to work in rehab so that he could regain enough strength, mobility, and independence to return home to live, his injuries were much too widespread and severe for him to realistically achieve that goal. Any vestiges of hope he held to go back to the life he once knew vanished as quickly as they'd appeared.

Because of how devastated Ted became after being "permanently transferred" to a long-term care facility, his once-robust will to live disappeared like a shadow in the night, and a referral was made to our gero-psych consult service to evaluate him for major depression and suicidal ideation. The geriatric psychiatrist on our team had already thoroughly reviewed Ted's medical history and had made recommendations for alternate antidepressant medications that could prove more beneficial in targeting his symptoms of depression than the current meds he was being administered in the nursing home.

As the social worker on the team, it was my role to meet with Ted to assess whether he posed a significant danger to himself or others and to create a safety plan if he did. It was the kind of visit I, frankly, dreaded because *I knew* from experience that the emotional intensity of such an encounter would not just be enervating for Ted but also for me as the clinician with a front-row seat to his pain and heartbreak.

The director of nursing informed me that Ted had almost no appetite since moving into the long-term care facility and had already lost ten pounds in his first week. She was quite concerned that Ted had been isolating himself in his room ever since his admission to the nursing home and that his affect seemed flat and expressionless most of the time. Ted had openly admitted to the facility social worker that "I wish I had died on the operating table so I wouldn't have to live like this."

Ted was so depressed at the gravity of his current situation and inability to take care of himself anymore that he had lost all motivation to do more than just go through the motions with the physical therapy services he received during his extended stay in the rehab center. Because of that, Ted's rehab services were eventually terminated due to a lack of measurable forward progress. In the Medicare payment system, "no progress" equals "no money" to continue to pay for ongoing physical therapy services. As a former collegiate athlete and lifelong competitor, Ted told me, "Flunking PT came as quite a blow to my ego and was the lowest emotional point yet. It represented a total failure on my part, and that is not something I've been accustomed to dealing with for most of my life."

I spoke with Ted for over an hour in his semi-private nursing home room, which was costing over $10,000 a month to reside in because he required two to three staff members just to move him from the bed to his wheelchair and needed assistance with all of his other activities of daily living, such as feeding himself, dressing himself, and toileting, due to the resulting paralysis from his neck fractures. Ted's wife was a petite woman in her early seventies who could not begin to provide the amount of skilled care her husband now needed, and the price tag to hire round-the-clock caregivers in the home was even more expensive than what they were already paying out of pocket for a shared nursing home room.

Ted told me about the series of events that had taken place over the prior two months since his fall and some of the subsequent losses he had incurred since then, including the loss of his home, his independence, his mobility, his privacy, his freedom, and the loss of control over his day-to-day life as he once knew it. Perhaps the hardest loss of all for Ted to cope with was the *loss of hope* he had for things to ever get better in the future. Now that Ted was completely dependent on facility staff to meet all his daily care needs since becoming permanently disabled, Ted's sense of confidence, pride, and resilience—once so strong and prevalent—had dissipated into a fog of overwhelming grief and despair.

Emphasizing that he needed two to three staff members to help him every time he moved from one place or setting to another because of his long frame and inability to help out in any way, Ted described to me how much pain he had been in the night before after being left upright in his wheelchair for multiple hours. He told me that what he desperately wanted more than anything else was for the staff to come put him to bed so that he could rest comfortably until the next morning. But from the time Ted turned on his call light for help the previous night, it was well over an hour before his head finally hit the pillow in relief—an unfortunately common phenomenon that happens in care settings across the country due to insufficient staffing patterns.

Ted disclosed how discouraging it was to have to wait endlessly for the facility caregivers to help him with a simple task that he used to do completely on his own until just eight weeks before. Ted stated: "This is a drastic change in my life. I never ever expected to be here. I just had that one terrible moment where I couldn't stop myself from falling, and now I am probably stuck in this place for the rest of my life. I still can't believe this is happening to me!"

We processed some of the numerous losses that Ted had been going through and the small but gradual progress he had recently been able to make since starting on an antidepressant medication while in the rehab center. Over the previous few days, Ted's appetite had started to improve and food was beginning to taste good again. He was sleeping less fitfully at night, isolating less, and his mood was slightly brighter, but his personality was still a far cry from the pre-fall, fun-loving man Ted had historically been. He told me he was having fewer thoughts about wanting to die and that he had become more resigned to the fact that he might never be able to return home to live—a painfully large pill for *anyone* to swallow, let alone someone who had functioned at such a high level for so long. Ted wistfully told me: "I have an obligation to my family to keep fighting and to not give up. I love them, and they love me, and that's where I am trying to keep my focus now. Not on everything that I have lost."

It didn't appear difficult for this gentle giant to admit to me that he had developed a serious depression over the past two months and that all the unfolding drama resulting from his falls, hospitalization, surgery, rehab experience, paralysis, and nursing home placement only made it harder for him to remain optimistic about his future. Ted wasn't sure if the new antidepressant medication our geriatric psychiatrist had recommended would work any better than the one he'd been taking, but he was willing to at least give it a shot in case it did. All those years of rigorous training in sports, business, and in life had conditioned Ted to not give up or give in easily when times were tough. Instead, he had learned to dig in, to face the challenges before him, and to focus on artfully resigning himself to what he couldn't change, while also working hard to change what he could—if not for his own sake, then for the sake of the family he deeply loved.

After the visit ended, I walked back to my car and reminded myself for the *millionth time* not to take my health and able-bodied status for granted. Ted's tragic fall clearly illustrated for me how quickly any of our lives can forever change in an instant and without warning. I wondered if I had it in me to be that vulnerable and courageous if I were suddenly faced with the magnitude of catastrophic loss Ted was enduring. Would I be able to find the inner fortitude to fight for every minute I had left to live, as my family would want, instead of giving in to my fearful, self-centered desires of wishing my life was through so my pain and suffering could end? What kind of faith, love, or Divine Intervention would it take for me to soften into some form of radical acceptance if I found myself in a similar situation, rather than choose to wallow in self-pity and resistance for the rest of my days?

I'd like to believe that my constitution is fundamentally as strong as Ted's and that I could somehow persevere if I incurred so much traumatic change in such a short amount of time. But to be honest, I have serious doubts about my ability to be that resilient at this point in my life. However, I've been fortunate enough to encounter a plethora of amazing teachers throughout my career who, like Ted, powerfully modeled for me what *real* courage, strength, love, vulnerability, and tenacity look like in the face of great misfortune and unthinkable loss.

Gleaning wisdom from their examples gives me hope that one day, I will be able to dig in that deep myself, to find the strength I need to cope with whatever challenges lie before me, and to resign myself to change what I can and make peace with the rest. I just selfishly pray that when it's *my turn* to discern such enormous, life-changing lessons, The Universe will grant me a little more grace and time to prepare myself for the tutelage than Ted was given.

Birthday Suit Departure

"I came into this world in a birthday suit,
and I plan to go out the same way!"

While I was working in the memory clinic, I had many opportunities to assist patients and families with completing their advance directives that outlined their wishes for future medical care. I was constantly surprised by the vast number of patients I met who had never taken steps to complete such important paperwork, despite the fact that they were between the ages of sixty-five and eighty-five years old and likely had more years behind them than in front of them. I've come to believe that most people fervently want to avoid thinking about the possibility of getting sick or old, and most certainly don't want to entertain the thought of becoming critically ill or dying. As a result, a large segment of our society actively circumvents those difficult conversations with their family members and friends and fails to chronicle their medical and end-of-life preferences in a manner that others can honor or follow.

Millions of people who are living with dementia in our country regularly miss out on the chance to share and document their wishes until it is much too late and they have already lost the mental capacity to do so. This is a real and avoidable tragedy that happens way too often and to far too many people—especially since Alzheimer's disease is currently the sixth-leading cause of death for people aged sixty-five and older in the United States, according to the 2021 Alzheimer's Disease Facts and Figures report.

As part of my standard clinical practice, I routinely asked patients during their first visit to our clinic if they had ever completed an advance directive, and if not, would they like to set up a time to meet with me to help with that task. One woman I posed that question to was named Peggy.

Peggy came to the intake appointment accompanied by her five lovely and doting adult children. The deep bond between Peggy and her kids was instantly apparent, as was the worry on their faces when it concerned the changes they had all been noticing in their mom's memory. It was also evident how much Peggy's family relied on their wicked senses of humor to discharge anxiety, cope with discomfort, and lovingly poke fun at one another. On the gentle but strong urging of her children, Peggy decided to take me up on my offer to assist her with advance care planning, and we scheduled a time for the seven of us to meet again the following month.

When Peggy and her kids arrived for the appointment, they entered the conference room laughing and joking as usual, and the warmth of their mutual connection was a beautiful scenario to witness. Many of the families I encountered in my job had much more conflicted and strained relationships, and sometimes the thinly veiled hostility emanating between them was disconcerting to watch and equally challenging to navigate. Most patients and families I engaged with were extremely emotional and nervous from the onset because of the sensitive nature of the topics we addressed during those intense consultations, so I found Peggy's family dynamic a much welcome change of pace. Their close, loving relationships made my role in facilitating an in-depth conversation regarding Peggy's future medical wishes a much more enjoyable task, and for that, I was immensely grateful.

After we had all exchanged the usual pleasantries for a few minutes, I asked Peggy what she had learned at the follow-up appointment about the results of her memory testing since I had not been present for that consultation meeting. The jovial mood in the room instantly dissolved into a long, solemn silence before Peggy finally broke the reticence by saying: "They informed us that the memory problems I've been experiencing aren't just normal aging as we'd hoped but are being caused by Alzheimer's disease in my brain and that I'm somewhere between the early to moderate stages of the illness right now. The nurse practitioner said that if I stayed socially engaged, mentally stimulated, and remained physically active, then I could hold the Alzheimer's at bay for as long as possible since there really aren't any other good treatment options or cures available at this time."

As soon as those words left Peggy's lips, her youngest son, Adam, choked back his tears and hurriedly excused himself from the room. Peggy's eldest daughter leaned over and put her arm around her mother's shoulders to comfort her, while the other kids at the table appeared to be at a loss as to what they should say or do next in that grief-laden instant. The pregnant pause that followed was agonizing and seemed to nearly suck the oxygen out of the room.

Just then, Peggy's eldest son, Thomas, got an impish expression on his face as he tried to interject some levity back into the situation by joking, "Mom, all of us kids have known since we were little that your brain wasn't wired like everyone else's on the block, and now we finally have proof!" At that, Peggy immediately broke out in peals of laughter, and the rest of the family quickly followed suit—grateful that Thomas had succeeded in transforming that sad and awkward moment into one that allowed them all to breathe a collective sigh of relief and refocus their attention on the matters at hand.

Adam re-entered the consult room just as I began to discuss the importance of Peggy completing her advance directives while she had this wonderful window of opportunity to do so. I explained that as the Alzheimer's disease progressed, it would impact Peggy's ability to comprehend and produce language and therefore make it challenging for her to communicate her wishes effectively. It would also impinge upon her ability to make complex medical decisions and to participate in salient conversations, like the one we were having that day, with the people who would benefit from it the most. What I *didn't disclose* was how this incredible woman and her family were just beginning to get a glimpse into how the dementia would gradually infiltrate every aspect of Peggy's life and therefore, their own. I didn't need to dash their hopes for the future or overwhelm them with such depressing news at a time like that. They had been through enough shock already.

While I helped Peggy complete her living will, I asked a lot of questions regarding her background and belief system. Peggy informed me that she was a devout Catholic and that her faith and religion had always been a guiding force for her throughout her eighty years of life. When we finally reached the last section of the living will that addressed questions regarding Peggy's preference for being buried or cremated after she died, Peggy stated that her faith dictated she choose burial. At that moment, Peggy's oldest daughter, Donna, suddenly became quite serious and asked her mother if she would like to be buried in her best dress along with her rosary.

Peggy got a mischievous look in her eyes and immediately quipped: "I came into this world in a birthday suit, and I plan to go out the same way!" Without missing a beat, Donna quickly retorted, "Then it's decided, Mom. You're *definitely* having a closed casket!" Uncontrollable laughter permeated the room and magically dispelled the raw tension and grief that had engulfed that same space only seconds before. That is what I have always relished about the power of laughter—its ability to rapidly transform our human experience and connectedness and therefore, all of us in the process.

As the poet August Wilson once wrote: "All you need in the world is love and laughter ... To have love in one hand and laughter in the other." On that memorable day, Peggy's hands were abundantly overflowing with both.

Don't Put Off Until Tomorrow

"My memory changes have really taken a toll on my self-esteem. It's hard to feel confident when you can't remember things from day to day."

We had multiple new people scheduled for intake appointments in the memory clinic on a particular Tuesday, which always made for a long and emotionally taxing day for everyone involved. All the new patients had been referred by their primary care physicians for identified memory changes or concerns, and every one of them arrived in a state of anxious apprehension, as usual. The same was true for the family members and close friends who accompanied them to their appointments; as was common, they were just as nervous about what was going to transpire.

The last person on the docket that day was a man in his early sixties who was joined by his wife of thirty-five years. With a single glance, I could see the worry written all over both of their faces. When I sat down in the consultation room to gather background information, I learned that Jeremy and Ruth used to work together until Jeremy's retirement two years earlier.

Jeremy made sure to let me know that he had voluntarily chosen to depart from his prestigious position at the university, but when I met with Ruth alone for the family interview, she alluded to the fact that her husband had been strongly encouraged to "bow out gracefully" before he was at risk of being fired due to progressive memory changes that had negatively impacted his job performance.

Jeremy was extremely bright and well-educated and had been among the elite in his scientific field of study for over two decades. He had a job that required a high level of precision, and he was known for his attention to detail and work ethic. Jeremy prided himself on being an innovator and had a long-standing reputation among his peers for excellence. But all that began to slowly change a few years back when Jeremy's razor-sharp mind began to dull.

At first, it was small details, like forgetting the name of a friend or the kind of coffee he always ordered at Starbucks. Then it progressed to forgetting how to implement some systems at work that he himself had helped design and had known like the back of his hand. Ruth also informed me that she now had to prompt Jeremy to remember to eat on occasion and to talk him through driving to familiar places that he had frequented for as long as she could remember.

When I turned to ask Jeremy if he noticed any significant changes in his short-term memory or abilities, he stated: "My memory changes have really taken a toll on my self-esteem. It's hard to feel confident when you can't remember things from day to day. Instead of feeling smart and capable like I always used to, I now feel like an idiot half the time, and it's demoralizing!" When Jeremy said this, Ruth burst into tears for the first of many crying episodes throughout the ninety-minute evaluation that day. Her anticipatory grief was palpable in the room, and I was sure that shedding tears had become more the norm than the exception for her over the past twenty-four months since her husband's decline began in earnest.

When Ruth and I were alone in the room, she described a long list of cognitive and functional changes she had observed in her partner that were heart-wrenching for her. Jeremy could no longer remember the date of their anniversary or consistently recall when his three children were born. He was struggling to stay on top of their finances and needed cueing to remember his social engagements. Jeremy had become quieter, withdrawn, and more short-tempered than ever before. The part that seemed the hardest for Ruth to handle was the way her spouse seemed to be slowly retreating into a world of his own that she didn't know how to access, and that was incredibly onerous for her to handle. Ruth clearly loved her husband and was terrified about the possibility of losing him to some neurological disease that she had no control over.

Ruth was also quite worried about how Jeremy's relatively young age of sixty-two factored into what was happening to him. She had done a lot of her own research on Alzheimer's disease before coming to the memory clinic because she secretly suspected that it was the root cause of the changes she had been witnessing in her husband. Ruth had read that most people who were diagnosed in their fifties or sixties tended to progress faster in the trajectory of their illness than if they were diagnosed at age seventy-five or eighty. The amount of cognitive ground that Jeremy had already lost over the proceeding few years was shocking to Ruth, and she could not bear to think of it accelerating even more rapidly from there.

As the appointment was wrapping up, Ruth shared that she and Jeremy had a trip planned overseas in the coming month to visit their daughter in Switzerland, whom they hadn't seen in over a year. Ruth and I conversed about the kinds of risks that international travel can have on someone who has been experiencing the type of marked cognitive decline that Jeremy had been going through. I'd learned over time that even well-seasoned travelers who develop dementia can eventually find such adventures far more stressful than enjoyable as their disease advances.

Ruth became solemn as she explained how circling the globe was a deep passion that she and Jeremy had always shared together—far before either of them had retired. Ruth's voice shook as she described how depressed she felt at *just the thought* that she and Jeremy might no longer be able to traverse to new and distant lands the way they had painstakingly planned when they plotted out their "bucket list" of vacation destinations on the world map in their living room just three short years before.

As we talked further, Ruth admitted that she had been apprehensive about the idea of journeying all the way to Switzerland alone with Jeremy, as he was no longer the reliable and capable traveling companion he'd always been in the past. However, Ruth didn't know how she could break the news to her soulmate that going abroad was no longer a feasible option for them without completely devastating the man she loved.

While I made my long drive home after work that day, I had ample time to reflect on my interview with Ruth. I felt bad that Jeremy's brain changes were bringing their wayfaring days to an end, but I also thought about how incredibly fortunate they were for having had the abundance of time and financial freedom to visit so many corners of the world while they were in the prime of their lives.

I couldn't begin to count the number of people I'd known in my life who pined for the day when they would finally be able to stop punching the clock and start traveling to the places they'd always wanted to go. Those same people had been much too busy in their younger years—working long hours, saving their pennies, and raising their families—to trek to the alluring locations their hearts were yearning to see. Unlike Jeremy and Ruth, most folks I've encountered have had to delay their gratification for exotic travel until they reached their mid-sixties or seventies (if *even then*) to have the commodity of time and money necessary to execute their globetrotting plans. Regrettably, for the hundreds of patients and families I have worked with, those aspirations were ripped away from them by the vagaries of serious illnesses they never saw coming or anticipated. As a result, their long-awaited dreams went up in smoke like a raging Colorado wildfire, and there was nothing left for them to do but take cover or run.

It struck me that so often in our future-oriented society, we get caught up in planning ahead for what I call the "someday syndrome"—a syndrome that is so insidious, we often delude ourselves into thinking we have all the time in the world to make plans for "someday" and to execute those plans when it is convenient and timely for us to do so.

What we fail to factor into our logical and somewhat "magical thinking" is that none of us *actually know* what is going to happen as the years unfold, and it is erroneous to believe that we have complete control over how the events in our lives will play out. All it takes is one unexpected fall, illness, death of a loved one, or global pandemic to wake us up to the fact that what we *thought* would happen as we gazed ahead to our future may, in fact, end up looking drastically different from the vision we once held for ourselves in the past.

As I wound my way closer to home, I wondered how long it might take for Ruth to work through the intense grief she was experiencing on so many levels and to be willing or able to adjust her paradigm to a radically different picture of her golden years than the one she had held in her mind's eye for so long. I genuinely hoped that this amazing woman would find a way to maintain a sense of gratitude for the time she and Jeremy still had left together. I prayed that Ruth would be able to navigate the duality of "both-and thinking," which would require her to grasp the notion that the brilliant man she married is *still here* with her, but at the same time, is *also gone* from the way he used to be before all of his brain changes.

As the great writer F. Scott Fitzgerald once said: "The test of a first-rate intelligence is the ability to hold two opposing ideas in mind at the same time and still maintain the ability to function." *That* ability is a tall order for *any of us* to accomplish in the best of times, let alone for the unseen, overwhelmed heroes on the front lines who dutifully care for their loved ones for years on end with little fanfare or support from the rest of us.

As I pulled into my driveway, I reflected on the deep respect I've gained for care partners like Ruth who somehow manage to rise to the challenges before them, despite the magnitude of grief and loss they have to contend with inside themselves to accomplish such a feat. And in that quiet moment, I was overcome with thankfulness for the profound lessons I have been privileged to learn from people like Jeremy, who continually set an example for all of us about how to live our best lives—even in the midst of unexpected brain changes and dementia.

For the past two decades, I've accumulated a wealth of firsthand experiences with patients and families who have had their hopes and dreams pulverized in the blink of an eye due to a new diagnosis that changed the trajectory of their twilight years forever. Because of witnessing this dynamic so often from such an intimate and painful vantage point, I've developed conflicted goals for my own future.

On the one hand, I am highly aware of the exorbitant costs of care in our country and realize that I should save every nickel I can for my eventual medical needs and retirement. But, on the other hand, I don't want to put off until tomorrow what calls to my heart today. I don't want to wait to see the world until I've banked "enough" money to enjoy this beautiful life I've been given and delay my thirst for adventure until some far-off time in the future. I want to live my dreams *now* while I'm still healthy and strong enough to relish the ride. And perhaps, most importantly, I've learned the value of encouraging the individuals and families I serve who are facing life-threatening illnesses, yet still capable of pursuing their dreams, to enjoy life while they can. Because, as millions of others who have gone before us had to learn the hard way, that "someday" may never come.

Rosie and Vince

"Why is our first instinct to find a magic pill?"

R osie was a vibrant woman who arrived for the memory clinic intake appointment dressed to the nines, right down to her designer glasses. She looked at least a decade younger than her seventy-two years would suggest. Rosie came accompanied by her husband of forty-five years, Vince. You could tell by one look at them that they were still madly in love after all that time together, and it was inspiring to witness. Rosie was referred to the memory clinic for diagnostic testing due to the cognitive changes she had been experiencing.

As a highly educated woman who held many advanced degrees, Rosie had been at the top of her game in the field of higher education before her retirement four years earlier. According to the note we received from Rosie's doctor, her memory changes had greatly accelerated since she quit working, and her short-term memory had become severely impaired. Rosie was admittedly nervous about coming in for testing because dementia ran in her family, and she was petrified that her mental decline could be leading to that same eventual outcome.

Within minutes of arriving, Rosie tearfully disclosed that a lot of her current distress was related to concerns about her husband's health. Vince had recently been diagnosed with incurable cancer and was "living on borrowed time." Rosie was deep in the throes of anticipatory grief—that unique kind of emotional pain and sadness that arises far in advance of an expected loss or death. She was already contemplating how she could possibly survive such a devastating loss if Vince were to die and how she would be able to care for herself without the constant aid of her longtime companion, whom she'd become increasingly dependent on due to her own cognitive deterioration.

Vince listened to his wife's disquiet with a sad and tender expression on his drawn face. It was hard to know if his somberness was due to his worries about his life drawing to an end or if he was in despair because of the dramatic changes he'd been observing in his wife—changes that had reached the point of impacting not only her memory and functional abilities but also her role as an equal partner in their marriage. *That*, for Vince, was the most excruciating part of all. Vince explained that frequently in recent months, Rosie could be sitting right next to him on the couch, but despite their close proximity to one another, she seemed more and more "checked out" and distant in a world of her own that he didn't understand or know how to penetrate.

Psychologist and author Pauline Boss refers to this phenomenon as "ambiguous loss." It is a less-recognized type of loss that commonly happens when a person living with cognitive impairment or dementia is still physically present with us but at the same time, is socially disengaged and psychologically absent compared to how they were before their brain changes began.

Ambiguous loss can last for a few months or many years and can be incredibly difficult for dementia caregivers to navigate alone. Part of the reason is that care partners like Vince are frequently surrounded by people in their lives who have no firsthand knowledge, experience, or true understanding of what it's like to lose someone you love piece by piece to a disease like dementia—it can be devastating to learn there's nothing anyone can do to stop it. Vince unquestionably had a lot on his plate to contend with, but by far, his reverence and dedication to Rosie's well-being took precedence over his own mortality concerns in our clinic that day.

When Rosie and Vince returned for the follow-up appointment two weeks later, the news they dreaded the most was delivered. The nurse practitioner informed Rosie that her testing results indicated she had a probable Alzheimer's disease just like her mother and grandmother before her, and it had unfortunately advanced to the moderate stages already. Even though Rosie and her husband had both secretly suspected that such a diagnosis would likely be given, hearing those words spoken out loud nevertheless pierced the fragile bubble of denial they had cautiously been living in and catapulted them into the indisputable awareness that their darkest days were yet to come.

Ten months after that heavy and dispiriting follow-up appointment, I received a gero-psych referral regarding a resident in a memory care facility in Denver whose story sounded eerily familiar to me. The assisted living staff member on the phone explained that they were requesting a consultation on one of the newer residents in their building. The woman in question had Alzheimer's disease and was constantly pacing up and down the hallways of the unit, calling out for her husband and saying that she had to "go home to take care of him because he's sick." Every time the facility caregivers would try to comfort this resident with assurances that, in fact, this *was* her home and that there was nowhere else she needed to be and no one she needed to take care of, the "dementia patient" would become even more agitated and try to "escape" out of the secured doors of the memory care unit.

The staff went on to tell me that she was referring their resident Rosie to our service, hoping that our geriatric psychiatrist could prescribe some type of psychiatric medication that would reduce her anxiety and hopefully mitigate her "elopement attempts," which were becoming increasingly problematic for the staff to manage. It had already gotten to the point where Rosie was at risk of being moved to another place to live other than the $10,000 a month specialized Alzheimer's care facility where she was currently residing.

When I hung up the phone, I suddenly found myself overcome with tears, remembering that last heart-wrenching appointment with Rosie and Vince in the memory clinic a mere ten months earlier. I recalled how worried Rosie had been about losing the love of her life to cancer and how she feared that she wouldn't be able to survive without Vince by her side to anticipate her every need. She needed Vince to be the working brain that would get her safely through the mixed-up world around her when she could no longer trust her own brain to do that job anymore.

And I vividly recalled how sad and disconsolate Vince had seemed as he struggled to come to terms with his own terminal diagnosis and the painful realization that he would soon be unable to care for Rosie as the Alzheimer's disease continued its deadly march across her failing brain. He was powerless to stop the cancer inside his body from truncating his life at a time when he still had so much to live for and do on behalf of his beloved spouse.

I thought about the phone conversation I'd just had with the care facility staff who, out of ignorance about her resident's background, didn't comprehend why Rosie was so desperately searching for her husband along those lonely and confusing corridors. She wasn't privy to Vince's electronic medical record that I could see. After receiving the referral on Rosie, I investigated Vince's chart and was greeted with a bright red flag on the top of his medical record, warning me that I was about to enter the chart of a deceased person. When I clicked to look inside, I discovered that the love of Rosie's life had lost his battle with cancer eight and a half months earlier.

The staff member obviously didn't know or understand Rosie's significant life history, including the excruciating grief and loss she'd been going through ever since the untimely death of her beloved husband, caregiver, and best friend—only six weeks before her admission to the memory care facility. Besides Vince, Rosie was *looking for* a place to escape to that felt familiar, safe, and welcoming—a place where she could be loved unconditionally despite her dementia—just like her *real home* with Vince felt not so long ago.

I wondered why our first instinct is often to find a "magic pill" that can alleviate our displaced anxiety and mask the grief and loss we are going through so that others around us feel less threatened by our imperfect displays of mourning and our overwhelming and tumultuous human emotions.

Ultimately, Rosie's predicament brought me to the larger question: How will we ever begin to change the culture of care so that we can focus on a person's underlying *humanity* instead of so easily labeling those who function differently from us as some sort of "behavioral problem" to throw a pill at or eliminate from our communities when they don't conform to our expectations in the way we think they should—especially when they are trying their best to do so with a dying brain and $10,000 a month out of pocket?

The Sandwich Story

*"My husband used to design and build the most
beautiful custom homes you've ever seen, and now
he can't even build a sandwich by himself."*

I was just three months into my new position as a social worker within the palliative care department. I had recently vacated my previous job in the memory clinic in order to accept the hot-off-the-press internal promotion that awaited me on the open road. My novel role as the home-based dementia specialist allowed me to escape the confines of the sterile consultation rooms that the memory clinic team was based out of and instead drive myself from one end of the Denver metro area to the other to deliver services to those members with identified cognitive impairments, as well as to the families and friends who supported them.

My new post in palliative care afforded me the opportunity to make home visits to individuals referred to me who had a documented dementia diagnosis, including Alzheimer's disease, vascular, frontotemporal, alcohol-related, and Lewy body dementia, as well as dementias that resulted from traumatic brain injuries or other causes. My position was unique to the department, as I was the only staff member in the organization whose function was to work exclusively with patients and their care partners who were impacted by some form of dementia. I was fortunate enough to spend time with these individuals in the intimacy of their living rooms and kitchens and provide disease education, counseling, resources, and caregiver support. As far as I was concerned, I had landed my dream job!

I received a new referral for a sixty-one-year-old gentleman named Sam, who had been diagnosed with frontotemporal dementia two years earlier. Sam's primary care doctor referred her patient to our service out of mounting concern about the strain that Sam's progressing dementia was having on his wife, Lily. Sam's physician thought that Lily could benefit from the dementia education and emotional support I could provide in my palliative social work role.

When I arrived at their home in the foothills of the mountains, Lily greeted me warmly at the door and ushered me inside. Lily then introduced me to her husband, who was standing in the entryway beside her with a beaming smile on his suntanned face. Sam didn't attempt to speak to me or shake my hand, but his quiet presence was inviting, nonetheless. Sam looked quite youthful for his age and resembled a shorter version of the actor Tom Selleck during his younger days. I don't know what I expected Sam to look like, but after reading his complex medical record before this home visit, it certainly *wasn't* the man I saw standing before me!

Lily led me into the living room, where the three of us sat together and talked for the next hour. When I tried to engage Sam in the conversation, I quickly realized how much damage the dementia had done to the language centers of his brain, as he had almost no functional verbal or receptive communication skills left, despite his outward appearance. My initial conversation with Sam was circular in nature and went something like this:

Me: "Do you like sports, Sam?"

Sam: "Yes."

Me: "What sports do you like?"

Sam: "Golf!"

Me: "Are there other sports that you enjoy, Sam?"

Sam: "Yes!"

Me: "What are they?"

Sam: "Golf!"

You get the picture.

Lily described to me how she had to fight Sam's doctors and the medical system for well over a year before Sam was finally and accurately diagnosed with frontotemporal dementia, after going to great lengths to rule out numerous other "more obvious" illnesses first.

"Everyone kept blowing me off and minimizing what was going on with Sam. They acted like I was crazy when I would tell about the things that Sam said and did at home that were so bizarre, because to them, he appeared so normal."

Lily told me that after a particularly terrifying incident, the doctors *finally* started to take her complaints seriously. Lily had looked out the kitchen window one afternoon and observed Sam in the backyard, holding a can of gasoline in his hand. There was a tree stump just a few feet away from their house, and Sam had doused it with gasoline and was getting ready to light it on fire when Lily came screaming out of the house to stop him. When Lily breathlessly asked Sam what the hell he was trying to do, he calmly replied, "Burn down the dead tree. I thought it'd be easier than chopping it."

Frontotemporal dementia is a less-recognized type of dementia that attacks the frontal and temporal lobes of the brain and can severely impact language, personality, reasoning, and behavior. It is known to strike people at a much younger age than Alzheimer's typically does—with the average age of onset being fifty-four. That is one reason why Sam's medical team repeatedly misdiagnosed his disease for over a year because Sam did not fit their mental image of what a "dementia patient" is supposed to look and act like, and besides, Sam was far too young at fifty-nine to have that "old person's disease."

Lily's problems certainly didn't end when Sam was diagnosed with FTD, but at least she felt better knowing that she *wasn't losing her mind after all* when it came to Sam's inexplicable changes of behavior the previous two years. She now understood that the vicissitudes she had been observing in her husband were indeed related to an underlying medical condition in his brain. Lily felt a great sense of relief to actually *know* what was wrong with Sam so she could start educating herself about the disease instead of flying blind through her days with absolutely *no clue* what was happening to the man she loved or how to possibly intervene.

I listened intently as Lily told me about another event that had taken place a few weeks prior to my visit. It was in the early afternoon, and Sam had come up to Lily and asked, "When's dinner?" Lily replied: "Sam, dinner is hours away. If you're hungry, go into the kitchen and make yourself a snack." Sam took himself into the kitchen, only to return moments later to ask again, "When's dinner?"

Lily explained to me that this exact scenario repeated itself three times before she had an "aha moment" and realized that Sam did not know how to initiate making his own snack anymore. She accompanied Sam back into the kitchen and then got out the bread, meat, cheese, mayo, a butter knife, and a plate, and said, "Here you go, honey. Make yourself a sandwich." Then, she returned to the living room.

Lily told me that Sam eventually emerged from the kitchen with the proudest look on his face, carrying a colossal sandwich, which was eight slices of bread high! Lily laughed in a sad kind of way and said, "Kay, it's like he was a bricklayer. Sam just kept adding one layer of ingredient after another until he ran out of bread, and then he was trying to figure out how to eat the sandwich that he couldn't even begin to get his mouth around!"

The levity in the living room quickly dissipated when Lily spoke her next sentence. She said, "Kay, my husband used to design and build the most beautiful custom homes you've ever seen, and now he can't even build a sandwich by himself anymore. It's like having another child in the house, only he is sixty-one. How am I supposed to handle this all by myself while trying to hold down a job so that I can keep our health insurance? How *in the name of God* am I supposed to keep my sanity and go on living as if everything is 'okay' when not a damned thing in our lives is *remotely okay* anymore?"

I glanced over at Sam, sitting silently in his recliner a few feet away from us with a look of relaxed contentment on his handsome face—oblivious to the conversation going on around him or the utter despair his wife was in. It struck me in that moment how juxtaposed Lily and Sam's lives had become—living side by side under the same roof but experiencing *entirely different* realities at the same time.

Like the vast majority of dementia care partners with whom I had previously worked, Lily existed in a world where she felt utterly invisible and invalidated. She told me just how resentful and misunderstood she constantly felt in her caregiving role: "What I've learned is this: Unless someone has *walked a mile in my shoes* as a caregiver, or has at least spent a great deal of time around someone they love who is afflicted with this horrible disease, then they have *no concept* of the personal hell that people like me are experiencing every day—often alone and isolated—in the merciless Land of Dementia. But those *same people actually believe* they can truly relate to the kind of unrelenting stress I am living under, when the plain fact is, they don't have a frickin' clue about *any* of it! For me, *that's* the most maddening part of all!"

I had no miracles in my bag to give to Lily and Sam that day. No tricks up my sleeve that would dramatically change the course of Sam's illness for the better, and no words of comfort to extend that could possibly begin to palliate the pain of unimaginable loss that Lily was experiencing because of how her husband's dementia had permeated every aspect of their lives. What I *did have to offer* was the ability to listen deeply and compassionately to Lily's stories. To validate the complexity of her life and caregiving role without trying to mollify her in the process. To provide disease education about frontotemporal dementia, as well as some tools and strategies for Lily to use with Sam based on the brain changes that were happening to him.

Most importantly, I was able to hold sacred space so Lily could begin to safely explore her feelings of grief and ambiguous loss that were profound and raw. What I was able to do as a social worker during that meeting was deliver the best possible care I could to that family in the most authentic way I knew how.

As I was leaving Sam and Lily's home that day, Lily walked me out to my car and tearfully thanked me, saying: "I didn't know what to expect when my doctor arranged for this palliative care visit with you. I didn't even know what the word "palliative" meant, let alone how having someone come out to the house could begin to help my situation with Sam, but I was wrong. Talking to a professional like you who *truly understands* what I am going through in a way that most people, even my own family, can't begin to fathom was such an unexpected gift for me today. You've given me some helpful information, reassurance, and hope this morning that I desperately needed, and that means everything to me right now. Bless you for the difficult work that you do, Kay. Because of it, you are making the world better for people like me."

From the Outside
Looking In

"Who are you and when are you leaving?"

W hile working as a social worker and home-based dementia specialist, I received a new referral from a primary care physician for his patient named Mrs. Valdez. Leticia ("Lettie") Valdez was seventy-six years old and had been referred to our palliative care department because of concerns regarding her advanced dementia, which, over time, had resulted in her complete dependence on her husband, Rico, to meet and anticipate all of her daily needs. Rico's health and well-being were growing steadily worse because of the sustained stress he had been living under, and her doctor knew this fact only too well since he had been serving as both Rico and Lettie's doctor for thirty years.

In his referral note, he expressed disquiet that the living will Lettie had completed a decade earlier needed review and possible revisions, given the severity of the physical and cognitive decline she had sustained since first completing that important document. During the past ten years, Lettie had suffered three small strokes and had later been diagnosed with mixed dementia—a combination of a probable underlying Alzheimer's disease "mixed" with the brain changes caused by the series of strokes. I was asked to set up a home visit with Rico to provide education, support, and resources around Lettie's disease trajectory, and to offer assistance to update her advance directives if Rico agreed with his doctor's assessment that the paperwork Lettie had completed years earlier no longer accurately reflected her wishes for future medical care, given the state of her overall diminished health and advanced dementia.

While reading through Lettie's medical chart to prepare for my visit, I learned that she had legally chosen her husband to be her appointed medical durable power of attorney a decade before while she still enjoyed robust health and the mental acuity to make all of her own decisions independently. Back then, Rico was his wife's "designated" medical proxy *on paper only* because he wouldn't be empowered to act as her medical spokesperson until she reached the point, either temporarily or permanently, where she was unable to communicate her wishes or make complex decisions for herself cogently or safely. *Only then* would Rico step in as Lettie's surrogate decision-maker and adopt the crucial role of being her medical advocate and watchdog.

By the time our department got the referral on Lettie, the damage to her brain was so widespread from the dementia that she struggled to make even the simplest of choices for herself, like which color shirt to wear or whether she wanted ice cream or pie for dessert. At this point, making complex medical decisions regarding her current or future medical care was completely out of the question. Because of that, Rico not only had to make *every* decision for himself and their household without any help or meaningful input from his wife, but he also had to make nearly *every other* decision on his partner's behalf as well. Rico's physician was concerned about the long-term impact this kind of unrelenting stress and caregiving responsibility was having on him and hoped I would be able to provide some kind of concrete intervention that would help ease the heavy burden Rico had been shouldering by himself.

When I called Rico to introduce myself and offer to set up an appointment with him and his wife, I could instantly hear the hesitation in his voice. Being a social worker and a dementia specialist was not exactly a calming combination for a lot of people who were in great emotional upheaval and denial, so getting myself in the door was always one of the biggest challenges I routinely faced in my work. I'm pretty certain that the *only reason* Mr. Valdez ultimately agreed to let me come at all was out of respect for his beloved doctor who, in advance of my call, had expertly greased the wheels with Rico about the need for my services. I set up a home visit with the Valdezes for the end of the week.

My job took me over a wide expanse of the Denver metro area where I oftentimes had never been before, and the home visit to Rico and Lettie was no exception. They lived in an exclusive development in a part of the city that people like me only entered by invitation—the "doormen" at the entrance made certain of that. When I told them who I was there to see, the gates magically opened so that I could drive through to the address on my GPS. My car looked out of place parked in front of the stunning three-story mansion, but I was well-versed in navigating through neighborhoods of opulent wealth, as well as through regions of town that more closely resembled urban ghettos.

One dramatic lesson I've learned as a social worker is this: Life-threatening and terminal illnesses level the playing field in countless ways between the rich and the poor. It doesn't matter if you live in a trailer home or in the most exclusive part of the metropolis; serious diseases like dementia are an unlikely equalizer of sorts among all who face them, and no amount of money, power, or privilege can change that difficult reality. For a longer period of time, money may serve to shelter those with great wealth from the inevitable storm that a tragic illness can leave in its wake, but it can never protect them from having to go through the same excruciating pain and grief that those who are less prosperous experience.

Rico answered the door quickly and greeted me with a smile and a firm handshake. I was immediately struck by his kind and gentle manner and by the weariness in his dark brown eyes. Lettie shuffled her way toward the door to see what all the commotion was about. When she saw me standing in the front entryway, she got a look of startled alarm on her thin face. I could tell that this family was no longer accustomed to having outside visitors in their home, and Lettie eyed me with deep suspicion from the instant Rico introduced me to her as "the nice gal that our doctor sent out to help us."

By the look on Lettie's face, she didn't give a damn *who* sent me out or what I had to offer! She clearly didn't want any strangers in her home, and I represented a threat to her routine and family. Her first words to me were memorable, as *no one* had ever greeted me in quite the same way before. Lettie peered at me from behind Rico's side and bluntly asked, "Who are you and when are you leaving?!"

It took everything in my power not to laugh out loud in that moment. I was used to people with dementia saying and doing "socially inappropriate" things, so I wasn't fazed in the least by Lettie's reaction. But one glance at Rico's face, and I knew that he didn't find his wife's words funny in any way— he appeared embarrassed by her behavior. So, I stifled my laugh and simply replied, "Hello, Lettie. My name is Kay, and it's such a pleasure to meet you." It was obvious that Lettie wasn't at all pleased to make *my* acquaintance, but she reluctantly moved her body out of the way just enough for me to enter her beautiful abode anyway.

Rico directed me to sit next to him and Lettie in their side-by-side leather recliners that faced a picturesque view of the mountains in the distance. Rico was welcoming and hospitable to me, but it was extremely challenging for us to try to converse while Lettie constantly interrupted the conversation. She had long ago lost the ability to understand or follow a thread of dialogue like the one her husband and I were attempting to have. I asked Rico if there was anywhere else in the house where he and I could chat more privately, as trying to "talk in code" in front of Lettie was only proving to trigger her paranoia even more. Rico summoned his teenage granddaughter into the living room and asked her to "entertain Grandma while I talk to this nice social worker for a few minutes alone." As Angelina attempted to lead her grandmother into the adjoining room, Lettie turned around and loudly inquired again, "Who *are you* and when are you leaving my house?"

Rico led me down the hall to his spacious office, where he filled me in about what had been going on with his family over the previous year. He described how Lettie was often up for most of the night, wandering the house and looking for her parents, who had died long ago. Rico teared up when he told me how close Lettie and Angelina had always been, but how, in the past six months, Lettie no longer recognized her own granddaughter and would yell at her to "get out of this house and never come back!" Rico was trembling as he told me how Lettie's treatment of Angelina was ripping him apart because Angelina's mother had been killed in a motor vehicle accident fourteen months earlier, and Rico had to fight the courts to get custody of their only grandchild after losing his daughter in such a sudden and tragic manner. Rico stated: "I feel like I'm having to choose between caring for my wife and my granddaughter, and that's no choice *any person* should ever have to make!"

As our discussion continued, Rico admitted how exhausted he had become from trying to survive on three to four hours of sleep a night and then spending his days tending to the long list of other responsibilities he had on his plate. Some of his many duties included coordinating and providing *all* the care for Lettie, Angelina, his home, and his family business. At seventy-eight years old, the immense stress that Rico was under as a husband, father, and grandfather was taking a toll on him both mentally and physically.

For months, their doctor had urged Rico to hire in-home help or maybe even move Lettie into a memory care facility where all of her needs could be provided for so Rico could return to being Lettie's devoted husband instead of her 24/7 caregiver. It was obvious that money was not the barrier to accessing outside assistance and resources for the Valdez family. Despite that fact, Rico would not entertain the idea of placing his beautiful bride in any other setting, nor was he open to hiring any assistance in the home because, "No one else can care for my wife like I can, and even if they could, Lettie would never let them get close enough to try!"

After my brief interactions with Lettie that day, I could understand Rico's reasoning, but I also knew that delaying help and support for himself as a caregiver also posed potentially serious consequences for his life. When the entire household, business, and family system are reliant upon the health and determination of one single individual to keep the ship afloat, the ripple effect of what can happen if the captain of that vessel becomes sick or dies is catastrophic, no matter how devoted, dedicated, and committed a caregiver might be.

During our discussion, Rico shared how he methodically timed his visits to the grocery store and other necessary errands so he wouldn't be gone from the house for more than fifteen minutes; otherwise, Lettie was beside herself with worry when he returned. Over the years, Rico had essentially become Lettie's "working brain" because of her progressed dementia, and without her husband nearby to constantly assure and guide her moment by moment through the day, Lettie got lost in time and space—even in the house where she had lived for decades. Consequently, when the man Lettie was dependent upon for nearly everything in her world was out of her sight for more than a few minutes, she became paralyzed with fear and anxiety, and this vicious cycle kept Rico even more tightly tethered to his caregiving role, and even less able to attend to any of his own needs as a result.

Rico told me he was trying to lose weight and lower his blood pressure in an effort to prevent having another heart attack, but since he had no extra time in his hectic day for any self-care, the pounds just kept piling on. Rico was also trying to find a counselor for Angelina because her emotional meltdowns were becoming more extreme in the context of losing her mother and being the regular target of Lettie's rage and paranoia. Angelina couldn't begin to comprehend how Lettie's dementia was damaging her brain and functional abilities or why she had changed so dramatically from the loving and doting grandmother Angelina had always known.

Angelina was distraught, heartbroken, and confused, and the brunt of her teenage anger was directed at her grandfather who was doing everything in his power to control a situation that was utterly untenable. I've heard it said that "If one person is living with dementia inside them, then *everyone around them is living with dementia*." In the case of the Valdez family, that statement could not have rung any truer.

I had reached the final point in the visit where I was beginning to review the contents of Lettie's living will with Rico. I asked Rico a series of questions about what he thought Lettie would want or not want in terms of her future medical care as her health continued to decline.

In the middle of that conversation, Lettie suddenly burst into the office in a frantic search for her missing husband. Before I could do anything to stop him, Rico invited Lettie to join us at the table, and he began asking for her opinion as to whether or not she would want a feeding tube, to be on a ventilator, or receive any other kinds of life-sustaining treatment as her condition worsened. Rico was clearly trying to involve his wife in the dialogue out of respect, but Lettie could not understand her husband's words enough to grasp the complexity of the questions he was asking, and her frustration skyrocketed. Because Rico was too close to the fire to fathom how obliterated his wife's communication skills had become, his act of kindness ended up backfiring badly.

Lettie got up and began to pace the floor of the office like a trapped animal looking for an exit. She started yelling at us to "Just stop talking and leave me alone!" and began crying so hard she was hyperventilating. Angelina ran into the room to try to help soothe her grandmother, but nothing seemed to calm down Lettie until I packed up my bag and headed for the front door.

Once Lettie could see that the object of her distress was leaving, she began to visibly relax and breathe a little easier. However, the look in Rico's eyes as I shook his hand goodbye was even wearier than when I had arrived only an hour earlier, and that weighed heavily on my heart as I made my way to my waiting vehicle.

I got into my car and drove away from that palatial home, grieving for the unique and difficult journey that every one of those family members was experiencing through no fault of their own. I felt deeply saddened that I wasn't able to assist the Valdez family in more concrete and helpful ways during our time together and disappointed that I couldn't achieve the goals their doctor had hoped for when he placed the referral to our department on Lettie and Rico's behalf. As I passed through the guardhouse gates on my way back to the office, I reflected on how the Valdezes' lives may have appeared "perfect" from the outside to people like me who passed by such majestic residences in silent ignorance and envy. I was reminded once again how wrong our made-up assumptions and judgments can be when it comes to the lives of other people we truly don't know at all, yet somehow *think* we do.

I have discovered that many of the people we imagine living lives of absolute ease, grace, and bliss are actually more like the Valdez family, doing whatever they can, for as long as they can, to simply make it through another long and difficult day of human messiness, love, and strife. Because of that earned awareness, I try to be mindful and evoke the words of actor and comedian Robin Williams in my daily work as a vision for the kind of care I aspire to deliver to the people I am fortunate enough to serve: "Everyone you meet is fighting a battle you know nothing about. Be kind always."

Breaking Open to Break Through

Winding My
Way Home

By the end of my time as a home-based dementia specialist, I had begun
to feel constricted once again by having only enough resources at my
disposal to make a single home visit to each patient and family. They
clearly deserved much more assistance than I was able to provide within the
scope of my job. In much the same way I had experienced the discomfort of
system-imposed barriers that limited the ability of our memory clinic team
to provide ongoing services to the patients and families beyond two clinic
appointments, I found myself facing that same issue.

As much as I had tried to tune out that still little voice inside, it became
more challenging as the message being broadcast to my heart and head
continued to grow louder. It was telling me that it was time to trust the process
and take another huge leap of faith outside my comfort zone—to take all the
knowledge and experience I had accumulated over my career and combine
them with my passion for improving the lives of individuals and care partners
impacted by dementia. Holy shit! It was telling me to start my own business!

I had set an intention back in 2015 that by the time our son, Eli, was eleven,
I would be able to cut back to part-time employment so I could work toward
starting my own business and have a better work-life balance. It would be my

ticket to spending more quality time with my favorite boy who was growing up fast. I had no concept of how I would realistically pull this off since I had spent my entire career working for organizations that provided me with a regular paycheck every two weeks and benefits that made my life comfortable. The older I got, the scarier the prospect of going out on my own had become.

On a Monday morning in early October 2018, I received an email from a professional colleague in Wisconsin who had hired me to do a keynote presentation and a three-hour workshop six months earlier. Suzanna wanted to see if I would be interested in creating another five-hour workshop for her dementia certification program the following spring in Madison.

My initial thought upon reading her email was, *Yes! I love doing training and education on dementia! That will be awesome!* The next thought to enter my brain milliseconds later was, *Who the hell am I kidding? I was totally worn out after putting so much time and effort into creating those programs for Suzanna while working full time last spring. I don't have the emotional bandwidth to go through all of that stress again, and neither does my family.*

Suzanna's email made it nearly impossible for me to concentrate on my palliative care work for the rest of the morning; I was distracted by the host of mixed emotions and physical sensations coming up as a result of her request. I decided to take a break and call a social work friend of mine who had recently transitioned from working in the Alzheimer's field to becoming a manager within a local mental health agency. I knew I could safely process the myriad of thoughts and feelings I was experiencing and seek her wise counsel in the process.

While discussing the dilemmas I would face—between the competing demands of my current job and family responsibilities with the career aspirations I had for my future—Amber suddenly exclaimed, "Oh my God, Kay! The hair on my arms is standing up! I have an idea!"

Amber's idea involved hiring me for a part-time opening that had become available only three days earlier in her department. The job duties consisted of counseling care partners who were actively caring for a loved one living with dementia in the home. Amber informed me that the office space I could potentially work from was only five miles away from where I lived, that I would be able to do parts of my job from home, and that she would be my boss. If I decided to take that leap of faith, it would give me the necessary time to start working on a strategy for building my own business while also providing the security of a predictable paycheck. It sounded like a perfect steppingstone to work toward that elusive work-life balance I had been longing to find—even though when I got out of bed that morning, making a sudden and drastic career change had *not* been a part of my agenda for the day!

Prior to calling Amber that morning, I literally felt like I had a volcano erupting within the depths of my gut. But after she told me about her idea, the sensation completely dissipated, and a feeling of absolute peace and know-ingness passed through me. The sudden and profound 180-degree shift that happened within my body was my *still little voice's* way of cueing me that it was time to move on from my "dream job" in palliative care. Although I would make 50 percent less per hour working for Amber, which was a terrifying prospect for me to even consider, I was able to reframe my fear. *Just look! The Universe has provided me with the ideal bridge to have the time, flexibility, and space I need to work toward my Big Dream at last!* I knew I had hit spiritual pay dirt! However, that fact didn't make the process of leaving my job and jumping off that metaphysical cliff into the Great Unknown any easier.

I interviewed with Amber and was offered the job in her department in record time. By the end of that month, a going-away party was thrown in my honor, as my colleagues and I laughed and cried together and toasted my next exciting adventure. Three days later, I said goodbye to the organization that had employed me for over eight years and left behind the final pair of golden handcuffs I would ever wear.

Looking back now, granting myself only seventy-two hours of time off between leaving one job and starting another was a terrible idea. It didn't give me nearly enough time to process the enormity of the step I had just taken into the abyss. It didn't allow my ego the chance to grieve the loss of the professional identity I had worked so hard to achieve or to come to terms with the massive psychological effects that such a change would have on my sense of self and my place in the world.

From my first day at the mental health center, things started to go terribly wrong. Every time I turned around, it seemed I was running into barriers, including the "computer system from hell" that instantly became my personal nemesis and source of overwhelming frustration. I found myself totally isolated in my new role, which was in stark contrast to the exceptionally supportive large team environment I had just left behind in palliative care. In addition, the job duties I was assigned did not match the written job description I was initially given.

Before I knew what was happening, I began spinning out of control with anxiety and depression that I had never before experienced. I became unable to sleep through the night, to hold down my food, or to learn and absorb the wide berth of information required of me as a brand-new employee in a system that was completely foreign. My brain was in flight-or-fright mode from the internal and external stressors bearing down on me like a cosmic two-by-four to my head.

One day, I couldn't stop crying in the parking lot outside of work, and I called my friend/boss. I told her I was sick and needed to take the rest of the day off, without going into any details. I cried so hard as I drove home that I could barely see the road in front of me. Once home, I hunched over, hyper-ventilating alone in my kitchen, and wailed so hard I could barely breathe. I just wanted to make it all *stop*, but I felt powerless to do anything except try to survive in the moment.

I called the minister from our church, whom I deeply trusted. Kendra advised me to immerse myself in a hot shower or bath before I drove over to meet with her, as warm water has a way of calming a body that is spinning off its axis. I followed her advice and arrived at her office an hour later.

Through my tears, I described in great detail the events over the previous six weeks. I told her how I thought I had been divinely guided to leave my full-time job in palliative care for the part-time one at the mental health center as a way to move toward my goal of work-life balance by starting my own business. I sobbed as I told her about the growing anxiety and depression that seemed to be holding my mind and body hostage and about how I hadn't managed to take a single action step toward building my business in the past six weeks because of the intense level of stress I'd been under. I wondered out loud if I'd just made the biggest mistake of my life and how to rectify it before I got any worse?

Kendra looked at me with deep compassion and understanding in her eyes and asked me if I would have ever left my job in healthcare if I had not been offered the part-time opportunity working for Amber. I quickly replied, "Absolutely not! That would have been way too risky for me! I wouldn't have ever left that job without at least securing another part-time position somewhere else first so I could have a safety net to fall back on, which is what I thought my job with Amber would provide."

Kendra leaned over, gently took my hand, and said, "Kay, I think all of this has happened because The Universe had to reveal a steppingstone to you before you'd have the courage to leave the comfort of your previous position and embark on a new path. Ever since you left, It's been trying in a variety of ways to let you know that you can't stay where you are any longer because you are being called to do far more important work in the world. Working for Amber only served as a portal to move you from one place to the next and was never intended to be anything more than that. Does The Universe have to give you a heart attack in order to get your full attention, or do you think you now understand what you have to do next, as hard as it might be?"

I sent a text to Amber as soon as I got back into my car. I knew I had to take swift action before I lost my nerve and wouldn't be able to follow through on what I needed to do. I asked Amber if she had time to talk with me the following day. I told her it was extremely important and that it would be best if we could meet in person. She immediately texted me back and said that we could meet at my office at 9:00 a.m. the next morning. Although I knew it was the right thing to do, I still cried for hours that night, worrying about how I would break the news to Amber that I was leaving and wondering if she would ever be able to forgive me.

The next day, I had an honest and extremely emotional meeting with my friend/boss. Through my tears, I explained why I was giving her notice that I needed to quit my job and how incredibly guilty I felt about putting her in such an awkward position after she put her reputation on the line to hire me. Having known me well over the past five years, Amber intuitively understood that I was suffering and needed to make an immediate change to save my mental health. She empathically acknowledged that the best thing for both of us was for me to vacate my position as quickly as possible, even though she hated to see me go.

A week later, I packed up the few belongings I had accumulated in my office during the seven weeks I had been employed at the mental health center, took them to my car, and slowly drove away. It seemed that The Universe had a different timeline in mind for my future than I had created for myself—a more accelerated one, to be sure. I arrived home that day in time to celebrate Eli's ninth birthday. My Big Dream was beginning to manifest two years ahead of my imagined schedule, and I had to figure out what to do next as I jumped off yet another cliff without a parachute in sight, with only the hope and faith that it was out there somewhere and that I was right where I needed to be.

Even though I was physically and psychologically exhausted from all the emotional upheaval and "cosmic two-by-fours" I had endured over the previous two months, I was also cognizant of the fact that it may have been spiritually necessary for me to go through the trials and tribulations that nearly took me under—it was becoming clearer, in fact, that I had to break open in order to break through.

Three months later, I launched my business called Compassion Works—a company devoted to empowering care partners and organizations impacted by dementia through coaching, education, and training. It has been the culmination of a dream for me, and a place where I would be able to support my clients without the same constraints or barriers that had been frustrating for me to deal with in all my past positions. Moving forward, I would be able to devote my time and talents to providing supportive services to care partners for not just one or two appointments, but for as long as they needed me. Just the thought of that felt like bliss to me!

The first coaching referral I received that spring came from a marvelous and unexpected source: it was from my friend and former boss, Amber. Her referral note arrived as I was putting the finishing touches on the five-hour workshop I would soon present for the students of Suzanna's dementia certificate program in Madison. The irony of that Divine Timing was not lost on me, and in that moment, I knew I had come full circle, and I was deeply grateful.

How Do We Fix
This Thing?

"After fifty-five years of marriage, I've become her worst enemy
and someone she despises. It's absolutely killing me!"

S ince I started my dementia coaching and training business, I've found it fascinating how new referrals find their way to me. Sometimes they come from providers in various medical systems, sometimes from a friend, and other times someone discovers me while surfing the internet. Regardless of how they come about, one of the most interesting referrals I've received was from a lady who was in the audience during a presentation I gave at an Alzheimer's conference in Denver. I never had the pleasure of meeting the person responsible for recommending me to her employer, but I am grateful she did. Because of it, I had one of the most memorable family meetings of my entire career.

I received a voicemail message one day from a woman who sounded both poised and panicked at the same time. She said she had gotten my contact information from someone her family employed. She wanted to talk to me about a situation that was going on between her mother and father and asked that I return her call at my earliest convenience. When I called her back the following morning, Bridget answered the phone on the second ring and sounded anxious to speak to me. She informed me that her parents lived in a gated community outside of Boulder. She explained that her dad still worked part time in the family business as a way to stay mentally stimulated, despite being in his late seventies. She went on to explain that her mom, Doris, had been diagnosed with dementia a few years earlier and that her dad, Peter, had been the sole caregiver for his wife until recent months when he decided he needed more assistance.

Bridget explained that her mom had a stroke about a year before she was diagnosed with dementia and that everything began to change following that event. To further complicate matters, Doris had experienced numerous falls over the past year, including one that resulted in a head injury and brain bleed. After that particular fall, Doris became agitated and paranoid and began hiding things all over the house, including her purse, wedding ring, silverware, and occasionally, the mail. Doris was convinced that her husband was trying to give away her prized possessions without her permission. To prevent that from happening, Doris tried to conceal the items in places she thought no one would ever look. Unfortunately, she would quickly forget about the objects she had so carefully hidden, and when she couldn't locate them again later, this only served to reinforce her distorted belief that her husband was behind the scheme—resulting in a vicious cycle of misguided and delusional thinking that is so commonly found among those living with advanced dementia.

As our conversation continued, the strain in Bridget's tone became increasingly apparent as she discussed other stressors her parents were experiencing. Bridget described a pattern of behavior her mom had developed that included throwing away or destroying all kinds of valuable objects in the home and being cruel to the family dog. Doris's personality had changed dramatically as well.

Before her dementia, Doris was calm and rarely lost her cool. Now, she got so angry with Peter that she even became physically aggressive and often told him she wished he was dead. Consequently, Peter was becoming incredibly stressed and had begun to experience daily panic attacks. He had become too frightened to leave Doris home alone. Fearing what she might do if left unattended, Peter reluctantly hired home health staff to stay with Doris while he was away. However, Doris would quickly turn around and "fire" those same caregivers after Peter left the house because she no longer had the cognitive skills to understand why she needed "a goddamned babysitter when I am perfectly capable of taking care *of myself!*"

With a quivering voice, Bridget said she'd like to hire me to facilitate a family consultation meeting between herself and her father. She wanted to discuss the escalating concerns in her parents' home and how to reasonably plan for the future as her mom's dementia continued to progress. We set a date for the following week, and Bridget requested that we meet at her dad's office in Boulder. The plan was set.

Three days later, I received a frantic phone call from Bridget. Earlier that day, her mom had become extremely upset and angry after being reminded by a caregiver that she was no longer able to drive a car when she wanted to go shopping. In her highly agitated state, Doris grabbed a letter opener and threatened to kill the caregiver with it if they didn't give her the car keys *now*! The caregiver was so terrified of Doris that she called 911 and had her taken to the emergency room to be evaluated. Bridget and her family were sick with worry and wanted to move the meeting with me up to an earlier date because of the current crisis they found themselves in. She gave me the address for the family business, and we agreed to meet there first thing the following morning.

For some reason, I had made up a picture in my head of what her dad's office would look like. I pictured a small mom-and-pop shop where Peter went a few days a week to putter around and pass his time. I imagined him reading the newspaper in his office, lingering over coffee, and maybe even taking an occasional nap in his chair before calling it a day. Needless to say, I was completely unprepared for what I found when I arrived at the appointed address!

The state-of-the-art office building was surrounded by huge trees and gorgeous landscaping. There were statues out front and a look of affluent elegance everywhere. When I entered the marbled lobby, I told the impeccably dressed receptionist at the front desk that I was there to see Peter. She immediately responded by saying, "You must be Kay. Come right this way," and she led me to an elevator that took me to the top floor of the complex, where I found Peter and Bridget awaiting my arrival in a large and elegantly decorated office suite. The walls were covered with business awards and family photos spanning many decades. I couldn't have been more stunned, as this was clearly *no* mom-and-pop operation! This was the central hub of a successful and powerful man who was waiting for me at the head of the long conference room table as his daughter walked across the room to greet me.

The small talk between us was brief, as Peter's style was no-nonsense and direct. It was obvious that he was accustomed to being in charge, orchestrating his universe in such a way that he had total and complete control over his dominion. Within minutes of being in Peter's presence, I couldn't believe how *far off* my preconceived notions of him had been!

It was crystal clear that Peter was a driver—a man accustomed to calling the shots and demanding solutions to any and all obstacles that came his way, no matter the cost. When Peter couldn't singlehandedly resolve the mounting problems with his wife's dementia, he agreed to enlist my aid.

As the three of us talked around the beveled wood table, I learned a great deal about Peter's history. Peter readily volunteered that he had been "tough and controlling" throughout most of his life—both in terms of running his company and "managing" his wife and six children. Although Bridget acknowledged that her dad had worked hard to become less domineering in his later years, the damage had already been done. In Doris's advanced dementia, she was not living much in the present moment anymore but rather back in time twenty to thirty years earlier, when Peter still ruled his wife and family with an iron fist. Doris was far too intimidated back then to stand up to her husband. However, given her current brain changes and lack of social filter caused by dementia, she was no longer fearful and lacked any insight or awareness about how her words now impacted Peter.

"Doris screams at me all the time, telling me how much she hates me. She has come to resent me and everything I stand for. After fifty-five years of marriage, I've become her worst enemy and someone she despises. It's absolutely killing me!"

We discussed the family history, Doris's behavioral outbursts, and the escalating dynamics between Peter and his wife. Bridget gently implored her father to "think about the big picture" and to realize that Doris required more care and intervention than any of them knew how to provide at home. Bridget was clearly concerned about the well-being of *both* of her parents— both mentally and physically—and was trying her best to carefully interject her opinions and concerns into the conversation without being too forceful. It looked like a dance that she and her father had performed for decades.

In the midst of it, Peter abruptly turned his head toward me and inquired, "So, how do we fix this thing?" There was a look of desperation on his face, coupled with an unmistakable air of authority from a man who was accustomed to working hard and having his issues solved at the snap of a finger or by throwing whatever amount of money was necessary at a problem so he could achieve the desired results. I instinctively knew that he wasn't going to like what I had to say next.

In an honest and straightforward manner, I explained the ways in which dementia can impact a person's memory, cognition, mood, personality, and functional abilities, and how researchers had not yet discovered a cure for this devastating brain disease. I reinforced the importance of Peter and Bridget becoming knowledgeable about dementia so they would know what to anticipate as the illness progressed, how to best support Doris through the changes ahead, and how to prepare for a future they never expected to face. Bridget wiped away tears and nodded her head in agreement as I spoke, while she simultaneously glanced across the table at her father to gauge his reaction to my words.

Peter sat with his head downcast so that I couldn't see his expression. I softly said, "Peter, I can tell that you're a man who has experienced great success and who is used to being in charge of the world around you. Unfortunately, dementia is not an illness that *anyone* can control—no matter how much influence someone may have. It is not something that *anyone* can conquer, outsmart, or 'fix'—no matter what your position in life. But there *are* some things you *can* do to improve this situation—beginning with gradually coming to terms with the reality of Doris's illness by learning more about it. I can help by providing education and resources to you and your family about the brain changes and challenges your wife is experiencing, from the perspective of someone living with the disease. I can assist you with being proactive as a care partner so you feel more confident and less anxious. I can be available for guidance and support along the way to navigate the emotional upheavals and grief that come with loving someone who has dementia. I will work with you to develop skills and strategies that will enable you to match your caregiving efforts to Doris's changing needs in a manner that will not only enhance her quality of life but also enhance your own in the process.

Peter sat in complete silence for a few moments before responding. Then he looked me right in the eye and said, "If that's all you've got, then we're done here," and he quickly dismissed me from the office. Bridget was visibly upset when she walked me out of the building to my car. As we chatted for a few minutes in the parking lot, Bridget thanked me for coming and told me how comforted she was to know there were people like me to call who "understand how crazy and out of control our family feels because of this disease."

Bridget said she would hang on to my business card for future reference and apologized that she and her dad were not on the same page when it came to what they thought was "best" for her mom. Then, in a resigned tone of voice, Bridget confessed, "As the oldest in the family, Dad always asks for my input, but my vote never really seems to carry much weight. In the end, my father's opinion trumps everything else."

As I drove away from that stunning office complex, I felt deeply disappointed about the way the visit had ended and sad that I wasn't going to be able to help this family in the way I'd hoped or intended. But I can't say that I was all that surprised either. Because, for people like Peter who fervently believe that "fixing the thing" is the only acceptable outcome, the services I had to offer would never be enough.

The Ghosts of
Dementia

*"I just want to tell them all off, but I can't! I'm fifty-
seven, I'm stuck, and I am furious about that!"*

S usan was referred to me for dementia coaching by a mutual acquain-
tance who was worried about her friend's mental health and desperately hoped I could be of help. When I first chatted with Susan over
the phone a year earlier to follow up on the referral, I learned a lot about her
family history—including her current role as the primary caregiver for her
fifty-four-year-old husband, Mark, who had been living with frontotemporal
dementia for over two years by then. During our call, Susan told me, "This
isn't my first rodeo. This is the fourth person in my family to have dementia,
and I don't know what I ever did to piss God off so much that He had to bring
all this grief into my life, but whatever it is, I am *over it!"*

I spent time during that first informal phone conversation explaining
to Susan what I do as a dementia coach and educator and the various ways
I could support her on her caregiving journey. Even though Susan sounded
interested in what I had to offer, she said that she was already involved in
an online dementia support group, so she felt she was "doing okay for the

moment." She said she would call me if and when she needed additional assistance in the future. I thanked her for talking with me and invited her to outreach me again if that time ever arrived.

A year later, I received an urgent email from Susan, stating she was feeling stressed out after a year of caring for Mark in almost total isolation due to the global pandemic of 2020. Susan explained in her email that she was ready to pursue working with me because of how overwhelmed and exhausted she had become. "I need coaching because I feel like I'm losing it! Between living with a man whom I can no longer communicate with and being in quarantine for months without the support of my family and friends due to COVID-19, I am *spent!* The quarantines are finally starting to lift now, and other people around me are beginning to move on with their lives once again, but not me. I am trapped and can't move forward at all because of my caregiving responsibilities for Mark. He has become incapable of discussing anything, comprehending anything, or helping with anything, so *everything's* on me! *Everything!* I feel like I'm tanking in depression and really need help before I sink any lower!"

I emailed back and set up a ninety-minute coaching session in my first available time slot a few days later. Just minutes into the start of our virtual coaching session over Zoom, Susan's lighthearted expression suddenly changed, and the tears and anger she had been holding in poured out of her like a spring thunderstorm. Susan told me how devastating the past year had been for her because of COVID and how she felt as if she had aged ten years in the past twelve months as a result of being physically cut off from her support system due to lockdown orders and social distancing.

Susan explained that it used to feel like "getting a break from Mark" when she went to the office to work for twenty hours a week. But after the pandemic began, she had been further isolated and alone since nearly all of her fellow employees had elected to work from home. Susan added that Mark's cognitive and functional abilities seemed to worsen over the past year, and she had begun to wonder how much longer she could withstand the enormous amount of stress she was living under without some assistance from the outside world.

Susan shared that Mark had been formally diagnosed with frontotemporal dementia by a neurologist three years before, but she thought the first signs of trouble began at least a year prior to that when Mark's personality started to change and Susan had no idea why.

"I thought my husband was turning into some kind of alien being right before my eyes. The kind and gentle man I've always known started becoming verbally belligerent and acting like he didn't give a shit about *anything* anymore—including me! In twenty years of marriage, Mark had never behaved like that before, and when I tried to ask him what was going on, he told me he was perfectly fine and that I just needed to mind my own damn business. I knew something was terribly wrong, but I tried to convince myself that it *couldn't possibly* be dementia because Mark was too young for that. I prayed that he had a brain tumor or something that could be cured. *Anything but dementia!*"

Susan went on to describe how multiple members of her family had been impacted by various forms of dementia in the past and how she just couldn't handle one more person that she loved being diagnosed with that awful illness—especially if that individual happened to be her spouse. Susan told me that her mom had developed vascular dementia after having a stroke, her grandfather got Alzheimer's disease in his seventies, and her aunt was diagnosed with Lewy body dementia in her early sixties. Susan had helped care for them all until the end, and she simply couldn't stand the thought of having to do that again with her husband, whose brain was now dying from the calamitous effects of FTD.

Susan sighed deeply and said, "Dementia has turned four people I've loved so deeply into ghosts, and the injustice of this disease has become unbearable for me after so many years of heartbreak. *How much* grief and loss is one woman supposed to bear, after all?!"

Tears began flowing as Susan told me how she had come to find out about Mark's diagnosis. The neurologist who conducted the battery of cognitive tests on Mark had called Susan on the phone when she was out running errands one day to give her the results of Mark's memory evaluation. "I had absolutely *no* warning! The doctor just called me out of the blue. I had him on speakerphone in my car while I was driving sixty-five miles an hour down I-25. He didn't preface the conversation by telling me that he had some hard news to share or that maybe I should pull my car over to have a discussion with him on the phone. He just told me that the test results indicated that Mark had a disease called frontotemporal dementia and that he was sorry there was not much he could offer in terms of treatment, as there was no cure for the disease at this time. The doctor suggested that I call the Alzheimer's Association for help and resources and basically hung up. I was sobbing so hard that I couldn't even see the road in front of me. What *the hell* was he thinking, delivering a bombshell like that to me without any preparation? I'll never forgive him for his callousness as long as I live!"

As we moved further into our coaching session, I asked Susan what kind of a support system she had available to her to deal with all of the incredible loss she was going through. Susan replied, "That's part of the problem! When people find out about Mark's diagnosis, they immediately start talking and acting differently. It's so annoying! No one really knows *what* to say, and most people have no clue what frontotemporal dementia even is, let alone possess the skills to comfort someone like me in my distress. Ultimately, they've all disappeared from our lives one by one to avoid having to feel so awkward and uncomfortable themselves. The only people who actually seem to truly understand the kind of hell I am living in are the ones in my dementia support group, but none of us in that online forum even live in the same city, so those relationships only get me so far."

Part of what made Susan's predicament even harder to contend with was the fact that she and Mark had been experiencing serious conflicts in their relationship for at least two years before he was diagnosed with dementia. Mark's alcohol abuse had gotten out of hand, and despite all his promises to quit drinking, Susan continued to find empty liquor bottles stashed all over their house and garage. She also discovered that Mark had been keeping a loaded pistol in the drawer next to their bed, when she didn't even know he owned a gun. Susan had been vehemently opposed to firearms her entire life, which Mark was well aware of, so she was livid when she discerned that her husband had broken her trust in such a reckless way.

"I had come to the realization that Mark was *not* the man I thought I married, because he has *no* integrity, and integrity is *everything* to me! I was ready to start divorce proceedings when I found out that Mark had fronto-temporal dementia. I now believe that the disease was part of the reason for the problems we were having, but I didn't realize it back then. For years, I just thought that my husband was lazy because he only put minimal effort into our marriage, and I resented him for that. But even if we had split up, I would have probably ended up taking care of him anyway because Mark has no friends, and his family is famous for running the other direction whenever there's any kind of problem that needs addressing—even if it involves one of their own. I just want to tell them all off, but I can't! I'm fifty-seven, I'm stuck, and I am furious about that!"

I listened intently as Susan described how Mark had long ago lost the ability to communicate with her in any kind of meaningful way because of his brain changes and how his loss of language skills made their relationship and Susan's caregiving situation even harder and more complex. "Mark just sits in front of the television for twelve hours a day, watching shows that he can't even follow the plots of, and only leaves his chair long enough to eat some food that I prepare for him. Mark can only speak in one-word sentences, and he rarely comprehends a single thing I say to him now, so I've given up really trying to talk to him much either. It's like his mind and spirit have flown away to some distant place, and all that remains is the shell of his body that no longer has the capacity to really connect with another human being or to even care. The man I once loved is *gone*, and I am left living with a ghost."

There was a long pause in our conversation after Susan spoke those anguished words. Years of practice have taught me that silence and holding space for another person's pain are often the most appropriate responses at such a time and are a far more respectful intervention than trying to offer words of comfort that sound hollow and disingenuous when someone is in that much inner turmoil and angst.

So often, caregivers like Susan are on the receiving end of unsolicited advice or empty platitudes from well-meaning friends and family members, making statements such as, "You should be thankful that Mark is still here to care for," or "God never gives you more than you can handle." Those kinds of sentiments tend to infuriate many care partners, making them feel guilty or simply reinforcing their belief that *no one* understands the reality of their unrelenting losses, the depths of their despair, or the utter helplessness they actually feel.

When Susan finally broke the silence between us, she looked up at me and tearfully said, "I know this may sound terrible to say, but at fifty-seven, I'm hopefully far from finished with my own journey on this planet. I just want this horrendous chapter of my life to be over so that I can start a new one where I only have myself to worry about, where I can find love, friendship, and happiness to sustain me, and where I can get far enough away from the ghosts of dementia that they will never be able to find or haunt me again."

I couldn't get Susan's story out of my head for days afterward. I am good at what I do, but to be sure, I am no miracle-worker! If I were, I would offer some kind of money-back guarantee to Susan and millions of other care partners just like her, informing them that they would *never* have to face such tremendous grief and pain again. I would give them an embossed certificate with a lifetime warranty that protected them against someone they love ever getting dementia till the end of time. And then I would wave my magic wand and transform all the senseless suffering and sad endings into uplifting stories of hope, where *everyone* gets to dance with angels, and *no one* ever becomes a ghost.

The Lightbulb
Incident

"I'm getting better at letting go of the mistakes Dad makes without getting bent out of shape every time he does something wrong."

I was in the middle of a virtual coaching call with Jasmine—one of the care partners I had been working with for many months. She had made the difficult decision to quit her job and move into her father's home after he was diagnosed with vascular dementia following a stroke. Jasmine's father, Michael, was a sixty-eight-year-old African American man who divorced Jasmine's mother twenty years earlier. He had been battling obesity, high blood pressure, and diabetes for a long while before the stroke finally hit, and when it did, life as he knew it came to a screeching halt when his independence and ability to care for himself literally disappeared overnight.

One of the many themes Jasmine and I discussed during our coaching calls was how frustrated she would get with the inconsistency of her dad's widely vacillating ability to complete day-to-day tasks correctly. "One day, he can easily figure out how to load the dishwasher and make himself a cup of coffee, and then the next day, he is utterly *clueless* about how to do either! Or, he gets partway through a job, but then it's like he doesn't know how to finish what he started. What the hell is going on in his head? Sometimes I feel like he just wants me to do everything for him, instead of doing anything for himself. It's maddening!"

I shared a lot of information with Jasmine to help her better understand the brain changes that were happening inside her dad's head. I described the permanent structural changes caused by brain cells that were damaged or had died as a result of the stroke, and the widely variable chemical changes that can make life so damned confusing in the "on-and-off world" of dementia care. We discussed how the chemical fluctuations that frequently occur in the brains of people living with dementia can impact their skills and abilities in such a way that sometimes they *can* and sometimes they *can't* do a specific task for no apparent reason.

Care partners often can't predict from one hour, day, or month to the next when the person they're caring for will be able to successfully accomplish a task or when they won't have the faintest idea how to go about it. That dynamic can drive folks like Jasmine crazy if they don't understand the reason behind those cognitive changes and instead jump to the conclusion that the person they're caring for is being lazy, manipulative, or just plain difficult. Educating and supporting care partners around these brain changes can make all the difference between a family member who feels emotionally equipped to handle the ever-changing world of dementia caregiving and those who feel trapped, overwhelmed, guilty, and resentful.

Jasmine recounted a story to me about a recent blowup she had with her dad, and she referred to it as "the lightbulb incident." Michael was getting ready for bed one evening when one of the lightbulbs in his bedside table lamp suddenly burned out. He called out to Jasmine for help, but instead of automatically replacing the bulb herself, Jasmine assured her dad that he was fully capable of putting in a new bulb without her assistance. She pointed him toward the hall closet where all the fresh lightbulbs were kept and stood back to watch what happened.

It took multiple tries, going back and forth between the hall closet and his bedroom, before Michael finally managed to find a bulb with the correct wattage for his lamp. With some difficulty, he then removed the burned-out bulb and successfully replaced it with the new one. But what he did next was what caused the fight. Michael took out the old lightbulb and promptly stuffed it into his underwear drawer—having no awareness that the final step in the process was totally wrong. That's when Jasmine hit the boiling point. "I just lost it when I saw what he did. I mean, *how hard* is it to just put the frickin' lightbulb into the garbage can where it belongs, instead of some random place where he'll never find it again!?"

Jasmine and I talked some more about how people living with dementia often have great difficulty sequencing tasks, and like the rest of us without cognitive impairments, they have more problems doing so successfully when they are tired and at the end of their day. So, when Jasmine asks her dad to do something that requires multiple steps to complete, such as changing a burned-out lightbulb, he may not remember how to initiate the task at all. He may also get lost in the middle of the sequence, forget steps along the way, or not be able to figure out how to correctly finish what he started.

I tried to normalize for Jasmine how becoming upset and exasperated with her father was to be expected, given the stressful conditions in which they were living—especially since Jasmine had never known anyone who had suffered through a life-changing stroke before, let alone been a hands-on caregiver for them. Jasmine visibly bristled in response to my comments and looked like she would start crying at any moment. But when I began to acknowledge how I *truly understood* how overwhelming it can be for someone in Jasmine's shoes to give up their life in order to provide round-the-clock care for a loved one with a disease as confusing and unpredictable as vascular dementia, her defensiveness dissipated as quickly as it had come. I went on to explain the importance of Jasmine learning the simple art of breaking down tasks into individual steps for her dad to complete one at a time. By doing so, she would give him the opportunity to experience more successes each day, and she would likely find herself a whole lot less frustrated and stressed as a result.

During the following weeks, Jasmine continued to focus on her goal of slowly and intentionally changing her approach with her dad. She gave me numerous examples of how she took the extra time to break tasks into manageable steps for him and how she became aware that rarely had she done this in the past. She also discovered the power of adapting her expectations to her dad's changing brain and even developed a new mantra that she told herself many times a day: *"Dad is doing the best he can, and so am I."*

Jasmine stated that although she still became frustrated and angry with her dad at times, she no longer automatically presumed he was acting out of laziness or spite. That slight shift in her mindset helped her become more patient with her father. Jasmine realized that by tweaking the way she mindfully interacted with Michael, he seemed more content, she felt less stressed out, and most importantly, their relationship was far less contentious because of those subtle but profound changes.

During our final coaching call the following month, we reviewed the content and skills we had covered together over the previous few months and some of the "nuggets" that Jasmine gleaned from our coaching sessions.

Jasmine told me, "I've made a lot of progress when it comes to picking my battles with my dad, and I'm learning not to go to the mat with him over something as stupid as putting a burned-out lightbulb into his underwear drawer. It seems like a small thing, but it has actually made a huge difference in terms of our day-to-day interactions. I'm getting better at letting go of all the mistakes Dad makes without getting bent out of shape every time he does something wrong. I'm also slowly improving my ability to adjust my expectations and approach so that I don't ask more of him than he can realistically deliver.

"The issue I continue to struggle with is figuring out how to be more patient and compassionate with myself when I don't always show up as a daughter and caregiver in the way I'd like to, and the guilt I feel when I don't live up to *my own* expectations. I guess I'm still a work in progress when it comes to that! But my biggest takeaway of all is coming to terms with the harsh reality that I truly don't have any actual control over what happens to Dad and his dementia, but I *do* have control over the choices *I make* and the actions *I take* when it comes to caring for him. So, from here on out, *that* is where I'm going to put my focus."

Save It for a
Rainy Day

"I wish you could just tell us what to do.
It'd be so much easier that way!"

received an email from a gentleman in a nearby state who had attended a
dementia workshop I'd presented a year before in his community. He had
saved my contact information for a rainy day, and that day had come in the
form of a deluge—much sooner than he had ever anticipated.

Norman explained to me that his seventy-nine-year-old mother, Angela,
had taken a fall a few months back, and it resulted in multiple fractures and
a hard bump to the head. It had appeared his mom was slowly on the mend
when she suddenly developed an unexpected embolism—a blood clot that
formed in one part of her body and traveled to her heart. It ended up taking
her life and in so doing, changed the lives of everyone in her family overnight.

Angela had been the primary caregiver for her husband, Frank, for many
years since he was diagnosed with moderate-stage Alzheimer's disease.
Norman and his siblings had been helping out with their dad here and there,
but their mom was the bedrock of the family and had always been in charge
of her husband's well-being, until her untimely death. Ever since that tragic

event, Norman and his sister and brother had been madly scrambling to piece together daily care for their father, who could no longer be left alone because of his advanced dementia.

Norman and his sister, Joanne, lived in close proximity to their dad, but their brother, Conrad, lived five hours away, which made caregiving even more complicated for him. All three of the adult children and their spouses still worked full time, so trading off spending seven nights a week with their father for the past three months had already led them to utter exhaustion, as did trying to hire consistent in-home help with the COVID-19 pandemic in full swing in 2020.

I spent time on the phone collecting preliminary information from Norman about the caregiving challenges his family was facing and where they could use my help and expertise. We set up an introductory coaching call via Zoom for the following week with Norman, his siblings, and their spouses. In the meantime, I emailed Norman a coaching questionnaire form so I could collect more background information and get clear about the family's goals for our first coaching call.

The ninety minutes we spent together virtually the following week proved to be fruitful but also extremely heavy. The family had three main choices ahead of them in terms of providing 24/7 care for their father—none of them remotely straightforward or anywhere close to easy:

Keep doing what they were doing—piecing together hired caregivers during the daytime hours, supplemented by various family members spending the evenings and nights with Frank on a rotating basis.

Place their dad into the one or two less-than-desirable nearby nursing homes, while facing the brutal reality that if they did, they would likely not see Frank face to face again for the next six months, except through a "window visit," due to safety precautions put in place because of the pandemic. This decision would also result in placing Frank at a significantly higher risk of contracting the coronavirus himself.

Move Frank in with his daughter, Joanne, and her husband, Mark, and hire caregivers forty hours a week to supervise Frank while they both worked their full-time jobs outside of the home.

We discussed the pros and cons of each difficult choice in depth. The option to continue piecing together care in the home for months or years, although it was the choice Frank would undoubtedly pick for himself, was probably not realistic for much longer due to the level of burnout the family had already experienced in just a few short months. Placing Frank in a nursing home in the midst of COVID-19, when a significantly large portion of the 230,000 US deaths thus far were nursing home residents and staff, was nearly unthinkable, not to mention fraught with incredible emotional baggage. Moving Frank in with Joanne and Mark was not a slam-dunk choice either. It also came with a high price, which we discussed in honest terms. The demands of that kind of daily caregiving would impact their marriage, finances, freedom, quality of life, and mental and physical health. Besides, everyone unanimously agreed that "Frank is going to hate *any* place that isn't home, and he's not going *anywhere* without a fight!"

Despite the stress and intensity of that family coaching session, I was incredibly thankful that everyone was respectful and loving toward one another, which made my job so much smoother. Facing chronic health conditions and end-of-life issues can result in enormous caregiver stress and bring out the best and the worst in a family system. Luckily for me, the crisis in this family was bringing out the good in everyone assembled, but that didn't mean they weren't suffering a great deal in the process.

All of Frank's children and their spouses were clearly struggling with making such heart-wrenching choices about Frank's care, which would be challenging even in the best of times but was nearly impossible in the midst of a global pandemic. Not to mention that none of them had even begun to grieve Angela's death, being thrust into crisis caregiving mode with Frank after Angela passed away. For this family, there literally hadn't been time to process their feelings of grief and loss over their mother's unexpected death three months earlier, and that in and of itself was awful.

Tears were shed, admissions of guilt spoken, and feelings of hope and despair addressed. Norman kept saying to me, "I wish you could just *tell us* what to do. It'd be so much easier that way!"

Like so many other care partners I work with, Norman wanted me to direct him to the "right decision" for his father and their caregiving situation, but it wasn't nearly as simple as that. I'd long ago come to the realization that what *I personally thought* was the best choice for a family to make on behalf of a loved one with an illness as insidious as dementia wasn't always the decision that proved to be the *best choice* in the end. The complexity of these situations was far-reaching and often literally came down to a family being forced to choose the lesser of their perceived "evils," leaving them feeling as if they had no real satisfying options to choose from at all—only shitty, arduous, and painful ones at best.

I was transparent with Norman about *why* I couldn't just tell him what to do. I explained that part of my job as a dementia coach was to facilitate a dialogue between Frank and his siblings so that, together, they could brainstorm, explore, and discuss the options of care available for their father and thoughtfully weigh out which ones seemed most aligned with their goals and values, or at least were the most tolerable.

I informed this concerned son that I was happy to offer my opinion and advice about the difficult choices his family was grappling with, based on the competence I'd gained from assisting hundreds of others through similar dilemmas over the years, but that *the truth* of the matter was this: When it comes to caring for someone with advanced Alzheimer's disease, there are rarely any cut-and-dried decisions to be found. Being a care partner for someone with dementia means learning to live in the gray and uncomfortable world of ambiguity—where obvious answers of "right and wrong" are replaced by educated guesswork, wise counsel, trial and error, and following your instincts for what you resolutely *pray* is the "highest good" for the collective whole. Because of that, it's outside of my professional purview to dictate to clients like Norman and his siblings what they should or shouldn't do for their father, given the ramifications of their unique caregiving circumstances. Ultimately, *they* will be the ones who have to endure the consequences of such onerous decisions on their lives, relationships, and psyches.

Although I completely understood where Norman was coming from in terms of wanting "an expert" to guide him to the perfect answer, I told him there were inherent limits and boundaries to my coaching role. I can spearhead a discussion about care decisions, provide education, resources, emotional support, and ample compassion, but deciding what is *right* for someone's family and unique caregiving needs was not a decision I felt ethically comfortable making.

Part of me felt guilty that I didn't have the panacea Frank's children were looking for, and another part of me was deeply frustrated and angry that there weren't a plethora of better options readily available for wonderful, committed families like these across the country, when Alzheimer's disease is a major leading cause of death for elders in our nation and in the world. I had to remind myself, as I do every day, that I can't possibly solve every problem that families bring to me. I can only promise to show up authentically and to genuinely provide the most effective interventions and assistance I can to each client I serve and then try to let go of the rest.

So, for now, Norman and his family would need to come together, dive deep into heart-to-heart dialogue, and discover *for themselves* what was ultimately the "best" choice they could mutually agree upon for their father's care and future, knowing they could adjust the sails if and when the decisions they made led to more turbulent waters than they had anticipated. I knew only too well that another "rainy day deluge" would likely come for Norman and his siblings—probably sooner than later. Until that day arrived, I would remain available with my virtual door and heart wide open should they need to return for my counsel again.

Everything in
Its Place

"I have no idea what I'm supposed to do next, but there must be some intervention to implement that can turn things back around!"

When Howard first called to explore the possibility of hiring me as a dementia coach, I could hear the reluctance and suspicion in his voice from the first word, "Hello." Howard explained that he was contacting me on the strong recommendation of his wife's doctor. He admitted that he wasn't sure why he had dialed my number that day because he was quite convinced that "a dementia coach" would never be able to help him with his situation at home anyway. I took a deep breath and tried to gently ease my way into building some rapport and trust with the guarded and overwhelmed gentleman on the other end of the line.

Howard informed me that his seventy-five-year-old wife, Rebecca, had been in a serious car accident eight months earlier in which she had sustained a number of broken bones and other injuries, but the worst outcome of the wreck, by far, was a severe traumatic brain injury. When Rebecca's compact car was struck at high speed by a pickup truck on a highway near her home, the impact of the crash caused Howard's wife to slam her head into the windshield so hard that it shattered and caused her to lose consciousness. The ramifications of that crash left Rebecca with permanent changes in her ability to regulate her thinking, mood, behaviors, and movements; the accident essentially left her with a permanent, trauma-induced form of dementia resulting from the severe damage that was done to her brain in that collision.

For the past eight months since the accident, Rebecca had been struggling with changes in her short-term memory and regulating her emotions and executive functioning skills, including her ability to follow a recipe, balance the checkbook, tell time on the clock, or stay on top of her daily schedule and appointments. Howard and Rebecca's union was a second marriage for both, but in the thirty years that they'd been together, Howard had never felt so frustrated and upset with his wife or so completely out of sorts himself.

"It's a complete disaster at our house! Since the accident, Rebecca struggles with things that she never did before. She screws up her pill box every time she touches it and is constantly losing things like her purse and phone when we have *designated places* in our house where all of those objects belong. My wife forgets her swimming suit in the locker room nearly every time she attends her water aerobics class, and we have to keep buying her new suits every week because of that issue. How is that even possible?!"

I asked Howard some questions about his background, and he shared with me that he had been employed by NASA in the aeronautics field before his retirement. "I am an engineer. Give me a problem, and I'll solve it! But when it comes to Rebecca, all the logic and reasoning skills I have don't seem to work one bit these days." Howard told me that he tends to be "very exacting by nature," which was part of what made him so successful in his career.

"In my home, everything needs to be in its place. There's not a single blade of grass in my front yard that isn't green and not a dandelion to be found anywhere on my property. I keep everything in perfect order, or at least I did until this happened to Rebecca. Now, I'm lucky if I can even find a bowl to eat out of because my wife keeps moving our dishes to odd places around the house that don't make any sense. I thoroughly believed that my wife's thinking would eventually improve as time went on, but it's already been over eight months, and it only seems to be getting worse instead of better. I have no idea what I'm supposed to do next, but there must be *some intervention* to implement that can turn things back around!"

As he told me all the ways he had attempted to help his partner become more organized at home, Howard methodically explained how he created a large, detailed calendar for their kitchen wall. It included, in a color-coded format, every activity each of them had coming up in their daily schedules. Howard painstakingly wrote out every item on their schedules a whole month in advance so that Rebecca could easily know what she had to do on any given day without constantly asking him about it.

"The calendar takes up most of the kitchen wall. You can't miss it! When Rebecca asks me for the umpteenth time if today is the day when she is supposed to go to her class at the rec center, I should be able to just point her toward the calendar for the answer. The problem is, she either doesn't remember to look at the calendar or she can't seem to make sense of what it says when it's right in front of her. It's enough to drive me completely nuts! Is there anything *you* can do to help my wife? I'm all out of ideas, and I don't know how much longer I can live like this!"

We discussed how the TBI had impacted Rebecca's brain in such a way that her short-term memory was impaired to the point that she couldn't retain new information for more than a few minutes before it disappeared somewhere into the ether. The trauma to her brain made it nearly impossible for Rebecca to organize her thoughts, sequence tasks, or correctly decipher written and verbal language in the way she had great mastery over before her brain became so muddled. It wasn't that she was *trying* to be difficult or to sabotage her husband's perfectly organized world; it was just that Rebecca no longer possessed the cognitive skills to meet the unrealistically high standards

Howard still expected of her—no matter how hard she tried to please him.

A few more minutes into our call, Howard disclosed that he and his wife had experienced more conflict in the past six months of their marriage than in the entire thirty years that preceded it. Howard admitted that the marital stress was, in large part, a result of Rebecca's memory changes, and they had impacted not only *her ability* to function "normally" but his own as well.

"I've tried to solve this problem with my wife from every imaginable angle," he shared with me, "and I keep running into brick walls at every turn. Can *you* help me find a way to get Rebecca to utilize the systems I've put in place for her so that we can get back to living our lives without all this disorganization and chaos? If that's a task a dementia coach can assist with, then I'm thankful that her doctor gave me your number, and I'll gladly hire you today."

There was an extended silence on my end of the phone as I carefully pondered how to best respond to Howard's question. How do I tell someone who is so dependent on using logic and reasoning to control every aspect of his environment that dementia is not a disease that *any of us* have dominion over—*especially* the person living with the disease? How could I make him see that the one who needed to change in this scenario was actually *him*, because Howard was the one who was still capable of adapting his expectations to Rebecca's changing needs, shifting his perspective from "losing control" to "learning new skills" and coming to terms with the hard reality that there is not always a clear-cut answer for every problem when it comes to dementia, but there *is* always the hope of making things better?

After my long pause finally ended, I said, "Howard, I may not be able to help you get Rebecca to comprehend or follow all of the systems you have so lovingly designed for her, but I *can* help you work toward reaching a place of understanding and acceptance regarding the changes in your wife's cognitive and functional abilities that you've been trying to navigate alone ever since her crash."

I went on to share how I could appreciate what a huge paradigm shift that would be for Howard, as it was for the many other family members I supported every day in my coaching practice. Even if a care partner didn't have the propensity, as Howard did, to apply logic and reasoning to every aspect of their lives and caregiving efforts, it still took a significant amount of education and sustained effort on their part to continuously adapt and adjust their way of thinking and approach to caregiving, regardless of how their own brains were intrinsically wired to respond.

I assured Howard that with time and practice, he, too, would be able to implement new interventions and ways of being that would promote Rebecca's success in her day-to-day interactions and leave him feeling less distressed and overwhelmed as a result. I couldn't see Howard's expression on the other end of the phone, but I could easily envision the perplexed and confused look on his face in response to my words. I could hear the muffled sounds of his breathing, feel his frustration emanating through the phone line, and sense the anger and helplessness he felt regarding his wife's progressive illness that couldn't be stopped, analyzed, or easily solved.

I wanted to reach out across the invisible expanse of distance between Howard and me to impart to him that I would *never* be able to restore everything to perfect order again when it came to his relationship with Rebecca, but that I *could* help to improve their quality of life through coaching and tailored support along the way. If Howard was amenable to the terms of *that* kind of agreement, then a dementia coach might be just the solution he was looking for.

Mending Fences

"I think I can live now! I actually think I can live!"

In addition to providing dementia coaching and education to care partners in my business, I also offer coaching services directly to people who are in the early stages of dementia. These clients are usually trying to come to terms with their diagnosis, grappling with the concept of how to live the rest of their lives with their progressive brain changes and how to plan for a future they never envisioned. One of those clients was named Gavin. We met at a dementia workshop I delivered in Lexington, Kentucky, and Gavin was the last person waiting in line to talk with me when my presentation ended.

Gavin was a distinguished-looking man who was smartly dressed in a button-up shirt and sports jacket, and he had an unmistakable air of authority about him. Gavin greeted me with a firm handshake and a warm smile, but his eyes held a look of sadness and worry. He explained to me that he had been diagnosed with early-onset Alzheimer's disease a year earlier at the age of sixty-four and had been struggling ever since to figure out what was happening in his head and what to do about it.

Gavin asked me if I would be able to help him understand his disease, as he had never met anyone with dementia before and had no idea what was in store for him. He bemoaned the fact that his doctor had delivered the Alzheimer's diagnosis in a fifteen-minute clinic appointment and then simply advised him to not waste any time worrying about what the future might hold but to instead "go live each day to the fullest, and everything else will take care of itself." Gavin admitted that he resented his doctor for not providing him with more information, support, and assurances during that office visit. At the very least, Gavin felt that he deserved to be given some direction, resources, or a plan that would assist him in understanding his new diagnosis and where he should go for help to prepare for the uncertain path he was just beginning to embark upon. I agreed to schedule a coaching appointment with Gavin over Zoom when I returned home to Denver the following week.

Our first coaching call consisted of gathering background information about Gavin's life and the specific goals he wanted to focus on during our weekly sessions. Gavin explained to me that he had three adult children— one daughter from his first marriage and two sons from his current second marriage to Joan. When I invited Gavin to include his wife on any of our coaching calls, he immediately responded by saying, "I don't think that's a good idea at all! Our marriage is in a state of crisis, and it's all because I can't remember shit anymore! Joan never imagined that 'for better or for worse' could possibly equate to one day caring for a spouse with a brain like a sieve. She is feeling angry and overwhelmed about how my Alzheimer's disease may impact our future and relationship, and I don't think she's emotionally ready to understand what's coming, and *that's exactly* what I need to know and understand the most. So, for now, let's just start by doing one-to-one coaching until my wife feels ready to join us in this process."

According to Gavin, part of what led to his divorce from his first wife was his "workaholism" and domineering style of parenting. "My mindset back then was that my primary job was to run a tight ship and to be the breadwinner for my family. Everything other than that was way down on my priority list—including being a good father to my daughter, Allison."

Gavin went on to explain that, aside from learning about his Alzheimer's disease and how to cope with the brain changes that were inevitable in his future, he also had a goal to try to improve his strained and tenuous relationship with Allison while he "still possessed the brainpower to pull it off." Gavin deeply regretted the mistakes he had made as a parent. Those mistakes came back to haunt him when Allison decided to completely cut her dad out of her life when she became a young adult.

It had only been in the past couple of years that Allison had begun to reach out to Gavin at all through an occasional email or phone call after she got married. But Gavin deeply grieved the fact that he was never invited to his daughter's wedding, let alone given the honor of walking her down the aisle on her big day. Gavin was aware that his brain changes were already starting to impact his short-term memory and ability to communicate effectively, so he was anxious to find ways to begin to repair the damage of the past and to make amends with Allison before his cognition got even worse. He referred to this mindful healing process as "mending fences," and Gavin wanted to mend as many fences as possible with his firstborn child before his window of opportunity permanently closed.

During our second coaching call, we reviewed the different paths to reconciliation that Gavin hoped would move him closer to his goal of mending fences with Allison. He carefully weighed his options and decided to start by writing his daughter a letter. He was initially terrified of taking such an action step but agreed to at least try to put his thoughts on paper. After all, if the letter didn't turn out the way he wanted, he could always throw it away and start again.

On the day of our third virtual coaching appointment, I could immediately tell how raw and emotional Gavin was by his quavering voice and the wistful look in his eyes. He told me that he had spent many days composing a long letter to Allison and asked if he could review it with me during our call before he sent it off. Gavin proceeded to read the letter to me line by line and frequently had to stop and regroup when he became overcome with tears before he could continue.

Gavin told Allison how much he loved her and how his heart had broken wide open when they were estranged for all those years. He discussed the mistakes he had made by focusing his time and energy on building his successful business while simultaneously losing the love and respect of his wife and daughter in the process. Gavin divulged how he had covered up his feelings of inadequacy as a husband and father by hiding behind his job and by being heavy-handed with his family at home, when inside, he felt out of control, jealous of the bond between Allison and her mother, and pretty damned unlovable himself. Hearing Gavin describe the highly guarded behaviors of his emotional "old self" and then contrasting them with the image of the man before me, who was being vulnerable and transparent about his feelings to his daughter, brought me to tears as well.

In the letter, Gavin owned his mistakes of the past and told Allison how much he longed for an honest and "real relationship" with her while he still had the mental capacity to carry on a good conversation. Gavin told Allison how frightened he was about the memory problems that he'd been experiencing, which made it hard for him to find the words he wanted to say, to retain information that he had heard only a short time before, and to make sense of things when his mind would grow foggy at times. Gavin described how frustrating it was for him to constantly misplace his keys, his phone, and his wallet, and how embarrassing it was for him to run into people that he had known for decades and be unable to come up with their names or to talk with them "without fumbling around and looking like an idiot!"

For a man who had built his life, company, and reputation on being an articulate communicator with a mind like a steel trap and a memory for details, Alzheimer's was bringing Gavin to his knees. By the end of that coaching session, Gavin proclaimed that he felt ready to mail his letter to Allison— with the fervent wish that she would receive it in the spirit in which Gavin intended and with a prayer that, perhaps, she might even write him back.

When we met again for our next coaching session, Gavin was as excited as a little kid at Christmas! With a huge smile on his face, Gavin immediately told me that Allison had written a lengthy letter back to him within days, and he asked if he could share it with me. With tears of relief and joy streaming down his face, Gavin read his daughter's beautiful words to me, and I was again moved to tears. In the lines scrawled across the page, Allison forgave her dad for his errors of the past, told him how deeply painful it had been for her to make the heart-wrenching decision to shut her dad out of her life for all those years, and how her choices were fueled by "self-righteous anger" born of feeling "abused and abandoned" by the father whom she both loved and hated.

Allison went on to tell Gavin that the fault did not lie solely with him but that she had her own part to play in their distant relationship as well. Allison confided that she had noticed her dad's short-term memory changes, increased confusion, and word-finding problems during their intermittent phone calls over the last couple of years. She wrote about how these changes in her father "scared the hell out of her." Allison said she didn't know what to do about her suspicions that her dad was developing dementia. She didn't know how to bring up such a sensitive topic with the man who had always appeared to be in complete control of his life and who now seemed to be losing his hold on the most vital part of all—his mind. So, rather than trying to talk to her father about her concerns, Allison instead opted to retreat into avoidance and denial about her dad's cognitive changes, while secretly hoping that if she didn't acknowledge his deterioration to herself or anyone else, then she wouldn't have to admit that her father was slipping further away from her just when she finally longed for a close relationship with him. I couldn't help thinking what a cruel irony the timing of Gavin's Alzheimer's disease was for the two of them.

After reading the remainder of Allison's letter, Gavin looked up at me across the virtual computer screen and simply stated, "Kay, I think I can *live* now! I actually think I *can live!*" We sat in reverent silence for a minute and just let that thought hang in the air like a bright cloud of expectant hope on the horizon. The happiness and relief I saw reflected in Gavin's face was one of the most sacred perks of my job that I get to experience on occasion. Gavin had truly begun the process of mending fences with his daughter. He left his ego behind, admitted his mistakes and imperfections, and invited Allison into a real and honest relationship with him while there was still time left. As for Allison, she got the wonderful chance to start healing the broken bond with her father before the progressive brain changes of dementia made that goal impossible to achieve.

I can't be certain what will transpire in Gavin and Allison's relationship in the future, but I feel confident that the resolution they are both looking for will eventually come. The sheer magnitude of Gavin's love for his daughter, combined with his deep-seated intention for *true* reconciliation, is nothing short of amazing. However, it also gives me pause as I reflect upon my own history, actions, and relationships.

Are there still places in *my life* where I have become so hurt, resentful, or guarded that I am filled with self-righteous anger and blame and rendered an emotional hostage to my pain and insecurities? Are there acts of open-hearted vulnerability that *I* need to take in order to garner healing with those I love and cherish most before the precious commodity of time runs out? Are there fences *I* have to mend before my time on earth is through so that I don't live in remorse and regret at some later date?

These questions haunt me periodically and regularly invite me to take a deeper dive into reassessing my choices, behaviors, and values. They inspire me to be honest with myself about *how* I am living my life to ensure that I am in alignment with the qualities I honor and cherish most. Because of that, perhaps the most crucial question of all is this: What actions can I take *now* to live a more compassionate, loving, and authentic life so I don't ever have to concern myself with mending fences at all?

One Step Removed

"To Tom's way of thinking, Charlotte may legally be our stepparent, but she is not our mother, so therefore, she's not our problem!"

I received an email from my website contact form from a woman in South Carolina who had heard about my dementia coaching services from a friend of hers in Colorado. Sheila wrote that she was desperate for any help I could give her to deal with a complicated caregiving situation that she was involved in with her elderly father and stepmother who resided in a senior living apartment five miles away from her Charleston home. I immediately responded to Sheila's email and set up an introductory virtual coaching session for the following week.

In advance of our first appointment, I sent Sheila a caregiver coaching questionnaire for her to complete and return to me before our Zoom meeting so that I could gather as much history as possible about the challenges she was contending with in her family. The questionnaire also provided useful information designed to enable me to understand my new client's concerns and goals, as well as how to prioritize our time together during our upcoming coaching call. As I read the four pages of Sheila's responses, I learned about her dad's second marriage to Charlotte fifteen years before when Andrew was seventy and Charlotte was sixty-seven years old. Both had been widowed for almost two years when they were introduced to each other through mutual friends, and they tied the knot just seven months later. The remarriage came as a shock to Andrew and Charlotte's adult children, who never seriously entertained the possibility that either of their parents would choose to become partnered again, and the news of their decision to wed went over like a lead balloon on both sides of the aisle.

In vivid detail throughout the questionnaire, Sheila described the incredible animosity taking place within her family, as well as her mounting frustrations that no one had stepped up to help her with all of the tasks. Sheila was keenly aware that she couldn't sustain her current level of stress without dire consequences to her health, and she spoke to this concern on the coaching form by stating, "Being a caregiver for both my dad and his wife has been devastating on my emotional and physical well-being. I am less active, more depressed, and I cry all the time. I've become more reclusive, which isn't like me at all. I've developed high blood pressure and severe migraine headaches, which I never had in the past. Last week, I thought I was having acute heart problems, so I drove myself to the emergency room, only to discover that I was so stressed out I had the first panic attack of my entire life, which was a terrifying experience because it felt like I was literally going to die any moment. Something has *got* to change!"

Within fifteen minutes of meeting Sheila over my computer screen, her warm personality and Southern charm won me over, but they failed to mask the look of sheer exhaustion clearly displayed across her weary face. Sheila explained that her stepmother's doctor had diagnosed Charlotte with "mixed dementia," which he believed was related to an underlying Alzheimer's disease, combined with the trauma Charlotte had sustained following two brain surgeries she underwent years earlier to relieve the pressure caused by hydrocephalus ("water on the brain"). Sheila remarked that her dad's wife continuously asked the same questions, was unable to recall events that happened just a few minutes before, and had a lot of trouble operating her flip phone.

Even more concerning for Sheila were the changes she observed in Charlotte's personality: "She has never been an especially kind or considerate person the way my own mother always was, but now she's worse than ever! Charlotte has become extremely irritable and short-tempered and often accuses my eighty-five-year-old dad of having an affair with the upstairs neighbor in their building whom he doesn't even know. She refuses to leave their apartment unless it's to go to a doctor's appointment and pitches a fit if my dad is out of her sight for more than a minute. He's become so beat down and depressed by all of this, and it just kills me to see him that way because the father *I know* has always been the life of the party!"

As the discussion continued, Sheila confided that she was extremely worried about her father's health due to the constant stress he was under from caring for his wife. Sheila told me that her dad had minor memory problems himself but that his main problem was his bad heart. Andrew had already endured two significant heart attacks in the past five years, and he also suffered from diabetes, chronic back pain, neuropathy in his feet, and macular degeneration, which caused his vision to be quite poor. Andrew had experienced two significant falls in the previous six months that resulted in hospitalizations and brief stints in rehab facilities.

Sheila continued, "I was already spending at least twenty hours a week before Dad's falls, going grocery shopping for them, taking Dad and Charlotte to and from medical appointments, managing their finances, and keeping all my family members abreast of the latest dramas unfolding between them. But in recent months, I've been spending closer to thirty hours each week attending to all those tasks, and I am just plain *worn out*! 'Popo' tells me all the time that he's sorry I have to put my life on hold for theirs, and I assure him that I don't mind at all, even though I *really* do."

When I asked Sheila to give me more information about the difficult dynamics in her family, she became visibly angry for the first time. "Don't get me wrong, I love my brother and sister, but they aren't worth shit when it comes to lifting a finger to help me! They are both comfortably retired and live out of state in Florida, but we rarely ever see them. My sister Barb never had a close relationship with our dad and basically wants nothing to do with him now. My brother Tom was always Mom's favorite, and he's never really gotten over her death seventeen years ago, let alone the fact that our father remarried a woman none of us can stand. To Tom's way of thinking, Charlotte may legally be our stepparent, but she is not *our mother*, so therefore, she's *not our problem!* What my brother fails to realize is that when it comes to the caregiving situation I'm stuck dealing with, Dad's wife is *most certainly* a problem *for me!*"

Sheila explained that her stepmother has three daughters from her first marriage. "One of them lives across town in Charleston, and the others reside just two hours away in Savannah, Georgia, but you'd think they lived across the ocean for as much as they ever come around. Charlotte's oldest daughter hasn't set foot on this side of the Georgia line in three years, so she doesn't believe there's a damn thing wrong with her mom since she disregards everything I tell her that's going on, like it's just my imagination or something! Her other sister in Savannah thinks their mother should be moved out of the apartment and into a memory care facility because she assumes that Dad and I are doing a crappy job of caring for her, even though she has no concept of how much we *actually do* or how expensive such a move would be. Our parents don't have the kind of money in the bank to pay for memory care. I should know; I've handled all of their finances for years, and *trust me*, they sure as hell don't have an extra ten grand a month sitting around to pay for Charlotte to live someplace like that!

"And last but not least, there's Charlotte's youngest daughter, Daisy. She's a *piece of work* if there ever was one! Daisy is a kindergarten teacher who thinks she understands everything about dementia because she works with five-year-olds, but she is actually *clueless* and in total denial about how bad her mom has gotten. It doesn't help that she can't seem to spare fifteen minutes of her precious time to drive over and lay eyes on her flesh and blood more than once every three or four months! Popo tells me his biggest fear is that he is going to die before his wife does and that no one will take care of Charlotte after he is gone. I must admit, he's got *good reason* to worry 'cause it's not like people are lining up for the job now!"

As our first coaching session drew to a close, I was struck by how many care partners I've worked with over the years who found themselves entrenched in similar caregiving situations due to the later-life remarriages or other choices made by the people who raised them. I've witnessed hundreds of adult children who never bonded with or even remotely *accepted* the new stepparent in their life and therefore, never felt like they had to take on any responsibility for their well-being—*especially* after their own family member had passed away. These complex relational dynamics would be challenging enough for anyone to navigate, but when you add the distressing element of dementia to the caregiving picture, things can get *even more* convoluted in a hurry.

From my perspective, it is often the Sheilas of the world who get the shortest end of the stick in these disconcerting predicaments. Because she was willing to bear the brunt of the caregiving burden for her dad and step-mom out of a sense of love and duty for so long, Sheila became a dependable scapegoat of sorts for her family members. They both relied on and blamed her for any issues that came up as they simultaneously washed their hands of any true responsibility for the welfare of either of their parents. And when someone like Sheila reaches the end of their rope and sends out distress signals, begging for assistance from others before they go under, it is often a caregiving ghost town they find awaiting them on the horizon instead of the cavalry coming to help.

I knew that I had my work cut out for me to coach this dedicated and exhausted daughter during the months ahead. We would spend our sessions brainstorming ways to engage her brother and sister, as well as her step-siblings, in the caregiving effort. We would strive to reduce the amount of stress that Sheila was experiencing by strategically delegating some of the workload onto other family members and professional caregivers whenever possible. We would create healthier boundaries for Sheila to maintain and find creative ways to improve her self-care regime while she continued to oversee her parents' daily needs, thereby mitigating the risks to her own health in the process. And finally, we would identify the specific kinds of emotional support and education Sheila needed most in order to feel confident and empowered as a care partner, rather than depleted and desperate. Because, in the end, vulnerable adults like Charlotte and Andrew may seem one step removed, depending on one's point of view, but their *very real* problems are always better off shared than ignored.

He Was My Rock

*"I guess when it comes down to it, I miss my relationship
with my husband more than just about anything else."*

I received an email from a person wanting more information about my
dementia coaching services. The correspondence came from a woman who
had been referred to me by a friend in her church community. Miranda
wanted to set up a time for us to talk on the phone, as she was hoping I would
be able to provide help to her family to understand her dad's Alzheimer's
disease and to learn how the family could provide better overall support to
both of her parents. Miranda was particularly worried about the impact the
caregiving stress was having on her seventy-year-old mother, Sonja, who
was becoming increasingly anxious and overwhelmed with the demands of
caring for her husband, Dirk, who was four years her senior.

The following week, I spent thirty minutes on the phone with Miranda,
gathering basic background information about her parents and discussing
her hopes and fears regarding her father's progressing dementia and the ripple
effects it was having on her mother's mental and physical health. We set up a
ninety-minute introductory coaching session a few days later with Miranda
and her only brother, Michael, over Zoom. During that call, I learned that
Dirk and Sonja had immigrated to the United States from Belgium in their

early twenties. Miranda's parents had always taken great pride in the fact that they came to this country with only fifty dollars and the clothes on their backs, yet they went on to become highly successful in their family-owned construction business where both Miranda and Michael had been employed in the past.

Miranda explained that her dad had been diagnosed with Alzheimer's disease in 2019 by a neurologist in Denver. The family first became aware that Dirk was having memory changes after Sonja had experienced a serious illness a few years before. After going through countless rounds of chemotherapy and radiation for her breast cancer, Sonja was unable to take care of her home and husband in the same way she had previously, so Miranda and Michael stepped in to help. They began to notice that their dad's speech was becoming more repetitive, he struggled to stay on top of all his wife's medical bills, and he occasionally got lost in familiar places when he drove. After Dirk was formally diagnosed with Alzheimer's disease, the family took away his car keys at the strong urging of the neurologist after informing Dirk that it was no longer safe for him to drive. Since that time, the family has had to repeat that conversation at least weekly, but he is incapable of recalling it for more than a few hours afterward due to the damage the dementia has caused in his brain.

Michael described his father as an avid outdoorsman who always loved to hike, fish, and camp in the mountains of Colorado. Even well into his seventies, Michael would go backpacking for a week or two alone in the Rockies, one of his greatest joys in life. Two years prior to Miranda outreaching me, Dirk was found by search-and-rescue teams after getting lost in a national forest for three days. The trail he had hiked a dozen times before suddenly looked unfamiliar to him, and Dirk became disoriented. He was found ten miles away from his intended destination—safe but incredibly confused and frightened about what had transpired and with no idea *why* such a thing had happened to someone like him.

By the end of our coaching session, Miranda and Michael asked if we could schedule future sessions on a one-to-one basis with Sonja only. They felt that Sonja was the one who needed the most caregiver support and coaching around her partner's illness. They explained that they first needed to convince her that working with me was a good idea since Sonja tended to be extremely private and hadn't told a soul outside of her immediate family that the love of her life was living with Alzheimer's disease.

I'm not sure what magical words Miranda and her brother used to persuade their mom to try virtual coaching with me, but two weeks later, we had our first Zoom session together. Just one look at Sonja's tense and worried face on my computer screen spoke volumes about how nervous she was in that initial meeting. For someone who was used to holding her cards close and was unaccustomed to sharing personal information with "outsiders," this was an exceptionally difficult process for her to engage in. But slowly over the hour, Sonja began to visibly relax as she told me about her background, marriage, and worries about Dirk. Sonja shared with me that after her husband had been diagnosed with Alzheimer's disease in the doctor's office, they had made a promise to each other that neither of them would ever speak of the "A word" again but would refer to Dirk's illness as "dementia" instead—a term they felt was somehow less threatening or taboo to mention.

Sonja tearfully explained that she and Dirk had always had a "wonderful kind of love affair" full of deep affection, fun, and mutual respect. She said that Dirk was her best friend and the rock on which she built her life. "I could always talk to Dirk about *anything* that was going on with me, and he always understood how to help me. Now, I have no one to share with because my husband can't remember the things I tell him for more than a few minutes, and I'm so lonely, even though he's still here with me. I know that sounds crazy, but it's true! I guess when it comes down to it, I miss *my relationship* with my husband more than just about anything else. I'm not sure how this 'coaching business' can really help me deal with all these challenges, but my kids think that it is a good idea, and you don't seem so bad, after all."

I broke out laughing and thanked Sonja for her vote of confidence and for her willingness to allow me the opportunity to help support her on her caregiving journey. Before our call ended, Sonja said she would talk to Miranda and Michael about setting up more sessions with me so she could "see if this coaching thing can actually make me feel any better or not. It certainly wasn't as bad as I thought it would be!" Sonja was clearly no easy sell, but I was thankful I had earned enough of her trust during our first meeting that she was willing to give me a second chance.

Over the next eighteen months, Sonja and I regularly met over Zoom to discuss, process, and strategize around her current caregiving stressors with Dirk and how to make small changes and adjustments aimed at increasing her caregiver confidence and skills while also decreasing the overall stress in their home. One theme we frequently hit on was how exhausting it can be to care for someone with dementia.

"I am tired all the time. I have to sleep with one eye open because I never know if Dirk will get up in the night and start rummaging through things or try to leave the house. I feel like I can never let my guard down with him, and I am constantly fatigued from having to do all the thinking for both of us these days. Dirk used to fix *everything* that ever broke in our house. For fifty years, I never had to depend on anyone but him. But now, he can't even remember how to replace a battery in the smoke detector, so *everything* is on me to figure out, and I've never been worth a damn at any of that stuff to begin with!"

Another topic we frequently addressed was the importance of asking for and accepting help, which also included being willing to let people know about Dirk's dementia so others could be of assistance. This was a tall order for Sonja to consider based on her experiences as an immigrant to this country: "As an immigrant, you are forced to adjust to a whole new language, life, and culture and to the prejudices against you based on nothing more than how you look or where you came from. Dirk and I spent our lives crawling out of holes over and over again—trying to prove that we *belong* here just like everyone else. I don't want my precious husband to be judged because of his dementia, so I try to keep it a secret to protect him. But I also feel weak because I can't seem to crawl out of the same holes all by myself. I just fall off the cliff instead—except for those times when my kids or you catch me."

One experience that Sonja most grieved about her husband's cognitive changes and functional abilities was that they could no longer have long, meaningful conversations like they'd enjoyed throughout their marriage. Sonja admitted to wallowing in self-pity at times but would then immediately chastise herself by thinking, "Why am I complaining when Dirk is *still here*? I should *be happy* that he is alive, but I don't always *feel* that way. I have guilt for even having those thoughts, but you help me to see that they are normal under these difficult circumstances, and I am grateful for that."

I introduced Sonja to the concept of "ambiguous loss"—a term that was coined by psychologist Pauline Boss to describe when people are still *physically* present with us but are no longer able to be socially or psychologically engaged in the way they historically interacted before their dementia. I explained the concept to Sonja like this: "When someone dies, there are typically built-in rituals like memorial services or wakes that mark the person's passing that serve to bring a sense of closure to those of us left behind. But we don't get that same sense of communal support or closure when someone we love is living with an advanced dementia because they are *still here* in the physical sense—even though, in many respects, they are also simultaneously *gone from us* because of the changes caused by their neurological disease."

Sonja nodded her head in agreement as I spoke—as if the unrelated dots were finally connecting. In the past, Sonja had volunteered for a number of agencies that served people with mental and physical disabilities, so she thought she *knew* what was in store for her when Dirk received his dementia diagnosis. But after our discussion, she realized that being a professional caregiver for other people who were disabled in some way was an entirely different animal than slowly losing the love of your life to a disease like Alzheimer's—especially when no one around her seemed to *truly understand* the losses she was dealing with daily.

As we talked further, Sonja disclosed that, although she had begun to let others know about Dirk's dementia and the changes to their lives, it was still challenging. "My friends who are taking care of a family member with other illnesses like cancer, heart disease, or lung disease think they *know* what I am going through with Dirk, but in reality, they don't *get it* at all! *Their* loved ones aren't forgetting the names of people they've known for decades or thinking they are living in another state or country other than the one they're in, and they aren't struggling to remember how to do basic tasks like dressing them-selves or using a razor because of their memory loss. On the rare occasions when people even ask me how *I'm doing* instead of always inquiring about Dirk, what am I supposed to tell them—that I feel *like shit* today?! Nobody wants to know that! So instead, I act like a clown and hide behind my mask. People think I am happy and doing well, when inside, I'm really falling apart."

As the months went by, it became more obvious that Sonja needed to have some breaks from her caregiving duties because of the increased stress, anxiety, and social isolation she was experiencing. But being in the midst of a global pandemic made finding such respite nearly impossible since all adult day programs for people with dementia had shut down, and hiring agency staff to come into their home felt too risky for Sonja because of her fear of contracting COVID. We dedicated one of our coaching sessions to brainstorming respite options Sonja would feel comfortable with, given the complexity of the situation. She finally decided she would ask an acquain-tance of theirs from church to come spend time with Dirk for a few hours on a Saturday so she could get away for some window-shopping and lunch with an old friend while Dirk was safely occupied at home. When Sonja later informed her husband of the plan, he was savvy enough in that moment to say, "That makes no sense at all! You are *inviting someone* over to our house, and then you are *leaving*?! That's the craziest thing I've ever heard of!"

During our next coaching session, Sonja told me that while she was at lunch with her friend, she became increasingly anxious and unable to focus on her meal or the conversation that was taking place because of her racing thoughts. Sonja was worried sick about what was happening at home with Dirk and was utterly distracted by the fear gripping her body. It was the first time she had physically been away from her spouse in over eighteen months. "It was just too drastic for me. It was like suddenly going from lukewarm water into freezing water. The shock was too much for me to handle all at once."

As a result of that painful learning experience, we developed a plan for Sonja to take shorter, more frequent caregiving breaks so she could get accustomed to not being constantly responsible for Dirk's well-being. Those respite opportunities, combined with other caregiving techniques and strategies that Sonja employed as a result of our coaching sessions, had a positive effect on Sonja's life, enhancing her ability to cope with the stressors of caregiving. Sonja decided to take a break from coaching since she felt she had gleaned sufficient skills and support to be more effective with her husband and to take better care of herself.

During our last session, Sonja recounted the benefits she received during the year and a half we had worked together. She shared that she had learned a great deal about the multitude of brain changes Dirk underwent because of his Alzheimer's disease. Sonja described how that newfound knowledge enabled her to be more thoughtful and successful in terms of the approach she used with Dirk, as well as to have more realistic expectations of both herself and her husband as his dementia continued to progress over time. Sonja told me how happy she was that her relationship with her husband had improved because she learned to break her self-imposed isolation by telling other people about Dirk's illness and the challenges they were facing and to reach out to others for help and support when she needed it. In addition, Sonja had become more compassionate with herself when she wasn't a perfect wife or caregiver, and to laugh at Dirk's mistakes instead of getting so impatient or angry with him for doing or saying things that were outside of his control due to his dementia. But the most valuable takeaway of all for Sonja was learning how to place her attention on what she and Dirk *still had left* rather than putting all of her focus on the losses they had accumulated along the way.

As we prepared to end our final coaching call, Sonja tearfully told me that "Talking to you has helped me so much. I always learn new things every time we meet, but the best thing is that you *really understand* what I am going through with Dirk, when most people don't comprehend the realities of our lives whatsoever. After spending an hour with you, I feel so much lighter— like I can go on with my day, knowing that I have given all of my burdens to you so I don't have to worry anymore."

In that tender moment, I was overcome with deep gratitude for Sonja's kind words and for the work I get to do as a dementia coach and educator. I have come a long way to arrive in this place, and I feel extremely blessed by the journey that led me here and by the people like Dirk and Sonja who continue to inspire me to keep growing my skills and passion so that I can support as many people as possible through my work, while hopefully making the world just a little better in the process.

Coming Full Circle

"That's not my mother! My mother died seven
years ago when the dementia hit. I don't even know
who the woman in that bed is right now!"

I t was a Tuesday afternoon, and I was on my way to meet a new patient who had just been admitted to hospice twenty-four hours earlier. Lucy could have easily qualified for our services a long time before then, but as so commonly happens in this industry, people are referred to hospice so late in their disease process that the hospice team is only able to provide their specialized brand of palliative care to terminally ill patients for a few hours, days, or weeks before they die instead of up to six months as allowed under the hospice Medicare benefit. I knew by reading the admission report on Lucy that her Alzheimer's disease was so advanced that she would be making her "celestial discharge" to Heaven before our team had much of a chance to support her or her family through all the ups and downs inherently involved with the dying process.

When I located the room number for Lucy's apartment in the memory care wing, I found that she was not alone. In a chair next to Lucy's hospital bed sat her only daughter, Justine. After hearing my knock at the door, Justine got up to greet me, and I could immediately feel her immense grief permeate the room and see the deep sadness in her green eyes. I introduced myself as the hospice social worker and asked if it would be okay if I came in and visited for a bit.

Justine seemed relieved by the distraction and immediately led me over to the bedside to introduce me to her mother. Lucy was curled up in a semi-fetal position with her eyes and mouth closed tightly to the outside world around her. Justine explained to me that her mom had not opened her eyes or responded to anyone or anything in her environment for the last few days. "It's like Mom is still here, but at the same time, she's already gone. The hospice nurse told me that Mom can still hear me, but she has slipped into a coma now, so she can't respond to anything I say or do. I never knew dying could take so long or be this grueling!"

After she uttered that last sentence, Justine started crying so hard that her whole body began to shake. I suggested that we move into the living room on the other side of the apartment, where we could sit and talk more comfortably away from her mother, and Justine nodded her head in agreement. After this grieving daughter was able to calm down enough to speak again, she picked up a photo album from the coffee table. She had put together the album for her mom as a "memory book." Justine repositioned herself on the sofa so I could also view the pages and proceeded to flip through decades' worth of images of her vibrant and beautiful mother smiling and waving at the camera like she didn't have a care in the world.

When Justine came to the last photo in the album that had been taken only eight years before, she looked over at her mom across the room and said: "That's not *my mother* in that bed over there! *My mother* died seven years ago when the dementia hit. I don't even *know* who the woman in that bed is right now! The parent who raised me has been slowly disappearing little by little right before my eyes for such a long time that all that remains of her is that tiny, withered body under the covers—just waiting to be released from this world. It's the most difficult thing I've ever been through, and *no one*, not even my mom's doctor, warned me how excruciating it could be or how it could change *every* aspect of our wonderful relationship, and of our lives."

Justine told me more details about the incredible bond she had shared with her mother and how devastating it had been for her to slowly lose her mother to a disease as cruel and unforgiving as Alzheimer's can be. For over two years, Lucy had not been able to recognize Justine as her daughter and had lost the ability to communicate her thoughts or feelings in any discernible way because of her dying brain. Justine described how isolating her caregiving journey had become because of how the people closest to her could not relate to or understand the trials she had been through with her mom.

Her friends and coworkers offered up their "well-meaning but useless advice" regarding how they thought she should handle her mother, when none of them had ever met someone who had dementia, let alone had ever cared for anyone with that illness. "They have absolutely *no idea* what my family and I are going through, and yet they seem to think they have the license to tell me what I should be doing with my own flesh and blood in spite of that! It is infuriating and such a damned lonely place to be!"

As she described all the losses she and her mother had endured for years because of Alzheimer's disease, Justine began crying in earnest again, and the pain emanating from her body was so visceral that I could almost feel it penetrate my own skin. Years of pent-up emotions came pouring out of her like a flooded river over-running its banks. She reached out to hug me, and my shoulder was soon soaked with her salty, wet tears. When we eventually walked back across the apartment to her mother's bed, I began to slowly see dementia in a whole new light.

I had worked in hospice less than a year by that time, and I was still too inexperienced and naïve to grasp the profound consequences that a disease like Alzheimer's has on a person who is living with it, or the ripple effects it can have on their family members and caregivers. Up until then, most of the patients I had encountered with dementia were in the latter stages of their illness, so I never personally witnessed the countless changes and losses those individuals had gone through for seven, ten, or even twenty years leading up to their deaths. I had only met them at the end of their long lives and often knew almost nothing about how they had lived, loved, or contributed to the world in their distinctive ways. That visit woke me up to the fact that I needed to learn as much as I could about the backgrounds of the patients I cared for in hospice, and I needed to change my personal social work practice as a result of that newfound awareness.

Because of the powerful lessons I gleaned from sitting bedside with Justine and Lucy, I gradually started to ask the families I worked with more questions about the history of their loved ones when the patients themselves were no longer able to remember or tell me. I began to probe more deeply during my conversations with families in order to understand how they had navigated all the dementia-related losses in their lives and how I could best support each of them in their grief based on that knowledge. In retrospect, it took me years of on-the-job training, error-activated learning, and a whole lot of specialized instruction in a variety of settings before I was able to hone my clinical skills to the point where I could effectively counsel and educate care partners around this often cruel and misunderstood illness.

My last twenty years spent as a social worker in hospice, the memory clinic, and palliative care ignited a passion in me around the disease of dementia that spread over time into a raging wildfire. The work changed me from the inside out—and for the better. Bearing witness to the ongoing emotional, physical, psychological, and financial burdens that families have to deal with in relative isolation has given me great empathy and insight into the crucial roles these caregivers play every day. My yearning to tap into the unmet needs of such richly deserving and overlooked caregivers accelerated over time, and I longed to apply my years of experience and unbridled enthusiasm to serve as a vessel of hope and healing for them all. I pined for the freedom to do more than just attend a few bedside, clinic, or home visits allotted by my employers when it was crystal clear to me that these overwhelmed and wonderful individuals needed *far more* ongoing and sustainable support than the systems I worked within were willing or able to provide.

I energetically felt as if The Universe were *pulling me* further and further away from my traditional nine-to-five job and *pushing me* out of my comfort zone so I could create a unique and better way of ministering to dementia caregivers. Observing the huge gaps that exist around providing adequate support and education to this population firsthand has further fueled my desire to dedicate my time and energy to patients and their loved ones living with dementia by improving their lives in meaningful ways.

Establishing my company, Compassion Works, in 2017 was the culmination of a dream for me. Looking back, I could have never imagined that all those past experiences would one day lead me to found my own coaching and training business, but it's by far the favorite "job" I've ever had and has become my mission and life's work. On my rough days when I feel like giving up or doing something "easier" with my career, I think of Lucy and Justine and the countless other patients and families who have been my most exquisite teachers and mentors over the past two decades. Their stories and memories continue to inspire me to keep moving ahead so I can provide high-quality services to families like theirs with compassion instead of indifference, with empathy instead of judgment, and with sound guidance instead of unwanted advice that they've so often been accustomed to receiving in its place.

At the end of the day, I hope the people I work with *know* that I truly "get it" when they tell me, out of a place of unadulterated grief, "That's not *my mother* in that bed over there." I hope they are able to *feel* the profound level of respect I have for them as care partners and to realize that I *see and honor* the messy, painful, and beautiful complexity of their humanity that I am humbled to be a part of.

Hitting Too Close to Home

"Kay, you are welcome to use my story in your book
if you think it would help anyone who may read it. I
only ask that you please don't use my name."

During my time in hospice, I worked as part of an interdisciplinary team made up of doctors, pharmacists, nurses, social workers, chaplains, nursing assistants, and trained volunteers. But within that larger team, our staff also functioned in smaller subsets typically comprised of a nurse, social worker, nurse aide, and a chaplain. I was often part of two or three such "mini-teams." As a result, I was fortunate to work with a cross section of colleagues in my work, and a few of them became some of my best friends.

I have never been in the military or in any situation that could be remotely compared to battle, but having worked with countless veterans of war over the course of my career, I've learned a great deal from them about the incredible bonds that commonly form among troops who serve in combat together. People who spend intense time with one another "in the trenches" seem to have a propensity for forming deep and long-lasting relationships with those around them who share the same experiences. Facing life and death together on a daily basis has a way of enriching friendships like no other kind of encounter can, and working in hospice most definitely fit that definition. That's why many of the people I worked with became more like family to me than colleagues or friends. One of them, whom I will refer to as Emma, was a team member I became close to, despite the fifteen-year age span between us.

Although Emma occasionally worked in tandem with a few other social workers on our team, I was the primary one she collaborated with during the seven years we spent together. Many of my social work peers tended to shy away from being paired up with Emma, as they were admittedly a bit intimidated to be partnered with her because she had a reputation for being direct and outspoken. She also held high standards for herself and her teammates.

I wasn't apprehensive in the least about being assigned as her social worker. After all the years I had spent working in corrections, I found Emma's straight-shooting yet warm and compassionate approach with patients and families refreshingly fun and easy to be around. Besides, working with someone who had such a deep sense of personal and professional integrity was invigorating to me after all the dishonesty and corruption I'd witnessed in my previous occupation.

Emma came to hospice toward the end of her long nursing career. She described feeling called to work in end-of-life care before she retired. She was relatively new to her role when we met, but that fact wasn't obvious—Emma adjusted to it as if she had been doing this work her whole life. As a hospice nurse, Emma exuded confidence, compassion, efficiency, and a quick wit that easily won over the patients, families, and facility staff members with whom we worked. Over time, the partnership and bond Emma and I formed was like a well-oiled machine. It got to the point where we could start and finish each other's sentences because we instinctively *knew* what the other person was going to say before they even uttered a single word, and at other times, language wasn't even necessary for us to communicate. It made working together a rich, delightful, and rewarding experience, and as a team, we were hard to beat because of that special dynamic.

My dad was nearing the end of his cancer journey when Emma and I met, and she was incredibly supportive of me during my grief leading up to his death—and long after he had passed. She was always available to listen when I needed to talk, to give me a hug when I was sad, and to be my friend through the ups and downs of losing such a significant person in my life. Likewise, I was there to offer support to Emma during her mom's long decline from Alzheimer's disease, as well as the events leading up to her dad's death. Going through those personal experiences together, while simultaneously companioning people who were sick and dying in hospice, only served to deepen the bond between us.

Emma broke the news to me of her plans to retire as I was preparing to start three months of maternity leave shortly before our son, Eli, was born. The timing ironically coincided in such a way that Emma would retire from hospice about the same time I would return to work after my leave. The idea of returning to my job after an extended absence and adjusting to work with a brand-new nurse was a depressing thought for me to entertain and one that weighed heavily upon me the whole time I was home with our new baby.

As luck would have it, The Universe had other plans in store for me, and I ended up staying at hospice for only a few months after my maternity leave ended before I started my new position as a mental health therapist for a health maintenance organization. As hard as it was for me to leave a job I loved, I must admit that my departure was easier because Emma had already retired.

Emma and I have remained close friends over the past decade. We frequently talk on the phone, meet up for meals, have deep conversations, and always share a lot of laughs each time we connect. But when the COVID pandemic began in the spring of 2020 and the world went on lockdown for months, Emma and I went for almost a year without seeing each other in person, even though we only live a few minutes apart in adjoining suburbs.

In the fall of 2021, Emma texted me. She wanted to know if I had time to meet up for breakfast the following week. I immediately responded that I would love to see her and asked if she would like me to extend the invitation to our mutual friend and retired hospice nurse colleague, Karen, who lived nearby as well. Emma texted back that she would like to have me all to herself for a change. Instantly, I knew that something significant was going on with my dear friend.

The following week, I had an uneasy feeling in the pit of my stomach as I drove toward the restaurant where Emma and I frequently met for breakfast. After hugging each other, getting seated at our table, and catching Emma up on the progress of my book, things took an unforeseen turn. Emma pulled a typed letter out of her purse and laid it on the table in front of me, along with a package of Kleenex to wipe away the tears that had begun to stream down her face.

The letter had been compiled at Emma's request by her husband and their three daughters. My dear friend tearfully explained that each of her family members had brought up concerns to her about the memory changes they had each observed in Emma over the previous year. Emma told me she had received the letter weeks ago, but she had been too depressed to call me—even though her family had strongly urged her to do so.

I scanned the letter that lay before me on the table. I read the descriptive words Emma's husband and daughters had written about their worries regarding changes they'd witnessed in Emma's short-term memory, listening skills, and attention span, as well as mood changes over the past twelve months. My friend explained that she had asked her family to write down their thoughts on paper because she honestly didn't understand *why* they were all so concerned about her when the subtle memory changes she was aware of in herself all seemed like "normal aging" to her and not anything to get worked up about.

Emma pointed to the burgundy sweater she was wearing and half-heartedly joked, "Look! My sweater isn't on backward. I must be okay!" and then told me about the first red flag she had witnessed with her mother before anyone knew she had Alzheimer's disease. Emma's mom had come to Colorado for a visit from out of state and was invited to attend a family outing to watch one of her great-grandsons play soccer. Emma's mother had been the kind of woman who took great pride in her appearance, but on the day of the soccer game, she arrived clad in dirty, wrinkled, mismatched clothing, and Emma shared with me how deeply embarrassed she had been about her mother's appearance. It was only later when her mom was diagnosed with dementia that Emma realized the cause of her mom's social faux pas back at the soccer field.

As so often happens when we retrace the elusive steps of an illness as insidious as Alzheimer's, it is only in retrospect that we can see the origins of the subtle brain changes that quietly began their silent destructive march years before. Emma knew *exactly* what dementia looked like from seeing it in her own family and in the hundreds of patients we had cared for in hospice. She did *not* want to venture down that same path herself because she knew *exactly* where it led, and it was *no place* she wanted to go.

As we talked further, Emma told me she was aware of occasionally forgetting someone's name or of misplacing things around the house, but other than that, she thought her cognitive changes went along with being in her late seventies. As a result, it was shocking for Emma to see in writing a letter that outlined in painstaking detail her loved ones' collective concerns. She told me she had been angry with her husband and daughters for weeks and had spent hours each day crying ever since. Emma said she was contemplating a call to her doctor to see if he could double her antidepressant prescription because she was feeling so deflated and hopeless about her future.

One theme highlighted in the letter was what Emma's family noticed about the conversations that took place with her—she no longer seemed to be as engaged in conversations as she had been previously. They noted that Emma often seemed more checked out or disinterested and would ask questions about subjects her family members had just been talking about only a short time before.

Emma looked at me and said, "I find myself really listening at the beginning of a conversation, but then I kind of get lost and drift away in my own thoughts after a while. So, when I realize that I have been off in my own world and not tuned in to what people around me have been talking about, of course, I have to ask a lot of questions. But then everyone gets upset with me and says things like, 'Mom, I just told you that, don't you remember?!' I always feel like shit when that happens! It's so embarrassing! I think I may be developing ADD at my ripe old age! Do you think that's possible, Kay?"

I looked across the table at my friend and asked her why she had invited me to breakfast that day. Did she just want to share the letter with me, or did she want to discuss her worries and get my feedback as well? I asked how I could be most helpful to her in this distressing time. Emma quickly responded, "Of course, I want your feedback! That's why I wanted you all to myself this morning. Tell me what you think."

I started out by saying that the information she had just shared was hitting way too close to home for me. It was one thing to work with people I had no past histories or personal ties with, but quite another to hear such heartbreaking news from my beloved comrade who was like a sister to me. I told Emma what an excellent hospice nurse she had been and how she always had such a wonderful and comforting bedside manner with the patients and families we worked with over the years.

I continued, "Emma, you've had a mind like a steel trap for as long as I've known you and have always been an incredibly skilled listener—both as a professional and as a friend. The differences in your ability to listen, retain information, and stay engaged in conversations that your family is describing are a marked change from how I have known you to be for the past twenty years. To me, that is definitely a cause for concern."

Emma's eyes immediately filled with tears. "Damnit!" she said. "I was afraid you were going to say that." And she began to cry even harder. In an effort to bring a little levity to such an intensely sad moment, I quipped, "I can tell you one thing for certain. When you and I used to work together, you sure as hell *never forgot* all the tasks you wanted me to accomplish for you on any given day, my friend," and we both broke out laughing in relieved unison.

I learned how Emma had come to rely more and more on her calendar and on the alarm settings on her phone to alert her to the tasks she had to do so she wouldn't forget. She also admitted that she was withdrawing more at church and in other social situations where she feared that others might notice she wasn't tracking as well as she used to. Emma explained that she would rather pull back from being around people than worry that they might notice something is amiss with her brain. When I asked my longtime buddy what frightened her the most, she replied, "I'm scared that if people know I'm having memory problems, they are going to treat me differently, and I don't want that to happen."

I told Emma that based on my experience, I believe the benefits of being open and transparent with others regarding an individual's memory concerns far outweigh the risks of becoming isolated for fear of being treated differently. "My friend, the truth is that people who are close to you *will notice* the changes in you whether you tell them or not. They may even be *more aware* of them than you are, which is a common symptom of brain change; the person going through it is often the last one to know. But, here's the thing. If you try to keep this all a secret, then the people around you will just make up *their own* reasons why they think you aren't paying attention or able to remember things the way you used to, and their conjectures may be completely off base. If you can be courageous enough to have more conversations like the one you're having with me today, then that will help the people closest to you understand the challenges you're facing and how to support you and your family in the best way possible. Emma, you don't have to go through this alone. You've dedicated your entire life to serving others. Now it's time to let people help *you* for a change."

After a lengthy pause, Emma finally said, "Maybe we could set up a Zoom meeting between you and my family after the holidays so we can all talk openly about what's going on and get on the same page in terms of what we should do next in this process?" I told her that I would be happy to help out in any way I could but that the *most important* role I hoped to play in her life was being her *friend* over anything else.

Emma's whole affect seemed to immediately change and soften. It was as if a huge burden had been lifted off her shoulders, at least for a time. She joyfully exclaimed, "Kay, look how well I'm doing today! I made it more than an hour talking to you before I had *any* word-finding problems at all! How awesome is that?" I celebrated that small but mighty victory with Emma and thanked her for trusting me enough to share her grief and difficult news with me.

Then, I decided to capitalize on that moment by poking fun at what our futures might hold. "I can just see it now, Emma. If you and I end up with dementia, you'll be like one of those old, retired nurses we used to have on hospice in the nursing home. You'll be stealing the med cart from behind the nurse's station and trying to push people around in their wheelchairs when they don't want to go anywhere! And I'll be over in the corner, trying to comfort patients who I think are distraught—oblivious to the fact that they don't *want* my help and not picking up on their social cues when they try to bat me away with their oxygen tanks! And God *help us* if you get *even more* stubborn than you already are in your old age! What the hell will we do with you *then?*"

We began to laugh so hard that tears streamed down our faces as we pondered those tragic but comical images of ourselves at some distant day and time. We laughed so hard, in fact, that the customers seated around us turned to see what all the commotion was about since only a few minutes earlier, tears of grief had been flowing freely at our table.

After our fits of laughter finally subsided, Emma's demeanor became more serious once again. She reached over and placed her hand on top of mine and softly said, "Kay, you are welcome to use my story in your book if you think it would help anyone who might read it. I only ask that you please don't use my name."

I was struck once again, as I'd been countless times before, by my dear friend's selflessness and generosity of spirit when it came to helping her fellow travelers on the road of life. To me, Emma exemplifies the *hope* we all have in our hearts when facing our uncertain futures, the *healing* that can happen when we are courageous and vulnerable enough to risk sharing our deepest fears and grief with one another, and the unmistakable thread of *humanity* that connects us all, despite our perceived differences, abilities, and histories.

Whatever the future may hold for my beloved friend, or for any of us who may one day face a life-threatening illness or situation that we never imagined possible, I sincerely hope we can all find the fortitude within ourselves to lovingly bear witness to each other's pain and to hold it with the respect, gentleness, and reverence it deserves. After all, as poet Mark Nepo so wisely reminds us, "Walk long enough, and we all trade places."

AFTERWORD

Freedom

*"The exquisite gifts I have received in the process of becoming
a 'bedside witness' are far better than any I could have
ever imagined manifesting in my social work career."*

As I reflect on my tenure as a social worker and clinician, I think back to what led me there in the first place. My time spent working with wayward youth at Lookout Mountain all those many years ago was the impetus for me to move into my life's work, and I'm grateful for it. I can still *almost feel* the bubbling tension, distrust, animosity, and misdirected anger that seemed to seep out of every nook and cranny of the Lookout Mountain facility, despite the incredible efforts of the dedicated staff who were employed there. Over time, I began to find it nearly impossible to make any substantial inroads with the juvenile offenders on my caseload, as every new kid who was court-ordered to our program for up to five years seemed more troubled and full of rage than the last. It was an endless source of stress for me, and the long-term consequences of that job left me emotionally drained, spiritually depleted, and cynical to the core. Psychologically, working within such an adversarial "us versus them" system almost killed me.

I remember facilitating a violent offender group by myself one day when suddenly, two boys in the class started arguing, "mean-mugging" each other (making threatening facial gestures), and puffing out their chests in an aggressive fashion. Before I could even say a word to intervene, they had whipped off their T-shirts, jumped across the table at one another, and proceeded to get in an all-out brawl right in the middle of our treatment room. I knew in that instant that I desperately needed to find another line of work, but I also had no idea what else I would do since I had spent the previous decade working in three different settings with high-risk teens. By my late thirties, I already felt stuck in terms of job options—if only in my head.

One of the young men on my caseload was named Shawn. Like most kids in my cottage, Shawn was a "violent offender," who, at age seventeen, had experienced more trauma and hardships than *any* child should ever have to face. All that Shawn knew about his father was that he had walked out on Shawn and his mom when Shawn was two and had spent most of his life locked up in a state prison somewhere. Shawn's mother had resorted to prostitution to pay the bills, and she became addicted to drugs and alcohol to cope. She was eventually charged with child neglect and abuse, and her five children were removed from the home by Child Protective Services and placed in foster care. Twenty-two failed foster placements later, Shawn found belonging in a street gang, and he got involved in committing serious crimes for years before he eventually ended up in the facility where I was employed.

To say that Shawn was fueled by rage is a gross understatement. He could be provoked into fighting by a simple look, gesture, or word, or by seemingly nothing at all besides his own distorted perception of "reality." Shawn's brain was in a constant fight-or-flight mode from years spent in literal survival, upheaval, and uncertainty. He operated on two major guiding principles: that no adult should *ever* be trusted and that "it's always better to get them before they get you" when it came to navigating his challenging peer relationships.

Everything else in Shawn's life was secondary to that belief system. It was the code of honor by which he firmly lived and, in all likelihood, would probably die.

Shawn went through a period over a couple of months where he got into at least two or three fistfights a week with other residents during his school day. He was constantly expelled from the classroom and sent back to the isolation room (think jail cell) in the cottage where my office was located. My supervisor decided Shawn was so out of control that he met the rare criteria of being placed on a restrictive regimen, which was referred to as a "special program."

As Shawn's appointed in-house mental health counselor, the program was the bane of my existence. There was a ridiculously long list of tasks that had to be completed and documented daily on Shawn's behalf, which I was put in charge of overseeing in addition to all my other job responsibilities. One of those "special program requirements" was for Shawn to meet with me at least every twenty-four hours for counseling that focused on building new skills for regulating his emotions and learning how to direct his anger in an "appropriate" fashion—which *didn't* include physically and verbally assaulting other people. I think I hated that special program and all the stress it caused me more than Shawn hated it. And *that's* saying something!

We were about three weeks into Shawn's special program, and he had made little measurable progress on his overall goals. I was weary from all the extra time and effort I had to put into this singular resident when I had at least a dozen other troubled teens on my caseload to contend with each day. I was already at the end of my rope when I got a call that Shawn had again assaulted a peer in school and was being sent back down to the cottage to be placed in isolation, according to protocol. It was my job to debrief the incident with Shawn in my office within an hour of his placement in the holding cell used exclusively for timeout purposes and then to document all my interventions in his special program log before I could go home for the day.

After Shawn had finally stopped screaming, pounding, and kicking the walls of the seclusion room, I retrieved the massive key needed to unlock him from the holding cell and escorted him to my office a short distance away so we could process his latest transgression. Because Shawn was so volatile and unpredictable, I kept my office door open in case I needed to call for backup. During the course of our conversation, Shawn began to escalate even further, and before long, he was in a state of all-out rage once more.

Shawn started screaming and verbally threatening me in ways I had never before experienced. At one point, he yelled, "When I get out of here, I'm going to hunt your white ass down and chop you into little pieces! And don't think I won't be able to find you!" For the first and *only time* in my entire life, I had a true out-of-body, or "dissociative," experience. I temporarily left my body and saw myself floating in midair above Shawn and me. I watched Shawn's face turn menacing, saw his fists clench, and witnessed my life in a whole new way in that terrifying instant. I remember thinking to myself as I hovered in midair, "They don't pay me enough for this shit! This is *crazy*! I am *done* doing this kind of work! I have had *enough*!"

Just as quickly as I left my body, I inhabited it again and felt myself once more sitting in my office chair. I took a long, deep breath and looked at Shawn's contorted, angry face, and said, "Shawn, I want to thank you. If you weren't such an ass just now, I wouldn't have come to the conclusion that I just came to, which is that I don't *want* to work with people like you in settings like this any longer. I want to work with people who care about their own lives and the lives of others around them. I want to work with people who aren't hell-bent on self-destruction or on trying to hurt everyone who crosses their path. I *want* to work with people who value kindness, dignity, and respect, and who are *open* to receiving help instead of always pushing it away. So, I want to *thank you*, Shawn, because now I *know* what I need to do next, and it starts with ending this conversation and getting you back into the seclusion room *now*!"

Shawn was so startled and caught off guard at my words of gratitude that he clearly didn't know what to say or do next. I mean, how do you continue to argue and threaten someone who just expressed gratitude for your totally unacceptable behavior? The best Shawn could do in that moment was to mutter, "That's cool," as he got up and walked calmly back into the holding cell. I locked the door behind him with shaking hands—the result of my brain's fully activated alert system—fueled by adrenaline, anger, and fear for my very existence.

I went home that Friday night, overcome by what had happened with Shawn and in my own personal existential crisis. I didn't have a lot of money in the bank to fall back on and had never quit a job without a plan of what I would do next. I had left other "golden handcuff" jobs in the past when they became too stressful, all-consuming, or just plain crazy-making, and that is *exactly* what my job at Lookout had become.

I spent the weekend talking through my angst with those closest to me and did a lot of soul searching. When I returned to work on Monday, I gave notice to my boss that I would soon be vacating my position, and although he tried diligently to talk me out of doing so, my mind was already made up, and there was no going back.

The first kid on my caseload that I informed of my impending departure was Shawn. When I explained to him that I would be leaving my job in a few weeks, he said, "Damn, Kay! Did you *mean* what you said to me in your office last week?" I looked him straight in the eye and replied, "Yes, Shawn. I meant every word of it. I want to thank you. I had thought myself into my own mental jail, and you made me realize that I had a *choice* not to stay. That I had a *choice* to leave this place and go explore other work settings until I find a job where I feel safe and valued. Where people treat each other with kindness, respect, and trust. Where I can receive more thank-yous than f-yous and get clear about *what really matters* in my life.

"You made me realize that I don't have to wait five months until I turn forty to 'parole,' as I've been talking about. That was just something I made up in my head, and it doesn't exist anywhere else. I realized that *I don't have to wait* to see what my future holds. I can go *now* and find out. In fact, in some strange way, you may have just saved me!"

Shawn looked puzzled at my words but also kind of proud—like he had finally done something to help instead of *hurt someone* for a change—however convoluted his abhorrent actions may have been. Judging by the smile spread across Shawn's face, I think he even surprised himself to discover how good that kind of foreign emotion could actually *feel*.

I didn't have an awareness of it at the time but would later come to understand that much of what I told Shawn I wanted was remarkably similar to the hospice philosophy of care. A philosophy that *affirms life* while also not hastening death. A philosophy that *honors people* on their journey by enhancing their quality of life through effective management of their pain—physical, emotional, psychological, and spiritual. And a philosophy that is based on the foundational belief that *all people should be treated with dignity and respect*, no matter what their prior histories or transgressions may have been. What was especially wonderful was that I didn't need to "don my emotional armor" to serve people who were sick and dying because they largely received the help I had to give them with outstretched arms instead of clenched fists.

More than twenty years have come and gone since I left my job in youth corrections and "paroled" to my new life as a medical social worker and dementia specialist. As I think back over the professional opportunities I've been fortunate enough to experience over the past two decades, I am amazed at how much I have changed, grown, and evolved personally and professionally since that distant time behind the barbed wire fences and locked doors.

In hindsight, I can now see that there have been countless occasions throughout my life when I literally thought myself into my own mental jail, as I did with my position at Lookout. So many times, when the door of opportunity was flung wide open for me to freely walk through, I lacked the insight to realize I *actually had* a choice. Because of that, I spent many years feeling trapped and bitter by the circumstances in which I found myself—never comprehending at the time that it was *I* who held the key to my happiness and freedom all the while.

When I began working in hospice and companioning people who were facing the end of their lives, I eventually awoke to how I wanted to live my life more authentically. I started to evaluate situations by a whole new standard of measurement: if I only had six months to live, would I choose to stay in this particular job, relationship, or set of circumstances, or would I try to make a change instead? That new paradigm led me to make some heartbreaking as well as liberating decisions along the way that were not always easily understood or popular with the people closest to me. However, they were choices I felt compelled to make in order to honor my spiritual path and intuition.

Spending years at bedside, listening to the regrets of people who were dying, motivated me to be mindful of the current choices I was making so I could work toward minimizing the number of regrets I would accumulate before my life ended. Having my dad die of cancer so early in my hospice career only served to reinforce how fleeting and unpredictable our time on earth can be and how I shouldn't take a single minute of it for granted—even though, oftentimes, I still do.

I have not escaped my well-worn pattern of being attracted to emotionally challenging jobs since leaving corrections, but my work in hospice, the memory clinic, palliative care, and dementia coaching have given me an entirely different perspective on my career, my gifts, and my purpose. I've come to find how life-affirming and energizing it is to work with people who, in their vulnerability, willingly open themselves to my assistance and expertise rather than put up walls of resistance. Those walls left me incredibly weary and devoid of all creativity and hope.

Over the years, I've diligently strived to find a delicate balance between my innate inclination to be overly empathetic and trusting in my work with people and my need to allow space for self-protection. It is a fine line to be as present and compassionate as possible while also shielding my heart from the ongoing grief and loss that I continuously contend with in my profession.

Looking back now, I am amazed at how wide and expansive my heart has become as I've developed the capacity to share my knowledge, skills, and gifts with the world in a way that is rewarding and life-changing. I have learned *so much* from the multitude of people I have had the opportunity to work with and serve. Every one of them has indelibly shaped me into a better human being, and for that, I am especially grateful. The exquisite gifts I have received in the process of becoming a "bedside witness" have been plentiful, humbling, inspirational, and *far better* than any I could have imagined manifesting in my career. I am *truly* living my passion, and *that,* for me, is freedom.

ACKNOWLEDGMENTS

To my dear friend RayLynne Cuzner and business coach Mary Gaul for encouraging me to move my collection of stories from a Word document on my computer into the world where they belong. Although I *never* intended to write a book in the midst of a global pandemic, your persistent faith in me and in the importance of sharing my stories with the people who need them most has made *all* the difference between simply *wishing* I could write a book "someday," and actually getting it *done!*

To my writing coach and editor, Donna Mazzitelli of Writing With Donna; to my publishing consultant, Polly Letofsky; to Victoria Wolf, designer, Wolf Design and Marketing; and to everyone at My Word Publishing who has helped take my story from a pipe dream on a thumb drive to a reality in print.

To all my friends and colleagues who have been supportive of this endeavor by cheering me on from the sidelines for the past year. Because of you, I was able to keep up my momentum until I wrote the very last page of this book.

And finally, to my incredible family, without whom *none* of this would have been possible. Without your ongoing love, support, and belief in my ability and dream, *Bedside Witness* would never have come to fruition. Special thanks to my amazing son, Eli. Being able to witness and enjoy the unfolding journey of your life has been the greatest gift I have ever received. And lastly, to my beloved Papa who continues to share his gentle wisdom with me from the heavens, and who is, was, and always will be my greatest teacher of all.

ABOUT THE AUTHOR

Kay Adams, LCSW, is a coach, educator, writer, facilitator, and speaker. She is the founder of Compassion Works, LLC—a company dedicated to providing individualized dementia coaching, workshops, and educational offerings to families, professional care partners, and organizations.

Kay is passionate about supporting people living with dementia, as well as the families, caregivers, and communities entrusted with their care. Kay's extensive background as a medical social worker in geriatrics, hospice, palliative care, and mental health has given her a unique perspective as a "bedside witness" to the plethora of needs that families contend with when caring for a friend or loved one who is facing a life-threatening illness or dementia.

Kay's mission is to empower care partners to navigate the wilderness of dementia by providing individualized coaching, education, coping strategies, and programs designed to improve communication, relationship dynamics, and caregiver support and confidence.

Known for bringing authenticity, humor, integrity, and a unique storytelling ability to her work, Kay connects deeply with those she serves and understands that it is a *privilege* to do so.

Kay and her family reside in Denver, Colorado. To learn more about Kay and her work, please visit: www.kaymadams.com.

INVITE KAY TO YOUR
BOOK CLUB!

As a special gift to readers of *Bedside Witness*, Kay would love to visit your book club either via video conferencing or in person.

Please contact Kay directly to schedule her appearance at your next book club meeting. Kay@kaymadams.com